Jerusalem

The Spatial Politics of a Divided Metropolis

Anne B. Shlay and Gillad Rosen

polity

Copyright © Anne B. Shlay and Gillad Rosen 2015

The right of Anne B. Shlay and Gillad Rosen to be identified as Author of this Work has been asserted in accordance with the UK Copyright, Designs and Patents Act 1988.

First published in 2015 by Polity Press

Polity Press
65 Bridge Street
Cambridge CB2 1UR, UK

Polity Press
350 Main Street
Malden, MA 02148, USA

ISBN-13: 978-0-7456-7103-1
ISBN-13: 978-0-7456-7104-8 (pb)

A catalogue record for this book is available from the British Library.

Shlay, Anne B., author.
  Jerusalem : the spatial politics of a divided metropolis / Anne B. Shlay, Gillad Rosen.
    pages cm
  Includes bibliographical references and index.
  ISBN 978-0-7456-7103-1 (hardback : alk. paper) -- ISBN 978-0-7456-7104-8 (pbk. : alk. paper)
  1. Jerusalem--Ethnic relations. 2. Jews--Jerusalem--Attitudes. 3. Palestinian Arabs--Jerusalem--Attitudes. 4. Jerusalem--In Judaism. 5. Arab-Israeli conflict. I. Rosen, Gillad, author. II. Title.
  DS109.95.S55 2015
  956.94'4205--dc23
                                        2014042514

Typeset in 11 on 13 pt Monotype Bembo by
Servis Filmsetting Ltd, Stockport, Cheshire
Printed and bound in the UK by CPI Group (UK) Ltd, Croydon, CR0 4YY.

For further information on Polity, visit our website:
politybooks.com

Figures and Tables		vi
Acknowledgments		viii
Map of Central Jerusalem		x
1	Introduction: The Politics of Space	1
2	The Jerusalem Story: Theory and Methods	18
3	What Is Jerusalem?	40
4	Who Is Jerusalem?	89
5	The Palestinian Challenge and Resistance in Arab Jerusalem	137
6	Downtown Place Making and Growth in Israeli Jerusalem	164
7	Conclusion	185
Notes		195
References		197
Index		211

Figures and Tables

Figures

1.1	Jerusalem's Old City and its downtown	2
1.2	Silwan, the City of David, and the Old City	4
3.1	The United Nations 1947 Partition Plan for Palestine	49
3.2	The Orient House	53
3.3	Greater Jerusalem	56
3.4	Areas A, B, and C in the West Bank according to the Oslo Agreement	70
3.5	Har Homa	71
3.6	The separation barrier/fence/wall that runs through East Jerusalem	76
3.7	City of David excavations	80
4.1	Haredi demonstration against their people being drafted	107
4.2	Signage in ultra-Orthodox neighborhoods enforcing dress codes	121
5.1	Subversive Palestinian graffiti on the separation barrier/fence/wall	147

6.1   Jerusalem Light Rail, Jaffa Center downtown   177
6.2   Mamilla under construction   179
6.3   Machane Yehuda   181

Tables

4.1   Defining social characteristics of people living in
      Jerusalem   103

Acknowledgments

Social research is by definition a community product. We relied heavily on a large number of people who provided data and information, interpretation and experience, and just plain time – a lot of it. Many people across the globe were generous as well as excited about what we were trying to study, even when we were not terribly clear about it or failed to understand it well ourselves. Since these research and writing activities span eight years, there was a great deal of time for others to be involved.

We thank our numerous respondents, over ninety, who gave us hours of their time over several years, some on multiple occasions. The information we collected reflects the enormous variation in individual views of Jerusalem. Our respondents shaped our thinking about Jerusalem, highlighting its eternal complexity. Our goal was to do justice to these complex renditions while writing an accessible Jerusalem story.

Many people provided counsel, advice, commentary, and support along the way. From the very start of our research activities, Chaim Fiakoff, former Director of the Ministry of Housing and Construction, was infinitely patient in explaining the intricacies and mysteries of housing development in Israel. We owe a special thanks to our colleagues in the Department of Geography of the Hebrew University, Eran Feitelson, Eran Razin, and Noam Shoval, for numerous meetings, dinners, and discussions. We thank the Germantown Jewish Centre for enthusiatically cheering us on from the very beginning. Others who contributed in various ways include Andy Clarno, Marsha Crawford, Nir Gazit, Lenny Gordon, Ayela Guy, Richard Immerman, Lori Lefkovitz, Laura Levitt, Aelon Porot, Malka Greenberg Raanan, Rickie Sanders, Hilary Silver, Yitzhak Sokoloff, Greg Squires, and Alan Walks. Julia Ericksen, now Professor Emeritus in Sociology at Temple University, gave essential guidance on the difference between writing a book and writing an academic article for a journal, and we expect our readers will be grateful for this as well.

Thanks are due to our splendid research assistants, Emma Giloth, Jennifer McGovern, Lauren Ross, and Matan Singer, who enthusiastically collected materials, managed and analyzed data, and helped with editing. A special thanks is due to the many Temple students who took Shlay's course on "Jerusalem: The Politics of Space."

Polity Editor Jonathan Skerrett provided the initial impetus for writing this book and gave critical support and guidance along the way.

Funded support for this work included a Fulbright Foundation Research Fellowship (2006–7), an Arie Shahar Fellowship (2008–9), a Temple University Summer Fellowship (2010), and a Lady Davis Fellowship (2013–14).

Over this period, three children were born (Rosen) and one graduated from high school and college (Shlay), with all providing endless richness and insanity in our lives. Our hope is for this book to be used as a vehicle to preserve Jerusalem for our children and for those across the globe, not just one group or another. Somehow Jerusalem survives, and we want it to continue.

Map of Central Jerusalem

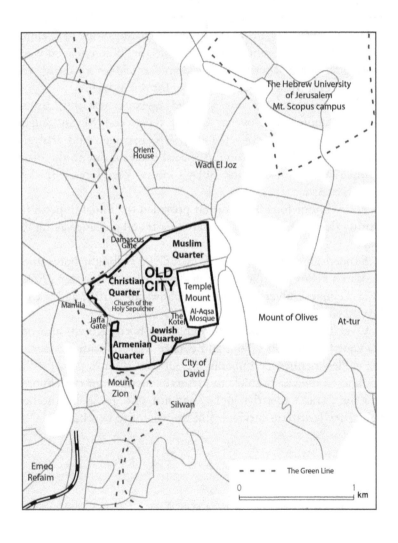

The Hebrew University
of Jerusalem
Mt. Scopus campus

Orient
House

Wadi El Joz

Damascus
Gate

**Muslim
Quarter**

**Christian
Quarter** **OLD
CITY**

Temple
Mount

Church of the
Holy Sepulcher

Mamila

Al-Aqsa
Mosque

The
Kotel

Mount of Olives

At-tur

Jaffa
Gate

**Jewish
Quarter**

**Armenian
Quarter**

City of
David

Mount
Zion

Silwan

Emeq
Refaim

- - - - -   The Green Line

0   1
                                      km

1

Introduction: The Politics of Space

The most dominant global trend today is the dramatic growth of cities. From the mega-cities of the third world to the sprawling hubs that define US cities, urban development has become rapid, irreversible, and endless. The question is not whether cities will grow but how will they grow and what form(s) they will take. Will city development practices embrace density, mass transit, and smart growth or will they hang on to the large, low-density homes that produce urban sprawl? The reigning definition of urban form in the twenty-first century is up for grabs.

The growing city is an increasingly unequal one. Escalating neoliberal urbanization has brought with it growing economic disparities and the heightened polarization of rich and poor. Gentrification has become a global force. The forces that transform urban areas into havens for the rich also create neighborhoods of concentrated poverty. Mirroring global trends, the city's rich are getting more affluent and the poor more destitute.

The growing city is more and more a contested one. Cities used to serve as spatial vehicles for upward mobility and assimilation. Now, increased immigration along with urban growth has not homogenized ethnic and racial identities but strengthened them.

Urban life is characterized by social and economic differences – differences that are both spatially visible and often polarizing.

The ultimate contested city is Jerusalem (Bollens, 2000; Nasrallah, 2003). Jerusalem is at the center of the geopolitical conflict between Palestinians and Israelis, who both consider the city to be their capital and integral to their respective national identities (see Figure 1.1). It is home for large numbers of ultra-Orthodox (Haredi) Jews – the Haredim, who battle for neighborhood dominance with secular Jerusalemites. Jerusalem is also a poor city in which its poverty is largely out of sight from its wealthy residents and the endless parade of tourists. It is an unusual place whose many divisions by religion, nationality, and class appear to define it as a place and community. Conflict over and within Jerusalem is its most prominent feature (Kliot and Mansfeld, 1999; Calame and Charlesworth, 2009).

At the apex of modern-day Jerusalem is its Old City – a place encased by thick walls of stone. The Old City is less than half a square mile in area but from the outside it appears much larger.

Figure 1.1   Jerusalem's Old City and its downtown (© Gillad Rosen)

Some people mistake it for a museum because it houses some of the most precious holy places for Muslims, Jews, and Christians. Although chronologically ancient, the Old City is very much alive, brimming with vital institutions for heathens and faithful alike and a place for tourists as well as local residents. It is a site for special occasions like Bar Mitzvahs but is also where everyday activities occur. Many people live in the Old City. Within its ancient walls a host of commercial activities take place. One can buy a wedding ring or cake, find a lawyer, buy shoes or a new dress, or have a festive meal. The Old City may be old, but it is still kicking.

On any given day, young children grace its walkways with their rambunctious energy as they go to and from the schools housed within its walls. Men of all ages rush to prayers. Young kids ride their bikes fast and furiously, almost hitting someone or something every few seconds. Old City rhythms keep time with the various calls to prayers, the bells of the cathedrals, and the setting of the sun. Sometimes the walkways appear dangerously crowded.

The Old City is formally divided into four quarters – Muslim, Jewish, Christian, and Armenian – each with its own sacred traditions. This is not some kind of Epcot Disney creation with imported authentic actors; it is the real deal. Shopkeepers routinely report that their business longevity encompasses two, three, and sometimes four or more generations of family commercial activity.

The Old City is a microcosm of and reference point for the Palestinian–Israeli conflict. With no resolution in sight, it is politically in the hands of Israel, which has absolutely no intention of giving up, dividing, or sharing it. Although political ownership of the Old City is theoretically up for negotiation, all wagers are on Israel to work to maintain its sovereignty and control. But good money is also on the Palestinians to effectively challenge Israeli sovereignty with their own political and religious claims.

Located on a hill, the Old City is bounded on its west side by the stone-encased Mamilla shopping mall, a collection of upscale chain stores and restaurants that provide panoramic views of the western part of Jerusalem. This view showcases the city's splendor, affluence, and beauty as a world-class locale for visitors and residents alike.

Figure 1.2   Silwan, the City of David, and the Old City
(© Anne Shlay)

On the other side of the Old City is a very large community of densely packed homes that appear to be built into the very hills on which they reside. This is the Palestinian village of Silwan, a long-established community of over fifty-five thousand people. Israel annexed Silwan to Jerusalem after the 1967 war, an illegal move according to international law. Silwan's proximity to the Old City, its militancy against the Israelis, and its location along a political faultline should Jerusalem ever be divided has propelled the village into the public eye (Pullan and Gwiazda, 2009; Mizrachi, 2012). This view of Jerusalem is one of many visible landscapes of the conflict between Jews and Palestinians (see Figure 1.2).

Immediately to the south is the City of David (in Hebrew: Ir David), a rich archaeological site that has produced evidence of the existence of a biblical Jewish city from many centuries ago (Reich et al. 2007). This place, according to biblical history, was captured for the Israelites from the Jebusites by King David (McKenzie,

2002). The conquest of Jerusalem by David is believed to have paved the way for his son, the future King Solomon, to build the First Temple.

The City of David has been designated a national park with the expressed intent to protect land outside the Old City walls. This park is officially known as the Jerusalem Walls National Park. The City of David also lies within the boundaries of Silwan, so parts of the village fall within the national park itself (Mizrachi, 2012).

Although the Israeli government is the legal administrator of national parks, for all practical purposes the City of David is run by a private entity, the Ir David Foundation, or, as it is called in Israel, El'ad. El'ad finances and controls City of David archaeological excavations and operates a center for educational tourism around the site. Over four hundred thousand people visit the City of David site on an annual basis. But in addition to the archaeology and tourist components of El'ad, it finances a residential program. El'ad purchases housing within Silwan and rents these homes to Israeli Jews (Pullan and Gwiazda, 2009).

The City of David nestled within the contours of Silwan provides another panoramic view of Jerusalem. This landscape is more complicated than the others. Closest to the Old City walls is the City of David visitors' center, a glitzy entrance to what is billed as the birthplace of Jerusalem's Jewish heritage. The glitz then gives way to the densely packed Palestinian homes of Silwan that are lined up along narrow streets. Dotted among the Palestinian houses are glimpses of Israeli flags that designate the presence of Jewish residents. This is contested space – a place of conflict between Palestinians and Jews; one managed by the Israeli government through its steward, El'ad (Greenberg, 2009). Here the public and private forces associated with money and power appear to gradually make their way down to the valley of Silwan, the location of the proposed King David's Garden, intended to be a Jewish-historical tourist site. For Israel, these developments are building up its tourism capacity by offering up access to the biblical heritage of the Jewish people. For Palestinians, they are nothing more than the Judaization of space – the process of conquering land, housing, neighborhoods, and communities through the in-migration of

Israeli Jews (Bartal, 2012). Many speak of this as Israel creating "facts on the ground" (Zertal and Eldar, 2007): the physical development of infrastructure, buildings, and people to create the "fact" of Jewish control of place (Abu El-Haj, 2001).

Jerusalem is best known as the spiritual center for the three largest monotheistic religions: Judaism, Christianity, and Islam. Yet other-worldly transcendence is far from its day-to-day reality. Jerusalem is a city bombarded by conflict. These disputes are largely about the city itself – about the land on which it is built, its roads and transit systems, its neighborhoods and homes, its places of worship, the social and ethnic origins of its residents, who may live with whom, who gets what and when, as well as any other permutation that speaks to issues of land, space, and power. Visible struggles take place when the Israeli government swoops into Silwan and demolishes the homes of the Palestinian families living there on grounds of illegal developments. Jerusalemites witness conflict when Palestinians protest the Israeli government's refusal to permit the residents of Silwan to build on their land or modify the physical dimensions of their housing. Jerusalem is filled with protests and demonstrations by everyone, about everything.

Yet some of the most important conflicts are latent or behind the scenes: for example, when the Israeli government transfers control over land and development to moneyed interests in the City of David. Some aspects of conflict are not manifested as battles at all, such as when people claim that an individual person (e.g. King David or the Prophet Muhammad) built a city or seized control of a place over three thousand years ago. Though no real proof of the activities of individual people can be obtained through archaeology, people accept false or nearly false claims and adopt them as true. The activities of the organizations around the City of David are able to manage conflict precisely through their ability to tell a compelling story about Jewish history – a story that mobilizes political acquiescence to the dominant point of view. In other words, Israeli Jews believe that Israeli domination of and destruction of the Palestinian village of Silwan is justifiable because Silwan sits in the way of Jewish access to their heritage.

The mobilization of public opinion is most powerful when it minimizes overt visible conflict and mimics consensus. The absence of overt conflict in situations of Israeli dominance over Palestinian development is precisely when the power equation is so one-sided that any explicit control is invisible. The flow of money from El'ad to ensure that archaeological efforts proceed unimpeded is one example of how global forces can work quietly and out of sight to move the conflict one way or another.

Jerusalem is the poster child for the divided city. It is divided over religion and religiosity as well as by race, ethnicity, and class. The battle over who owns and controls Jerusalem is the focus of national, regional, and international attention. Its fate in the world above may be the stuff of prophecy, but its destiny on earth is a fight that appears to have no limits. The struggle over who controls Jerusalem seems to be almost eternal. For those routinely engaged in this battle, there is little room for negotiation or conciliation. The struggle for Jerusalem is viewed as a zero-sum game, in which there are only winners and losers. Jerusalem is not a realm where compromise goes down easy, if at all.

Jerusalem is in the news internationally on an almost weekly if not daily basis. Sometimes it is because an American politician is visiting, usually a Secretary of State or someone else who is of importance. Sometimes there are complaints that the government is building housing in places deemed off limits by international law. The news focuses on Jerusalem because it is frequently the locale for violence, killing, battles, and war. Death and destruction do not get every country on the nightly news, but when Jerusalem is involved, its place in the media is virtually guaranteed.

Yet Israel as a country is an abstraction even to American Jews who are effectively initiated into the tribe of Israel from their moment of birth. People are citizens of countries but they live and love in cities. According to the old song by Roger Miller, "England swings like a pendulum do," but everyone knows that it is in the global city of London that the swings are swung. The United States is a melting pot but American blending happens in places like New York, Los Angeles, or Miami. Political demands for democracy occur in countries but the ground zero for fighting for these rights happens in cities like Moscow, Beijing, Kiev, and Cairo. Citizens pledge allegiance to nation states, but their experience of homeland occurs closer to the earth in large urban centers. Amalgams of memories call up the particulars of the places in which people reside. People may die for countries, but living takes place in cities.

There is substantial disagreement about the basic facts of Jerusalem and there are a large number of claims and counterclaims. Located in the middle of Israel, Jerusalem is claimed as the nation's capital. Yet the rest of the world does not recognize Jerusalem's political status as the sovereign center of the country. Land adjacent to Jerusalem has been politically annexed and developed by Israel while others testify that the land was occupied and then stolen by Israel and is really part of some other country. Jews maintain that it has a historical affiliation with Jerusalem dating back three thousand years and that Jerusalem was the site of the First and Second Jewish Temples, which were themselves in place for over three hundred years. Others, however, deny the importance of Jerusalem to Judaism, suggesting that Jewish duration in the city was brief and casting doubt on the existence of the First and Second Temples. People even claim that the Western Wall in the Old City was not part of the Jewish Second Temple but instead belongs to Islam (Reiter, 2008).

The statuses of particular places within Jerusalem are intensely disputed. Virtually every idea about the city's history generates a group or campaign that denies its legitimacy. Places deemed sacred by some are rendered profane by others, and vice versa. What some people might consider to be compelling ideas or simply facts about Jerusalem are treated as ideology and lies by others. There are virtually no truisms that hold about Jerusalem because anything that someone says is true about the city is immediately contradicted by someone else.

The most basic questions are political. Answers to fundamental questions that would seem politically neutral are not so easy to answer. For example, how big is Jerusalem? The answer depends on how one defines it. Whose definition of Jerusalem do you use? What parts do you include or exclude? Should settlements that encircle Jerusalem be considered part of the metropolitan area? How can one include places in Jerusalem when they are technically not even in the same country?

Inevitably the answers to basic questions reveal how people come down on one side or the other on the long-standing debate over who rules Jerusalem (Bollens, 1998; Friedland and Hecht, 2000). It is relatively easy to answer questions about the size of Chicago or Dallas because there is consensus over the boundaries of these cities. But no consensus exists over Jerusalem's boundaries because the question "What is Jerusalem?" is a political one. Arguing for a larger definition supports an Israeli point of view by recognizing the legitimacy of Israel's taking land acquired in the 1967 war as part of Jerusalem. Arguing for a smaller definition recognizes the Palestinian perspective that land occupied by Israel is not legitimately, or at least permanently, theirs. Debates over these fundamental questions associated with Jerusalem are nowhere near being resolved. The Jerusalem conundrum echoes the question asked by Pete Seeger in his famous song on the early violent days of union organizing, "Which side are you on?" And his declaration "There are no neutrals there" could also have been written about the city and reverberates across the globe. Should Israel's claims on Jerusalem be challenged? Is Jerusalem as outlined by Israel a fait accompli? Is a divided Jerusalem still physically viable? Agreement over what Jerusalem is will eventually signify the denouement of the conflict between Palestinians and Israelis. What is Jerusalem is the central dilemma to the conflict over the city.

This book is about the politics of space and the conflict over space in Jerusalem. It examines the battles over the ownership and control of what many consider to be the most important city in the entire world. New York, Tokyo, and London may be the urban hubs in charge of global capitalism (Sassen, 2001). Jerusalem, however, is the analogous urban steward of eternal deliverance or damnation. Wealth and poverty may be the outcome of good and bad decisions on the world's stock exchange. But good and bad acts that transpire in Jerusalem arguably affect what happens in the world to come. Macroeconomic trends, employment, and the cost of goods and services may depend on what occurs on the stock market. But at the end of the day, religion, as the source of human salvation, will trump capitalism every time.

Many people have heard of or know something about Jerusalem. It is often mentioned in songs and poetry in many different languages. Children grow up singing hymns and camp songs about Jerusalem. Some may not know why it is religiously important but most will certainly know that it is. Hands down, Jerusalem would win in terms of name recognition over Istanbul, Kabul, Amman, Beirut, and maybe even Toronto. Everyone everywhere has heard something about Jerusalem, and for that reason alone, they regard it as a special place.

Many have a one-dimensional understanding of Jerusalem, in part because the media deliver simplicity. People think of it as a holy place. Or they believe it is a dangerous place. Even those who pay a lot of attention to events in the Middle East may not be aware of Jerusalem's complexity.

Religious tourists form the bulk of visitors to Jerusalem (Cohen-Hattab and Shoval, 2014). Not surprisingly, their knowledge about Jerusalem is largely gleaned from their own Jerusalem-based religious experiences. People learn about their religion, not necessarily about those of others. Jewish tourists quickly learn about the destruction of the Second Temple almost two millennia ago. Christians go to the Via Dolorosa, travel the path Jesus took with his cross, and visit the church where he died. Muslims go to the Dome of the Rock, the site from where the Prophet Muhammad ascended to heaven. Jerusalem is sliced and diced into digestible morsels for each group of the faithful.

But religious nuggets do not tell the Jerusalem story. Visits to holy places cannot explain the travails that represent the regional, national, and international standing of contemporary Jerusalem. Religious homage alone explains little about the contested world in which the city operates.

Of course, tourism, even religious tourism, is not geared toward examining cities but toward consuming them through personal experiences in those places. Through tourism, most people learn little about the cities they visit because the experience of place does not necessarily yield an understanding of them. For example, think of a visit to Westminster Abbey, the Liberty Bell, the Lincoln Memorial, or the Sistine Chapel. These experiences in and of themselves yield little information or understanding of the cities they are in, in these cases London, Philadelphia, Washington DC, and Rome.

Through the eyes of religious tourists, Jerusalem may seem like an uncomplicated place. Yet its appearance of simplicity is deceptive. To be sure, no city is devoid of conflict and all have at least some issues to do with divisions, segregation, inequality, contested politics, and more (Allegra et al., 2012). But few cities rival Jerusalem in the intensity with which these divisions and conflicts are expressed both in the political sphere and in ordinary everyday life. Secular Jewish automobile drivers know that on Shabbat (the Jewish Sabbath) if they drive through ultra-Orthodox religious neighborhoods they risk having stones thrown at their cars. Palestinian youth learn to not frequent downtown haunts like Ben Yehuda Street where they are likely to be harassed or provoked. Tourists (religious and secular) avoid Haredi neighborhoods, particularly if woman are not attired according to Haredi customs of modesty. Advertisers do not employ sexualized images of women or men on billboards and often avoid using women models altogether, not just in religious neighborhoods but in secular Jerusalem neighborhoods as well. Non-kosher restaurants (i.e. those serving food not prepared according to Jewish law) close on religious holidays to conform to local neighborhood standards, even though, by definition, non-kosher restaurants may open whenever they want to. Jews avoid traveling through Palestinian villages and vice versa. Jerusalem businesses, residents, and regulars know the necessary spatial practices to avoid problems ranging from social discomfort to physical violence (Friedland and Hecht, 2000).

Visitors are often surprised by the racial and ethnic diversity to be found in Jerusalem. Unlike contemporary Jewish communities in North America or Europe, Jerusalem (and Israel writ large) contains a panoply of difference in racial and ethnic origins. Like the United States or any other liberal democracy, the Israeli government is explicit that all citizens have equal political and civil rights.

But the reality is that Israel privileges Jews over other religions and identities (Yiftachel, 1998; Yiftachel and Yacobi, 2003).

In Israel, greater privileges are granted to Jewish citizens because it is a Jewish state. The operation of a Jewish state by and for Jews holds ramifications for how race, ethnicity, and religion are perceived and evaluated. Overt discrimination is not legal, but preference along racial and ethnic lines is more or less the norm (Yiftachel, 1991, 2006). Instead of minimizing differences among varying races, ethnicities, and religions, Israel emphasizes and therefore reinforces difference. Difference is emphasized by virtue of the fact that Israel is a Jewish state, not a generic one. Israel is by definition a Jewish state to bring to the fore that Israel is by and for Jews.

Religious politics around differences seep into the broader culture. In everyday life, one often hears disparaging remarks about particular groups, comments that are made with relative ease. Every group is fair game – recent Russian immigrants, Ethiopians, Jews coming from North Africa and the Middle East, the Haredim, and more. Cultural stereotypes are often discussed as social facts in ways that would be far less socially acceptable within most Western liberal democracies.

The emphasis on social differences based on variations in Israelis' ascribed characteristics is in part an artifact of the orientation of the Israeli government. The plethora of political parties do not unify people but rather divide them by nationality, religiosity, class, and their position on settlements, the conflict, and attitudes toward peace. Israelis are less tolerant of social difference because Israeli politics are based on recognizing and upholding difference. Israel's acceptance of racial intolerance or that racial distinctions are normative legitimizes neighborhood segregation and renders it acceptable and even desirable. Racial and ethnic segregation is considered normal. The concept of socially mixed neighborhoods in Jerusalem is largely an anathema. The question is not why people would avoid racial and ethnic integration either socially or spatially. The question is why they would consider engaging in racial and ethnic mixing in the first place.

Independent of race and ethnicity, people across many groups are intensely committed to Jerusalem as a place. Unlike many American cities, Jerusalem has been the object of war and combat. Jews and Palestinians alike have died in armed struggles for Jerusalem in the last century and both sides claim it as the site for their nation's capital. Jerusalem's historical and religious history gives it very special significance. It is unique among cities and evokes unprecedented levels of sentiment and attachment.

The uniqueness associated with Jerusalem creates problems not only for those living in and governing the city but also for those trying to understand it. One reason why understanding Jerusalem is so challenging is that everything about the city is politicized. It seems as if every building, house, or location is claimed by one group or another. In Jerusalem, resource allocation and decision making are built into the organization and management of political and legal systems (Margalit, 2001). The government of the city does not transcend politics because the entire system relies on a politics of inequality.

This is a book about Jerusalem's spatial politics and the social processes that emerge from this constellation of competing interests. Spatial politics are the seemingly endless sets of claims, demands, struggles, debates, and challenges over the land, developments, neighborhoods, and communities that make up Jerusalem. Jerusalem's spatial politics are a window onto the world of the Palestinian–Israeli conflict because Jerusalem is ground zero for this struggle. Spatial politics explain the motivations for and organization around the battle for Jerusalem and illustrate the ways in which space itself is a weapon in this struggle. The activities operating on space, the constellations of interests around it, the ways in which different groups mobilize for action or fizzle out, and the use of various tactics, ranging from legal maneuvers to terrorism to simply staying put – all comprise the spatial politics that are evident in Jerusalem.

Like most cities embracing the neoliberal turn, Jerusalem is characterized by a large degree of economic inequality, which is manifested spatially (Choshen et al., 2013). These neighborhood-based wealth disparities vary not only with location but also with residency status, nationality, ethnic identity, religion, and religiosity. In other words, economic inequality has its origins in non-economic realms. How such characteristics are connected to and produce varied socioeconomic and political outcomes is a major concern of this book.

Jerusalem is not like other cities, which makes this examination of socioeconomic inequality a bit different. The outcomes with which this book is concerned are not solely economic. Struggle over space in Jerusalem is political, either overtly, covertly, or both. It is about power, control, nationality, and religion. Some of Jerusalem's battles are between people of the same religion, for example pitting Jews against Jews and Muslims against Muslims. Others are about the struggle for territory and national sovereignty: battles between Israel and Palestinians – including Palestinian Israelis whose identities and citizenship are in conflict. Moreover, Jerusalem's struggles are not simply internal to Israel or even to Muslim countries in the Middle East. Jerusalem has a world-wide following and is a spiritual global city. In many ways, Jerusalem can be seen as the epicenter of extremism, intolerance, and fanaticism. Explaining how one place can embody so many seemingly contradictory forces operating around a spatial area just about the same size as the city of Chicago is one of the many challenges of this book.[1]

Jerusalem is not only a complicated city; it is a controversial city, one that evokes strong reactions from many people across the globe. Not everyone may have an opinion about Jerusalem; but for those who do, their points of view are often very strongly felt.

Large numbers of people have strong feelings about Israel – about the conflict between Israel and Palestinians, over the legitimacy of Zionism and the right of Jews to have their own country, and about Israel's occupation of East Jerusalem and the West Bank. Opinions about Zionism, the occupation, the conflict, and so on, are also opinions about Jerusalem. Jerusalem is neither an idiosyncratic case nor is it incidental to whatever happens with Israel and the Palestinians, with the Middle East, and with the rest of the world. We hope to show that one of the greatest tragedies and mistakes associated with the Oslo Agreement (the landmark but doomed agreement between Israel and the Palestinians) was to defer negotiating Jerusalem. Any kind of negotiation to end the Palestinian–Israeli conflict requires that the boundaries and ownership of Jerusalem be definitively resolved.

The goal of this book is not to inflame or incite but to analyze and inform. The book is intended to provide a comprehensive look at the spatial politics associated with the recent development of Jerusalem to encourage discussion that depends not on rhetorical devices but on carefully assimilated knowledge about the situation. Of course, Jerusalem will remain an emotional and volatile topic for most, not because people are irrational or bad, but because there is so much at stake. For this reason and more, this book is committed to telling a contemporary Jerusalem story that is as rigorous and balanced as possible.

Jerusalem:
The Spatial Politics of a Divided Metropolis

This book is a social and political analysis of the spatial politics underlying the development of contemporary Jerusalem. The time period that we investigate largely begins with the creation of the State of Israel in 1947 with the United Nations resolution that stipulated boundaries to create two new states, one for Jews and the other for Palestinians. This initiation of what has been deemed "two states for two people" moved quickly into a war (1948) – what is commemorated as the Milhemet HaAtzmaount (the War of Independence) for Israel and the Nakba (disaster) for the Palestinians. Our work takes us through to 2014, a year that began with some hope for peace but descended into a war, relentless bombings and attacks, riots, kidnappings, murders, and violence.

The period we write about includes two intifadas (uprisings: 1987–93, 2000–4), many wars (the 1948 Arab–Israeli War, the 1956 Sinai War, the 1967 Six-Day War, the 1973 Yom Kippur War, the 1982 and 2006 Lebanon Wars, the 2008 and 2014 Israeli–Gaza Wars), and the massive upheavals that occurred in and around Jerusalem through neighborhood and settlement construction, the initiation and expansion of checkpoints, and the building of walls and security barriers. The myriad of spatial transformations reflect defensive and offensive development and infrastructure activities undertaken by public and private actors in and around Jerusalem as well as the spatial manifestations of resistance. Each development represents some aspect of the struggle between different groups at war over who rules Jerusalem. The material foundation of every structure embodies several sets of political and social relationships with the goal of establishing or resisting domination, or both. Rather than settle the conflict once and for all, each new physical development has allowed one side or the other to politically dig in a little deeper.

The chapters that follow show the spatial politics associated with each set of developments, how the conflict has escalated and waned, and the making and remaking of the Jerusalem quagmire through using land and development as tools for conquest and resistance.

Chapter 2 describes the research methods used and provides a set of theoretical perspectives used to interpret the activities described in this book. These perspectives include theories of political hegemony (Antonio Gramsci), the production of space (Henri Lefebvre), the city as a growth machine (John Logan and Harvey Molotch), and divided cities.

Chapter 3 asks what is Jerusalem. It examines the blurring, shifting, and redefining of Jerusalem's boundaries with the growth and development of Israel as a nation state and the intensification of a Palestinian national identity. This ever-changing Jerusalem is one of struggle by different groups not only for the land per se but also for the hegemonic narrative about the land.

Chapter 4 introduces the different groups that have come to make up the Jerusalem mosaic. No Jewish stereotypes can begin to capture the plethora of different social groups that keep moving into and out of the city. It is the people who underlie the physical infrastructure of Jerusalem, not the other way around.

Chapter 5 is about East Jerusalem. East Jerusalem has been the home to Palestinians since the 1948 war and is the location some intend for the capital of a future Palestinian state. But instead of being preserved as the capital of this Palestinian state, much of East Jerusalem has been deliberately absorbed into Israeli Jerusalem with its Jerusalem unification politics. East Jerusalem has become embattled with the politics stemming from the Oslo Agreement, the Judaization of space, settlement development, and the security barrier/fence/wall. The Palestinian resistance to Israeli dominance as it struggles for East Jerusalem sovereignty is a complex story of a Palestinian people with memories of and attachment to a Jerusalem they have known for generations.

Chapter 6 concerns recent Jerusalem development, a modern form of building and growth that is shaping a new Jerusalem and the old one as well. While Jerusalem's settlements originate in politics, they function in many ways like the typical suburban housing strategy used in many US cities. More recently, Israel has embraced neoliberalism, shed its welfare state veneer, and worked at using the public sector to build private sector development around housing, entertainment, tourism, and commerce. In addition to its efforts at staving off political divisions, Jerusalem is working at being a capitalistic city that encourages investment. But its desire to engage in the work of land and space commodification is complicated by the conflict as well as its age and historical relevance. The security barrier/fence/wall that has been built to deter terrorism functions to make Jerusalem safer for capital investment. At the same time, continual threats of violence are constant reminders of how unpredictable investment in the city can be. Whether Jerusalem's commercial development turn is sustainable given its spatial politics is a serious question.

In Chapter 7, we conclude this book by going on a twenty-four-hour tour of Jerusalem. Through this trip across the metropolitan landscape, we take a last look at the incremental yet important ways in which spatial politics are embedded in every crevice of the city.

2
The Jerusalem Story: Theory and Methods

Introduction

Walking through the Old City at twilight on a cool December night provides an intimate experience of the intensity of the three religions that call Jerusalem its home. Jewish men in black hats descend via the Jaffa Gate and meander through the Muslim Quarter on their way to prayer at the Kotel, the remaining wall of the Jewish Second Temple. Their focus is straight ahead, looking neither left nor right at the surrounding kiosks manned (and men they are) by Palestinian shopkeepers. Soon they will be bopping and weaving while they pray at the Kotel, a place of a Jewish historical and religious transcendence.

Muslim men rush through the Damascus Gate and race for the Al-Aqsa Mosque. This prayer space, adjacent to the Dome of the Rock, is just a few meters from the Jewish Kotel. The Dome of the Rock covers the Temple Mount, a place that for Jews is even holier than the Kotel. Muslim and Jewish holy places physically collide while the two groups of the faithful narrowly avoid running into one another.

Muslim prayers are relayed by speakers while church bells ring throughout the Christian Quarter. The Old City and its immediate surroundings contain more than fifty churches, effectively including most of the many variants that branched off from the mother faith hundreds of years ago. The Church of the Holy Sepulchre, where Jesus is said to have died and been buried, is the most holy church. But nearby churches pay homage to Christian faiths from almost every denomination, honoring Orthodox Greeks and Armenians, Lutherans, and more.

The Old City's centrality to religion cannot be overestimated. One can debate the nuance of sanctified places for this or that faction or argue that other places are more holy because of something that may or may not have happened long ago. But holy is as holy does and what matters most is what religious people think and believe. They believe that the Old City is the place for the faithful, and what truly happened when and how is almost entirely irrelevant. Besides, in the realm of the sacred, evidence is not necessary, just faith or belief.

Although the media often emphasize conflict in the Old City, particularly between Jews and Muslims, in many ways it is a space where the main represented religions are given a place of their own. This is because the Old City is divided into separate quarters: Christian, Jewish, Armenian, and Muslim. Each group, even the Christians and Armenians, has a space for the expression of its religion and does not need to compete for space with other religions. In the Old City it seems as if no religious group has precedence over another.

Step outside the walls of the Old City, however, and it is another world altogether. As a Jewish state, Israel privileges Jewish holidays, just as other religious governments privilege the holidays of the religions they represent. Unlike ecumenical societies such as the United States, there is no requirement to give equal or even any billing to minority holidays. In December 2013, a Christian Knesset (Parliament) member asked the Speaker of the chamber if a Christmas tree could be put up in public space within the building in honor of the holiday. The Speaker denied the request, saying it was "inappropriate" (JTA, 2013). In the Old City, all faiths are equal and "true." Debates over status occur within faiths, not between faiths. But in Jerusalem outside the Old City walls, the religious pecking order is a different matter altogether.

This chapter is about getting at variants of truth in the social science vernacular about the Jerusalem story. We shall move from heaven to earth and back again in order to present the theoretical and empirical foundations of this book.

This chapter has two parts. The first part examines the research methods underlying this investigation. It explains how we came together to study Jerusalem, our methods for collecting and assembling data, and the secondary data used. The second part of this chapter provides an overview of the theories used in this project: theories of political hegemony, theories of the production of space and the right to the city, theories about cities as growth machines, and theories of divided cities.

The Making Place Project: Methods and Motivations

Like many research efforts, this study of Jerusalem's spatial politics was born, in part, from intellectual serendipity. In August 2006, Anne Shlay, an urban sociologist from Temple University, Philadelphia, embarked on a Fulbright-funded sabbatical trip to Israel at the Hebrew University of Jerusalem. She knew nothing about Israel or Jerusalem. Six thousand miles and two months later, she was reading an article in her Israeli French Hill apartment about Jerusalem settlement construction (Parmenter, 1999). Settlements, the article said, were constructed on Jerusalem land that was previously part of Jordan, had been captured in the Six-Day War (1967), was illegally annexed to the Israeli Jerusalem municipality, and now housed Jewish Israelis by the thousands. The article listed the Jerusalem neighborhoods involved. The French Hill, the neighborhood in which Shlay was currently living, was on that list. She was immediately confused. Was she living in Jordan? Was she living in a settlement? Her main question was, "Where the hell am I?"

With only a couple of months left on her sabbatical trip, she realized that she would not be able to figure this out by herself. Thinking she needed to see more of Jerusalem, she put the word out that she wanted a driver to show her the city and she would pay someone to do this. A few days later, Gillad Rosen walked in the door.

Rosen was a graduate student in the final stages of finishing his dissertation. He and his wife were a month away from having their first child. Driving an American scholar around Jerusalem seemed a good way to make international connections as well as provide a distraction from the turning points in his life. He was willing to drive Shlay around but not for cash and would only take money for gas.

On their first trip, Rosen learned that the US State Department has told its Fulbright Fellows not to travel over the Green Line, a 1948 boundary that defined Israel's former borders with Jordan. He explained that it was not possible to avoid crossing over the Green Line, this former border, if you based your work at the Mount Scopus campus of the Hebrew University where he and Shlay both worked. She and everyone else at the university crossed the Green Line every day. And Shlay actually lived over the Green Line. The US State Department was obviously confused in its instructions, perhaps even wrong. But what was the source of confusion?

It is with this conversation that the Making Place project was born. "Making place" is about how people construct meaning, purpose, and identity around a location. A location is just that – a physical point or spot in space. A place, however, conveys how a location in space is part of the human social and political experience. A generic place might be "home," a location where someone lives, but also a place where they feel they belong. Neighborhoods have physicality, but their existence as neighborhoods depends on how they are collectively understood as places with which people identify and toward which they have feelings.

A place exists in the physical world but it is constructed in the social world. Places have borders or some variants of where they begin and end so people know when they are in a place or not. It is the construction of these borders around places that is part of the place-making process. While places may be demarcated by physical characteristics like rivers or mountains, all places are created in the social sphere. These social negotiations around place are most clearly seen in those frontier places where conflict over ownership is divisive (Kotek, 1999). Jerusalem is the ultimate frontier city, one of the most prominent global locations in which place borders and the meaning of these borders have been constantly renegotiated. In many ways, one could examine Jerusalem's history since 1948 as the world's most visible place-making experience because its borders, meaning, and identity have been the object of perpetual challenges.

As will become clearer in Chapter 3, place making rendered the Green Line a distant memory for many Israeli Jerusalemites. Yet it remained important to international actors, like the US State Department, who believed that it was a metaphor for the legitimate and legal boundaries of Israel. Going over the Green Line was "bad," implying, incorrectly or not, that one was crossing into occupied territory. Indeed half of the Jerusalem incorporated into and governed by Israel was occupied territory according to the US State Department and the international community. Shlay had been living in occupied territory for her entire Fulbright Fellowship experience in full violation of State Department regulations without either her or them being aware of this discrepancy. This was making place.

By shifting the Green Line, if only metaphorically, one increased the size of the land mass considered to be "legitimately" under Israeli control. The Green Line had metamorphosed from being a physical and real border to an idea. International law stipulated that Israel's building over the Green Line was bad, that some of the places that Israel defined as places in Israel were not in it and were unlawful to boot. To be in compliance with international law, the US State Department told its Fulbright Fellows to be good and to not travel over the Green Line, to effectively stay in the pre-1967 Jerusalem, which was impossible.

Everyday life in Jerusalem had already superseded the Green Line. International law spoke about a Green Line that should not be crossed. But no one knew exactly where it began or ended. International law had met the Alice in Wonderland world of post-1967 Jerusalem.

This Jerusalem boundary struggle in the body and mind of Israel spoke to our fields of study – the social geography and sociology of the urban world. We started talking research, a language we both understood well. We decided to study the process of how the Green Line had shifted. How had this perceived authentic boundary of Israel changed locations and moved from one place to another? What had been done to symbolically but powerfully alter the boundary definitions of Jerusalem? Studying the shifting Green Line meant studying Jerusalem's development politics and how different people viewed the city as a result of new development. Studying development or spatial politics required studying how development decisions were made. Who made development decisions and how were they made, particularly at the periphery of the city? And how were these decisions resisted?

To assess Jerusalem's spatial politics, we relied on a theoretical perspective largely used to study the growth and development of American cities. This paradigm was the "city as a growth machine" (Molotch, 1976; Logan and Molotch, 2007). City growth, according to this paradigm, which will be discussed in greater depth below, is the result of concerted activity by a constellation of growth actors who economically benefit from development. This constellation of actors is the city's growth machine. This theory views American city development, particularly large-scale projects, as the product of the concerted efforts of local growth machines. This is not good news for democracy, particularly for what passes as democracy in cities. In the United States, these alleged growth actors operate outside of public view, orchestrating development through shared networks. We hypothesized that the growth politics of Jerusalem were similar, and that it would not be empirically obvious either how development decisions were made, who was making them, or who directly and indirectly benefited from these decisions (Shlay and Rosen, 2010).

To examine the Israeli development process around the growth of Jerusalem, we decided to interview representatives of institutions involved in development decisions as well as proponents and opponents of these decisions. We also decided to interview people who had a reputation for being knowledgeable about or concerned with development.

Our research design had several phases. First we generated a comprehensive list of what we anticipated to be growth-oriented institutional categories. These categories included government, planners, think tanks, foundations, right- and left-wing advocacy organizations, newspapers, environmental organizations, peace organizations, religious organizations, universities, developers, banks, international organizations, and political parties. We compiled a set of key informants (both Palestinian and Israeli) to ask whether these categories were the correct ones associated with a potential Jerusalem growth machine and which individuals best represented the activities of these institutions. We relied heavily on their social networks and the networks of others to obtain a wide range of perspectives from people in the Middle East as well as outside of it. Based on this information, we determined whom to interview. Respondents were selected to represent a diversity of religious, ethnic, professional, and political perspectives. Appointments were set up to conduct in-person interviews that were timed to occur mostly when Shlay was in Israel. Interviews were conducted in the summers of 2007, 2008, 2010, and 2012.

The research goal was to outline perspectives on Jerusalem, which we believed varied significantly across different people based on their occupational and political positions as well as ethnic and religious origins. An interview protocol was developed that addressed issues specific to Jerusalem. This protocol contained semi-structured, open-ended questions. Several of our informants reviewed these protocols and provided feedback for revisions. We conducted ninety interviews over the course of five years. All interviews were conducted in person and most in English. Some people were interviewed more than once. Interview times ranged from one to two hours. We conducted most interviews as a pair. We each took notes and transcribed them separately. We then exchanged notes, cross-referenced them, and made clarifications of ambiguities or differences in perspectives. Interviews were enhanced with multiple on-site visits and field work. We visited most of the places discussed in our interviews.

Our interviews were supplemented with other questions and experiences that, in addition to the interviews, were important to developing an understanding of Jerusalem as a divided city. First, we realized that the nationality of and passport held by the researcher was important to the research. Nationality is a proxy for someone's political perspectives. Our subjects "read" who we were by virtue of where we were from. In addition, our passports gave us entry or became a barrier to conducting interviews. For example, Israelis may not legally travel to Bethlehem or Ramallah (Area A with full Palestinian autonomy), two important places where we conducted key interviews. But people with US passports may freely travel throughout the West Bank. How place matters was the subject of our research, and we learned that our place of residence mattered while conducting this research.

Our interviews focused on people defining their Jerusalem and explaining their views of and experiences with its development and growth. Topics included:

- definitions of "greater metropolitan Jerusalem";
- the most important places for Jerusalem's growth and development;
- the role of government in Jerusalem's development;
- the central social and political factors shaping urban investment and disinvestment;
- the role of various factors and institutions in shaping Jerusalem's development, including developers, environmentalism, religious groups, extremists and outside money (e.g. El'ad and Ateret Cohanim, the settlers' movement), Zionism, and ideology.
- the effects of the defeat of the massive proposed housing development known as the Safdie Plan (see Chapter 6);
- the effects of the security barrier/fence/wall;
- perceptions of East Jerusalem;
- perceptions of settlements in relationship to the definition of Jerusalem;

- sense of belonging and identification with Jerusalem; and
- the most important institutions shaping Jerusalem's metropolitan development.

We learned to read the politics of many of the people we interviewed by assessing where they chose to be interviewed. We discovered patterns associated with their choices, ones also noted by Hanna Herzog (2005), who argues that interview location is not only a technical matter of convenience and logistics, but also incorporates social and political statements. Where we met became both symbolic and political, reflecting, in part, our interviewees' perspective on where, beyond their national or religious identity, they existed politically and where they wanted us to "sit" politically. For example, a *Jerusalem Post* reporter rejected the idea of meeting at the Ambassador Hotel (in East Jerusalem), insisting on either the King David Hotel or the Mount Zion Hotel (in West Jerusalem). One *Haaretz* reporter, however, asked to meet at the Ambassador Hotel, where most of our interviews with Palestinians took place.

Interview data were largely compiled with the qualitative software Atlas TI. All interviews were coded. Major coding categories included: definitions of Jerusalem; urban growth and development; rights and social services; political Jerusalem; demographic Jerusalem; Jerusalem transportation; right to the city; politics, institutions, and actors; power struggles; and religious identities.

Secondary data sources included maps, historic documents, and the Palestinian and Israeli censuses. The secondary data were used to present the ways in which Israeli policy has established the material basis for altering perceptions of boundary legitimacy through boundary expansion, settlement development, and the construction of new neighborhoods as well as land use and transportation planning and developments. Maps and other data document the "facts on the ground" that are the physical foundation for place making.

The use of interview data permitted an evaluation of the different meanings attached to these policies, decisions, and plans. These narratives lay out the ideological battlegrounds over boundary legitimacy and demonstrate that land use and spatial development are intimately connected to the political struggle between Palestinians and Israelis, particularly over the future international status of Jerusalem, as well as struggles between religious and secular Jews.

As researchers, we also learned our topic experientially. Rosen had grown up in Jerusalem and as a social geographer knew the city very well. He was raised in West Jerusalem in an area mostly commonly known as the Ganim-Yuvalim urban district. This area, which comprises eight neighborhoods and is home to more than fifty thousand residents, is actually comparable to a small to medium-sized city in Israel. It has always been considered a heterogeneous socioeconomic environment. The district is home to affluent and underprivileged residents, religious Orthodox, ultra-Orthodox, and secular Jews. It has communities of European and North American origin (Ashkenazim) as well as of African and Middle Eastern extraction (Mizrahim). More recently it has attracted many Jewish families from the former Soviet Union who have been immigrating to Israel since the early 1990s. As a child, Rosen grew up in Kiryat Menachem and Kiryat Hayovel, two working-class neighborhoods. In 2010, after completing two years of post-doctoral training at the University of Toronto, he attained a position as lecturer at the Hebrew University of Jerusalem and moved to Ramat Sharett, a middle-class, largely secular neighborhood.

Shlay, a newcomer to Jerusalem, studied the city by living in very different neighborhoods each time she visited the city. Her Jerusalem resident neighborhoods included: the French Hill, an Israeli neighborhood that was part of Jordan until 1967 (2006); Musrara, a neighborhood at the Jerusalem "seam," the pre-1967 line that divided East and West Jerusalem (2007); Catamon, a middle-class, largely secular neighborhood in West Jerusalem (2008); Nachlaot, a gentrifying neighborhood in the center of the city with many religious families (2010); Machane Yehuda, in a building just above the famous large market that gives its name to the area (2012). While writing this book, she lived in Talbiah, one of Israel's wealthiest neighborhoods, on a street down the block from the residence of Prime Minister Benjamin Netanyahu. Taking buses and trains everywhere, she became fluent in Jerusalem.

Shlay is also Jewish, and her first visit to Israel was with a group from her Philadelphia synagogue, Germantown Jewish Centre. But her interest in Jerusalem was never explicitly motivated by Zionism, an ideology and politics she had self-consciously avoided. So when she decided to study Jerusalem, she came into the country as a solo academic with few friends or established contacts. With no ready-made community other than an intellectual one, the friends she ultimately made were all Israelis, a process facilitated because so many Israelis speak fluent English. For the purpose of doing this research, she simply took herself off and went to live in Jerusalem for a month or two at a time and just hung out in the city.

While not engaged in a deliberate form of ethnography, Shlay simply lived Jerusalem, and a lot of that living found its way into the book. She also wrote regularly about her Jerusalem experiences. From her first academic trip in 2006, she created a list of people whom she emailed regularly with stories about her experiences. These emails were initially a way of processing and sharing experiences with friends and family, but the audience grew to more than two hundred people who regularly shared her emails with other people. Two of her emails were published in newspapers, one in the *Jerusalem Post* and another in Philadelphia's *Jewish Exponent*. Some of these stories are also contained in this book.

We debriefed regularly on any and every Jerusalem experience. Morning coffees were brain-storming and nothing was off limits. We wrote chapters together over breakfast. While we came together as intellectual comrades studying a city, we collided over our interpretation of Jerusalem. Often, we each saw a different Jerusalem, one shaped by our respective lives – Rosen as an Israeli-born-and-bred Jerusalemite and Shlay as an American Jew not "making Aliyah" (i.e. "going up" or immigrating to Israel) but claiming Jerusalem anyway. Yet this tension over the interpretation of Jerusalem did not result in a set of compromised ideas but in collective clarity that would have been impossible to develop without the partnership. This synergistic part of the research methods used is impossible for anyone else to replicate.

Understanding Jerusalem: Theoretical Perspectives

Like a lens that focuses one's view of the world, theory makes
sense of and provides a perspective on how social science interprets
the activities and situations of people and places. When people
share theoretical ideas among themselves, they also share a view
of how they believe the world works. Theory shapes perceptions,
and those perceptions shape what we see. In this sense, theory and
culture are synonymous. They both provide the road map and
symbols for interpreting the empirical facts that are observed,
counted, and measured.

Political Hegemony

Antonio Gramsci, the Marxist theorist of cultural domination,
argued that all people are intellectuals or theorists because they
possess ideas that shape their world views (Gramsci, 1971, 2001).
Shared cultures represent a form of "common" sense – common
because it is both taken for granted and unchallenged.

Common sense represents a set of deeply held shared thoughts,
conventionally known as culture. But for Gramsci, common-sense
ideas are not neutral, because ideas are political. They are political because these shared and taken-for-granted ideas are a form
of domination; common sense produces political acquiescence.
Common-sense ideas do not generate conflict because they reflect
ideas over which people are in agreement. Gramsci believed that
common-sense world views are hegemonic because these shared
ideas shape expectations and have the power to control alternative thoughts as well as behavior. Hegemonic ideas render people
powerless to question the status quo. These ideas hold sway in
ways that make people adhere to prevailing authority structures
and less likely to think up alternatives to the present social and
political hierarchy.

Ideas about space are hegemonic. Discussed in Chapter 3 is
the way in which attempts are made to erase memories of places

through new Jerusalem development. Holidays like Jerusalem Unification Day are a celebration of spatial dominance and control. Ideas about people are hegemonic as well. As shown in Chapter 4, Jerusalem's Jews are as different from each other as one could possibly be. All are professed to be united as Jews living in Jerusalem. But their common identities as Jews cannot disguise the underlying antipathies that fuel divisions among these groups, despite shared nationalist goals. These divisions fuel secular Jewish residential mobility out of Jerusalem. The loss of these wealthier secular Jews weakens the economic and fiscal health of the city and undermines the image of Jerusalem as Israel's capital for both secular and religious Jews.

Theory as an antidote to all-encompassing common sense could, according to Gramsci, become a tool for political liberation. Alternative theories generate new ideas that challenge the prevailing order. They expose the failings of the social, political, and economic structures that are the fundamental foundations for society. Rather than becoming a tool for producing acquiescence and powerlessness, theory can lead to analysis of the prevailing social order and provide leverage for challenging the status quo. For example, as shown when discussing the resistance of Jerusalem's Palestinians, the perceived need for a Jerusalem Unification Day underscores how divided Jerusalem remains. If Jerusalem were truly united, no one would have to say one word about it.

This book uses theory as a prism for examining Jerusalem and for unveiling the common sense that appears in interpretations of the city's situations. What are the ideological truths that underlie how people look at and understand Jerusalem? What ideas cement a divided Jerusalem as well as rip it asunder? How do ideas about conflict mold for different people a sense of belonging to different parts of the city? Whose definitions of Jerusalem prevail ideologically and in the conflict between ideas about the city?

Jerusalem is a place defined by power – power that is experienced as coercion as well as ideological domination. In Jerusalem, there are always the visible signs of force and the less visible signs of the management of political and social acquiescence. How does power quietly mold ideological adherence to a constantly changing

Jerusalem? How is political acquiescence created and maintained in a divided city in which social, political, and economic inequality prevails?

Jerusalem is a place of bricks and mortar. It is a place where people traverse, live, and die, a place where people move in and out, and a place of the mundane regularities of everyday life. Jerusalem is a faith-based place, a place where symbols of deities and spirits capture the lofty and down-to-earth pleas of the religious masses, be they Christian, Jewish, or Muslim. It is a cosmopolitan place, where people of varying ethnicities, races, and nationalities mingle and get along – most of the time. It is a place filled with ideas, ideas about who should rule, what is wrong, what is right, who belongs and who does not – ideas with no absolute truth, only points of view held by the powerful and the subaltern. How do some ideas about Jerusalem prevail while others do not? How do the ideas about the prevailing Jerusalem manage to dominate over others? The theory undergirding this project is about connecting people's ideas about Jerusalem to that bricks-and-mortar city over which so much conflict exists.

These questions that connect power, the ideological, and the physical are inspired by Gramsci's theories. These theories give visibility to power dynamics – the power over space and place, the power over different social groups, and the power over the many ideas about what Jerusalem is, has been, and will become. We rely on four theoretical areas: (1) Antonio Gramsci's theory of political hegemony; (2) Henri Lefebvre's conceptualization of the production of space in everyday life (Lefebvre, 1991, 1996); (3) John Logan and Harvey Molotch's theory of the city as a growth machine (Molotch, 1976; Logan and Molotch, 2007); and (4) theories of divided cities (Marcuse, 1993; Kliot and Mansfield, 1999; Bollens, 2000; Silver, 2010).

Space, Everyday Life, and the Right to the City

As a Marxist, Henri Lefebvre viewed space as a social product – one produced like other commodities (Merrifield, 2002). Space is produced through the day-to-day activities that occur around, within, and on it. For Lefebvre, space is a product of everyday life. It is the creative product of the people whose lives are part of it. Bricks and mortar are incidental to the social activities that produce space.

Lefebvre argued that capitalism expropriates space by repackaging it as an abstract commodity that can be bundled much like manufactured commodities such as a bunch of vacuum cleaners, pencils, or sweaters. For Lefebvre, space in the abstract that can be bought, sold, and traded conceals the work of the everyday that is embodied in it. Space can never be abstract because it is a unique product that is part of everyday life (Lefebvre, 1991).

Lefebvre, the Marx of space, believed that, as a human creation, space belongs to the communities that produce it. The right to socially produced space is the right to the city – the right to participate in and control the spatial environment in which people live and work. The right to the city is a structural condition of human beings' existence as physical and social creatures (Gottdiener, 1987; Lefebvre, 1991). Space is the creative product of the everyday people whose lives are mirrored in it. Just because one cannot overtly see the place-shaping activities in space does not mean that they are not there. For Lefebvre, the right to the city is as intrinsic to the human condition as is labor (*à-la* Marx) or simply breathing. Space and the control of it can be taken away, but the right to it is always present (Purcell, 2002).

Movements for democratic control over land-use activities are connected to broader political strategies because land-use control, similar to control over the labor process, is intrinsic to the human condition (Harvey, 2003; Lefebvre, 1991; Purcell, 2003). Just as workers – the sellers of labor power – must rise up to reclaim this, city dwellers must rise up and reclaim the space they have produced. The right to the city is the right to reclaiming alienated space. It is also a powerful idea that provides the opportunity to examine people's everyday activities within the context of how space can and should be used to support their lives. These conflicts are expected to escalate as globalization forces and accompanying immigration intensify the cultural strife and divisions within cities.

Lefebvre's concepts are central to examining conflict over Jerusalem. The overt, covert, and even subliminal fights over Jerusalem reveal disputes that are quarrels precisely over what everyday activities have created these spaces and places. Jerusalem is the spatial life-blood of so many groups: secular Jewish Zionists, Orthodox Jewish Zionists, ultra-Orthodox non-Zionists, the Jewish Diaspora, Palestinian refugees, Palestinians living in the West Bank, Palestinians living in East Jerusalem, the Palestinian Diaspora, and, yes, even Christians. Each group believes that it owns some part of the Jerusalem city – not necessarily ownership in the conventional or legal sense, but the right to control and indeed embrace parts of the city as uniquely theirs. Whose right is more justified among the many who feel that their lives are embodied in the holy and not so holy spaces of Jerusalem? Questions over who has rights to the city are central to the Jerusalem dilemma (Rosen and Shlay, 2014).

The City as a Growth Machine

The political dynamics of Jerusalem are largely around the allocation, ownership, and use of space. As noted long ago by Harvey Molotch (1976), land is the stuff of place. Although control over land and space is central to how all cities operate, Jerusalem's focus on the control of development activity is both more intense and intentional than in other places. The politics associated with land use in Jerusalem are local, regional, national, and international in scope. In what other cities do plans to build or tear down housing appear on the evening news or headlined in newspapers and websites all over the world? Jerusalem's development decisions reverberate across oceans and continents. The pronouncement of building a house or locating a trailer on a plot of land in and around Jerusalem has geopolitical effects. The location of roads, bridges, police stations, parking garages, or almost anything that suggests an impending housing development or new neighborhood is a source of serious speculation and agitation. Building housing in Jerusalem is almost never just about building a place to live.

What is built, where, on what, and why is central to cities everywhere. But in Jerusalem more than elsewhere, the power to control development is the power to control the political, social as well as spiritual definition of the city. Besides controlling Jerusalem's size, growth, and population composition, the city's development is believed to affect messianic prophecy, world peace, the next world, and even to have the power to end the world altogether.

Introduced by Molotch (1976), the city as a growth machine was a rebuttal to the prevailing urban paradigm that city development is guided by uncontrollable economic forces. According to growth machine theory, city growth is orchestrated and controlled by a coalition of people representing institutions that materially benefit from growth and development. Growth coalitions are alleged to be engaged in unseen material politics over important development schemes while the bamboozled public is left in the dark.

Underpinning growth coalitions and development activities are questions of democracy and urban governance, considerations of who pays the costs of and who receives the benefits of growth, and the ideological support for growth-oriented development.

According to growth machine theory, groups involved in the planning and promotion of growth are neither elected officials nor specifically empowered to officially control building and development. Growth coalitions consist of economic actors associated with institutions which benefit from land-based growth, including banks, public utilities, universities, real estate developers, and newspapers (Logan and Molotch, 1987; Vessilinov et al., 2007). These people connect with each other over issues associated with downtown (re)development, sports stadiums, and other big projects that encourage land-use intensification, greater densities, and population growth (Strom, 2008). Project advocacy is invisible to the public, and the activities of growth coalitions are largely behind the scenes. Shared social networks permit growth coalitions easy and coordinated access to decision makers (Shlay and Giloth, 1987). In short, growth machine decision making is largely undemocratic.

Urban growth machines, the constellation of local actors promoting large-scale development, differ from place to place. Within large metropolitan areas in the United States, growth coalitions are largely members of the private sector who stand to benefit the most from large-scale development. In Jerusalem, by contrast, metropolitan growth is managed extensively by members of the public sector and, in particular, it is orchestrated by the national government (Shlay and Rosen, 2010). While the government has overt control over the organization of space and over how and when development occurs, its interest in space is not simply about money. Jerusalem's growth machine reflects national political interests as well as economic ones. Its national political interests are twofold. First they are ethnic, to the extent that Judaism represents a national ethnic identity, not simply a religious one. Second, the Jerusalem growth machine is motivated by a national agenda because it ties Jerusalem's metropolitan development to issues of Israel's security – security from feared attacks by Palestinians and different countries in the Middle East.

Growth in and around Jerusalem is local but it is shaped and promoted by national interests that use metropolitan development to hold onto and secure land, and therefore territory. Jerusalem's metropolitan growth does not simply expand Jerusalem as a metropolitan area, it expands Israel as a country. Building housing on land outside the borders of Israel, in the West Bank, is geopolitical for building the nation of Israel. As shown in Chapter 3, each settlement, small and large, has the goal of expanding Jerusalem's frontier as a mechanism for securing new boundaries for the State of Israel.

Religion and nationalism are important but complex components of Jerusalem's growth machine. At one level, building a Jewish state drives Jerusalem's metropolitan expansion as part of Israel's national political identity. While the vast majority of world opinion views settlement development around Jerusalem to be unjust and illegal, Israel justifies and defends these land-based activities as necessary for the preservation of the Israeli nation state and its Jewish people. Israeli nationalism becomes a tool for social control in Jerusalem.

But the overtly religious elements provide a different form of legitimacy to this settlement development. Some of the most politically active settlers are identified as National Religious. They view the settlement of the West Bank as a continuation of the biblical Jewish settlement of the lands of Judea and Samaria. Some of the religious settlers are zealous in their approach, militantly attached to the land, and are vehemently and often violently opposed to any maneuvers to rout them from these communities. Their Zionism is a religious one that is committed to the Land of Israel, the area described in the Bible, not the State of Israel, the most recent political incarnation of this part of the Middle East. The Jerusalem growth machine, as shall be seen, is Zionist but a National Religious form of Zionism. Secular Zionism has been swallowed up by Jerusalem's growth machine and cannot be readily identified as such.

These National Religious settlers are not the same as ultra-Orthodox (Haredi) settlers. The Haredi have moved to West Bank settlements largely because this is where the government has built housing for them. The Haredi West Bank settlements are essentially opportunistic ones inhabited solely for housing not for political purposes. They represent basic tools for relocating religious Jews out of Jerusalem to settlements with more affordable housing. Motivated by free or cheap land in the West Bank, Israel has shifted Jerusalem's population growth from the city itself to its hinterland (Shlay and Rosen, 2010). As such, Jerusalem's growth is also propelled by the economic motivations shared by US growth machines. In many ways, indeed, settlement construction may be viewed as a modern-day land grab (Zertal and Eldar, 2009) similar to the settlement of the Wild West in the United States, where the land was seen as available for the taking, either by stealing or by some other nefarious methods.

Theories of Divided Cities

Cities since the beginning of time have been characterized by the aggregation and amalgamation of different kinds of people. Social diversity is the constitutive element of city life. While urban life is about the spatial concentration of different kinds of people, urban spatial patterns are about the separation and segregation of different kinds of people from each other (S. Hasson, 2001; Denton, 2013).

Cities are effectively spatially divided along a plethora of characteristics: race, family type, income, ethnicity, nationality, religion, religiosity, and more. Land-use segregation compounds these divisions. Neighborhood segregation is so ubiquitous that it is considered a normal and expected characteristic of cities. So, asks Peter Marcuse (1993), "What's so new about divided cities?"

The typical city contains divisions produced by the interplay of housing market mechanisms that segregate land use and populations. Housing markets may be further segmented by race and ethnicity. City neighborhoods vary significantly from each other. But despite the overwhelming dominance of social spatial separation in cities, these patterns do not exhibit the types of divisions manifest in what may be called "divided cities" – the quintessential example of which, as will be seen, is Jerusalem.

Divided cities are socially polarized. Differences are often experienced as violence. The extent of polarization commonly leads to displacement (Bollens, 2000; Silver, 2010). People are not just separate or indifferent. As shown in Chapters 4 and 5, divided cities like Jerusalem emote strong feelings of antipathy bordering on hatred. Cities are also divided when the physical separation coincides with a national cause or some larger political issue that reinforces the social polarization. Divided cities do not need walls to be divided, as shown in Chapter 3.

Divided cities are physically divided (S. Hasson, 1996; Kliot and Mansfield, 1999; Silver, 2010). These boundaries can take on a life of their own. They often become symbols whose power is increased by social antagonism, thus further buttressing the divisions.

Not only do divided cities have social and physical characteristics, they have legal and political ones as well. For a divided city, the source of the separation is often official, legal, and authorized by a political body or group. As discussed in Chapters 4 and 5, the difference in the political rights of Jerusalem's Jews and Palestinians is mirrored and reinforced in Jerusalem's spatial divisions. Segregation may therefore operate largely as an additional process that results in increased divisions. These processes help create the underlying patterns associated with divisions. Segregation may have fluid boundaries but divided cities have clear demarcations, often with physical partitions that divide one side from another.

Theory and Method in the Making Place Project

People have been fighting over Jerusalem for thousands of years (Montefiore, 2012). The underlying reasons for battle keep changing, but a basic constant remains. Jerusalem engenders powerful feelings among its inhabitants and keepers. In part, this is because it is so materially connected to the spiritual world of religion. Yet some of the aura of Jerusalem cannot be explained. Jerusalem is a compelling place because, well, just because. There is magic in the air. There is something in the water. This is a nutty place.

To study Jerusalem, we interviewed and talked to many people. Our focus was not on the biblical or spiritual, although we knew this was important. We wanted to know how people perceived Jerusalem and how it is being shaped in a period where metropolitan development has taken over the world. We also moved around the city, lived with it and lived in it. While we read a myriad of books and articles, were media devotees, and pored over maps and data, we also hung out to take the city's pulse. We went to public spaces and stayed there for long periods. We walked through many neighborhoods. And we talked Jerusalem to everyone and anyone. What is Jerusalem's version of megalopolis? What drives it and defines it? How does this little place, in terms of comparative global city size, manage to shake up the world on a routine basis?

This book relies on analyses of what we call spatial politics. These represent the social and political struggles over ownership and control of each part of Jerusalem – not ownership in the legal sense but as a social and collective idea. We look at the shaping of consensus and divisions around Jerusalem, with a focus on land, location, and spatial communities.

To interpret what we have discovered, we rely on theory – theories of political hegemony, spatial development, growth, and divisions. What are the forces that spatially distribute people, how are divisions manifested spatially, and how does order prevail? For all sorts of good reasons, including poverty, social antagonisms, and political divisions, Jerusalem could be expected to be routinely on the brink of falling apart. Yet it does not. Or, rather, it has not yet. Nevertheless, the conflicts that hold Jerusalem together today could always cause it to fall apart tomorrow.

3

What Is Jerusalem?

Introduction

A space is not an authentic place unless it is mediated through a social world (Gieryn, 2000). No space is a place unless it is touched in some way by the people who move through it and make it theirs. In the social world of place creation, a space's users give it an identity, transforming it from an abstract thing where air and earth meet to a fully fledged part of the social world.

But place identities are neither static nor constant. In the realm of taking social ownership of space, places enter the disparate worlds of nationalism, political strife, ethnic tensions, neighborhood change, reinvestment, disinvestment, and more. Places are parts of economic systems and political regimes. Place identities represent the social ownership of different spaces. Developing a place identity is a critical part of place formation.

Social ownership, the claiming of a space as socially one's own, is not the same as political ownership of space. Political ownership is really a form of sovereignty or command over spaces. Places can be parts of countries, states, cities: that is, political entities. But how people take ownership of space is about how they use and think about it as a place – their place. Political and social ownership may or may not be compatible. Indeed, it is through the absence of congruence between political and social ownership of places that conflict emerges.

One of the major features of urban places is that differences can coexist, that distinctly different places can exist separately side by side. The spatial distribution of these place identities represents the social mosaic of ethnically and racially defined neighborhoods that make up the city. Place identities divide spaces into the different places that constitute the city as a whole. All cities have divisions based on diversity. This is a central feature of how we define urban places as cities. Being different is not a reason for conflict between places. It is how differences and divisions are politically and socially managed.

Theories of divided cities (see Chapter 2) purport that they are different from other cities. In the realm of divided cities, different identities collide with each other (Bollens, 1998; Kliot and Mansfeld, 1999; Silver, 2010; Dumper, 2014). It is this collision of identities that creates and shapes conflict, particularly in cities like Jerusalem.

An example of identity collision is seen in the recent spatial history of Al Quds University and the Parliament of the Palestinian Authority, both located in Abu Dis, a Palestinian locality adjacent to East Jerusalem. Al Quds University calls itself the "Arab University in Jerusalem."[1] Al Quds is the Arabic word for holy, which is also the Palestinian name for Jerusalem. Al Quds University is essentially the Jerusalem-based Hebrew University counterpart for the Arab/Palestinian community of Jerusalem. Next to Al Quds University is the Parliament building of the Palestinian Authority, the legislative body that is charged with governing the Palestinian-controlled areas within the West Bank.

In 2003, the Israeli government released a plan to locate its security barrier/fence/wall down the middle of the Al Quds University campus. This would have split the campus in two. Protests by the international community as well as Palestinian leaders ultimately led to an agreement to locate the barrier/fence/wall on the edge of the campus, effectively walling both the Parliament and the entire Al Quds campus out of East Jerusalem.

From Israel's perspective, the barrier/fence/wall works to shut out, and therefore eliminate, all remaining Palestinian institutions from Jerusalem. This continues the Oslo Agreement, which prohibited political organizations representing Palestinians from operating in Jerusalem. The political logic of this spatial separation from Israel's point of view is that an East Jerusalem devoid of Palestinian institutions cannot be claimed as a future Palestinian capital because it has ceased to function by and for Palestinians. For Israel, East Jerusalem's place identity is Israel because its boundaries are not shared by these important Palestinian institutions: Al Quds University and the Palestinian Parliament. How can a place be Palestinian if it is no longer part of the social world of Palestinians?

Although technically walled out of East Jerusalem, Al Quds and the Palestinian Authority continue to claim East Jerusalem as theirs. They may not be formally included as part of Israel's Jerusalem, but they do not purport to be of Jewish Jerusalem; they are of Arab Jerusalem. From a Palestinian perspective, a municipal boundary or even a wall cannot divorce these institutions from their Arab East Jerusalem constituency. These Palestinian institutions are disconnected from Israel by the barrier/fence/wall, but not from East Jerusalem, or really any Jerusalem, however it is defined. Abu Dis, the suburban home of these Palestinian institutions, is not outside of Jerusalem. It is as much a part of Arab East Jerusalem as any other Palestinian neighborhood in the vicinity. Israel may think it has walled out a place, but physical barriers cannot wall out memories of places, memories and dreams of the ownership of place. What we call Arab Jerusalem was created and shaped by the everyday life of its Palestinian inhabitants.

This example may be used to address several questions about Jerusalem. Have the definitions of Jerusalem shifted with the seeming expulsion of the Palestinian Parliament and the Al Quds University campus? By being walled out, have these Palestinian institutions left the place called Jerusalem? Has a physical barrier/ fence/wall reduced or eliminated the Palestinian claim on East Jerusalem? Has the Palestinian/Arab place identity remained stable over time, transcending seemingly minor physical obstacles like concrete walls? Is the barrier/fence/wall one of the many nails in the coffin for Jerusalem as the capital of a future Palestinian state?

This chapter asks the question "What is Jerusalem?" It lays out a process that has blurred and shifted Jerusalem's boundaries throughout the course of Israel's conflict as a nation state with Palestinians and their Arab world. It shows how Israel's development of the urban landscape has worked at altering perceptions of what Jerusalem's boundaries are and whether these boundaries are considered legitimate, politically suspect, or both. In the language of Lefebvre, this chapter examines Israel's challenge to create an everyday life from the manipulation of place and space from above. Israel's attempts to mold its new Jerusalem is an attempt to create abstract space out of places that have been socially owned for centuries. It is a fight for control over Jerusalem. And the visibility of the struggle shows clearly that the fight is far from over.

Jerusalem's growth politics in the name of nationalism and the security of its national territory have been fomented by the Israeli government. Jerusalem has a growth machine that takes political ownership of contested space by building housing on it. The process and ultimate result are considered to be a not so silent war on the Palestinian community and its government, the Palestinian Authority. From Israel's perspective, the territory on which they build belongs to them. But because this ownership is contested across the globe, they build on it so there are no illusions of who owns what. Building for Israel is an assault on Palestinian social ownership of land, space, and ultimately place.

Jerusalem's nationalist growth machine is behind the settlements, gaining legitimacy because it purports to support the desire by the National Religious to gain control over what they consider to be their biblical home – Judea and Samaria. Settlement expansion appears to be motivated by ethno-national-religious interests represented by the ever-increasing more right-wing segments of Israel's government and population.

By constructing settlements, Israel also builds housing, a lot of it. The housing component of the settlement development around Jerusalem is, however, often overlooked. As will be discussed, by building inexpensive and new housing, settlements also fulfill a huge pent-up demand for living space in Jerusalem, thus cementing support for these developments. Jerusalemites who take advantage of this subsidized housing view themselves as making an economic decision, not a political one. By being the location of new, cheap housing, settlements appear similar to their North American sub-urban counterparts, which offered up cheap housing to the masses moving out of central cities. But in addition, having cheap housing available in settlements takes some of the heat off the push for gen-trification of Jerusalem's city center. The city's growth machine builds expensive and enormously profitable condominiums for the wealthy while shifting its less affluent population into settlements.

The resulting shifts in the distribution of population and housing have increased political tensions in the region. Settlement development, however construed, fuels Palestinian rage, Israeli extreme right-wing vigilantism, intense international disapproval, and serious threats of political and economic sanctions. At the same time, talk about peace plans almost always zeros in on which Palestinian-identified spaces will be expelled from Israel for what is termed a final-status agreement.

Participants in the intensification of land development around Jerusalem appear happy about settlements as economic stimulants as well as political acts. Land and property values in the wake of Israeli development are increasing, no doubt because these areas become connected to the Jerusalem municipality. But unlike US growth machines, which live for exchange value, the Israeli growth machine has other fish to fry. In the name of Israel's politi-cal sovereignty, growth is about taking social control over land in order to retain political dominance.

Jerusalem's development has large and uneven effects on the spatial lives of different groups. This reinforces its divided city aspect. For example, Jewish Jerusalemites revel in the bubble created by a wall that encapsulates and seemingly protects their daily lives. Alternatively, Palestinian cohabitants struggle to live with and traverse the wall-like barriers which operate as per-manent obstacles to everyday life. A single difference between the everyday lives of Palestinian and Jewish Jerusalemites was crystalized for Shlay one evening on the bus coming into Jerusalem from Ramallah. At the busy Qalandia checkpoint, which services thousands of people every day, she was ordered off the bus, having misplaced her visa. Alongside many Palestinians, she then experienced a lengthy and nerve-racking entry process at the hands of army personnel who were part of the checkpoint security system. She walked through what seemed like a maze of concrete walls and metal gates before she was released to the other side. Half an hour after she was admitted back to Jerusalem, she stopped at her local upscale grocery store, where people shopped oblivious to the barrier/fence/wall. The incongruity was striking, and it brought home to her how inordinately different the everyday lives of these two groups are.

Each and every move that attempts to shift Jerusalem place ownership from one group to another wreaks havoc with the already withering prospects for peaceful negotiations. Everyday life cannot be wiped away with bulldozers and concrete. Palestinians and their advocates view Israeli development as illegitimate land grabbing. Any Israeli incursion into their land or villages is viewed as an element of political policy to reduce or eliminate the Palestinian presence in Jerusalem. Yet for Israelis, development and land-use policy in Jerusalem is advanced in the name of community building and security, Israel views Palestinians as obstacles to development that could yield archaeological finds about Jewish civilizations, as threats to security, and as getting in the way of building a Jewish state of, by, and for Jews.

For Israelis, the growth of Jerusalem represents the normal expansion of a thriving metropolis. For Palestinians, Jerusalem's development is nothing short of imperialism. This chapter addresses the spatial development activities that have been fundamental to shaping the conflict over Jerusalem. These are: (1) the post-1967 building of Jerusalem's new neighborhoods accompanying Israeli annexation of East Jerusalem; (2) the initiation and development of Jewish settlements over the Green Line, outside Jerusalem's municipal borders and in the West Bank; (3) Holy Basin development activities, including Jewish incursion into Palestinian neighborhoods and archaeological excavations; (4) the creation of the Israeli security barrier otherwise known as the fence or "apart-heid wall"; and (5) the development of the Jerusalem Light Rail system. It is through these place-making struggles that we examine the changing dynamics of power over Jerusalem.

International Jerusalem and the United Nations Partition

Students of globalization and world systems analysis portray global cities as the orchestrators of global capitalism (Sassen 1994, 2001; Harvey, 2003). Jerusalem's global importance, however, has little to do with managing the world's economy (Alfasi and Fenster, 2005, 2009). Pedestrian concerns with moving mere money are nothing compared to Jerusalem's spiritual capacity to move heaven and earth and arbitrate eternal salvation.

Jerusalem's political importance has ebbed and flowed over more than two thousand years and its rulers have built it up and torn it down with great frequency. The last several decades of the city's centrality to current Israeli politics are mere drops of sand in its past. Jerusalem has been the stuff of empire that includes the Egyptians, Persians, Romans, Ottomans, British, and more. Its contemporary physical make-up is the composite of the myriad of institutions that were destroyed or moved on as one group took ownership of the city from another.

Jerusalem is the birth- and death-place of powers that have come and gone. Its pittance of years spent with the modern state of Israel is nothing compared to the hundreds of years the city was held by the Romans or Ottomans. This historical perspective should make it clear that Jerusalem was never, and probably will never be, definitively owned by any group or civilization.

Jerusalem's fame is not as a city of peace but as a city of con-quest and conflict. Its symbolic and social prominence has inspired neither cooperation nor solidarity. Rather, its historical legacy is about divisions, conflict, violence, destruction, and separation (Montefiore, 2012). Given its role in world history, it should not be surprising that contemporary Jerusalem is politically messy. The city is now at the center of an international political quagmire, one probably no more convoluted than others in its long lifetime.

The Jerusalem of today is the capital of the world's only Jewish nation state, the State of Israel, a country founded immediately after the Holocaust decimated the large and vibrant Jewish communities of Europe. But Al Quds (Jerusalem) is the desired capital of a would-be future Palestinian state, a nation state that would represent and govern the Palestinian people. Yerushalayim/Al Quds, as it is known, respectively, in Hebrew and Arabic, has symbolic, historical, and religious significance for the reigning State of Israel and the current stateless Palestinians.

The conflict over Jerusalem is part of a much larger disagreement over the future of the Palestinian people in the Middle East. With the decline of the Ottoman Empire following their defeat with the Germans in World War I, the Middle East was divided among Italy, France, Great Britain, and the newly established Arab countries. Although these demarcated areas were called countries, the political boundaries often had no historical or "natural" basis, rendering the borders' defensibility questionable (Biger, 2008).

These countries were occupied by their victorious European powers. From 1917 to 1947, Greater Palestine (including Jordan), home to both Arabs and Jews, was under the British Mandate (Khalidi, 2010). The concept of separating Jews and Arabs was put on the political table, and gained increasing world legitimacy (Biger, 2008).

In 1922 the largest chunk of land was taken out of Palestine to establish the independent sovereign state of Jordan. Officially it was granted independence in 1946 and has been known since as the Hashemite Kingdom of Jordan East of the Jordan River. In 1947, Israel was partitioned out of a much larger area to create the first Jewish state in modern times (Dumper, 1997). Another area of land was partitioned to become a future state of what would later be called Palestine. A third area was the proposed international city of Jerusalem (Dumper, 2002). The anticipated municipality included the politically incorporated city of Jerusalem, its Old City, and the surrounding towns and villages. Alongside Jordan, Israel and

Palestine would become countries on their own. Jerusalem was to
be governed by the United Nations (see Figure 3.1).

Jerusalem and the 1948 War: Constructing the Green Line

Instead of accepting the partitioned areas allocated by the United
Nations, the Arab countries in the Middle East chose to wage war
against the newly created Israel. This war, while devastating to
both sides, was unsuccessful in defeating and annihilating Israel. As
noted in Chapter 1, Israel, which won the war, called it the War
of Independence. The Palestinians, who were the ultimate losers
of the war, called it the Nakba, the disaster. Israel became a state
for the Jews living in this part of the Middle East. Palestinians in
this part of the region did not become a country on their own.
With the Arab defeat suffered in this war, land that would have
become Palestine was instead allocated to Jordan and Egypt. Jews
received their own state including 61 percent of the area that
was originally intended to be for the Palestinians (Biger, 2008).
Palestinians did not receive a state. Over seven hundred thousand
left or were expelled from what is now Israel, moving to refugee
camps throughout the region (Morris, 2008; Shavit, 2013). This
Arab position to reject a Palestinian state and to maintain ejected
Palestinians as official refugees has come to haunt the region as well
as the rest of the world (Shiblak, 1996; Akram, 2002).

An Arab/Palestinian state and a regional definition of Jerusalem
officially died with the 1948 war. Jerusalem acquired a new border,
known as the Green Line. This border created a divided Jerusalem.
East Jerusalem (predominately Muslim) became part of Jordan.
West Jerusalem (predominately Jewish) was claimed by Israel and
became its capital city. The Green Line became the official boundary of the State of Israel from 1949 to 1967. Jerusalem operated as
the frontier border between Israel and Jordan (Kliot and Mansfeld,
1999; Lustick, 2004; Biger, 2008).

The Jordanian part of Jerusalem included the Old City. This

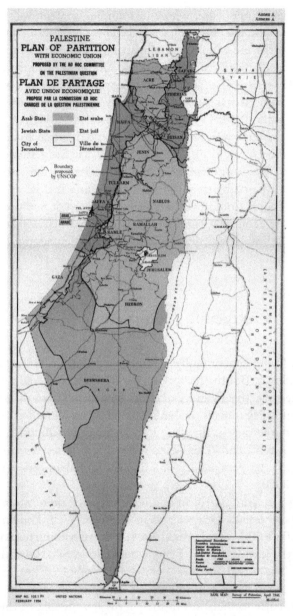

Figure 3.1 The United Nations 1947 Partition Plan for Palestine (United Nations)

was the city's inner core, whose surrounding ancient walls defined it as an important historical symbol. The Old City of Jerusalem contained the most important Christian, Jewish, and Muslim religious symbols, artifacts, and locations. Although small in area (less than half a square mile, as noted in Chapter 1), very old, and somewhat decrepit, it was the regional trophy associated with the war's end (Dumper, 2002; Calame and Charlesworth, 2009).

With the 1948 war, the concept of a united Jerusalem under the reins of the United Nations was tabled. What was Jerusalem after this war? Was it one city that had been divided into two parts, or was it two completely different cities, one in Jordan and the other in Israel? Could two Jerusalems coexist, not just as different political or economic entities, but as different places that people believed in? What was this place named Jerusalem after it was split in two?

Constructing a Jerusalem of Memory

Politically and economically, Jerusalem operated as two cities after the 1948 war. But the reality of a divided Jerusalem did not mesh with the collective memory of either Jerusalem's Jews (in Israel) or Jerusalem's Palestinians (in Jordan). Both sides identified with the part of the Jerusalem they had lost. Longing for the other side of Jerusalem remained. This desire by each group for the other half challenged the permanence of a divided Jerusalem (Friedland and Hecht, 2000).

For Israel, particularly among religious Jews, there was a yearning for the Jewish Quarter and its Western Wall, known as the Kotel of the Old City (Lustick, 2004) – the remaining foundational wall of the Jewish Second Temple built almost two thousand years earlier. The Kotel became a powerful symbol of loss not only among Israeli Jews but among the Diaspora as well. For Jews, this particular formulation of their Jerusalem devoid of the Kotel was unacceptable. This was emphasized by a long-time Jerusalem resident.

Jerusalem itself is a vague concept. I don't really care what it is. All that matters is the Kotel. We need unhindered access to Jerusalem. Not blocked and threatened. The importance of Jerusalem is tied to being part of the Kotel. The rest of Jerusalem is necessary only to the extent that the core is protected. (Interview, 2008)

Palestinians in East Jerusalem also longed for the Jerusalem they had left and lost. In the course of the 1948 war, many Palestinians left their homes and villages (Falah, 1996). Whether they left by force or voluntarily is still debated, although contemporary historians seem clear that Israel often used coercion (Morris, 2008; Shavit, 2013). A large number of Palestinians became refugees, took on the identity of being permanently in exile, and filled up the stateless United Nations refugee camps located in Lebanon, Syria, Jordan, and elsewhere. Insisting that they were routed from their homes by war and deliberate forms of Israeli mayhem, they held on to the memories of place – their homes, way of life, and the Arab villages that had now become Jewish neighborhoods: Malka (Arabic: المالحة), Baka (Arabic: بقعه), Ein Kerem (Arabic: عين كارم), Catamon (Arabic: قطمون), and more. These memories coalesced around their eventual demand for the right of return, to go back to their homes, but even more so to a way of life.

The two Jerusalems remained separate for almost two decades in which the memories of loss did not dissipate but instead grew stronger. The people of Israeli Jewish Jerusalem (West) pined for the Old City and the Kotel. Jewish Jerusalem (West) was only partial, while the other Jerusalem (the Old City) was lost to them. Arab Jerusalem (East), now part of Jordan, was also incomplete without the neighborhoods in West Jerusalem they had lost and left behind (Tamari, 1999).

But for the moment, war had settled the borders of Jerusalem. Israel got on with developing the political and social infrastructure to govern from West Jerusalem. The Jordanian government largely ignored East Jerusalem in favor of its capital Amman (Klein, 2010). The two Jerusalems existed side by side divided by a border known as the Green Line.

In 1967, another war erupted. In six days, the geopolitical

landscape of Jerusalem, Israel, and the Middle East dramatically changed. Israel, the victor in war, took over huge swaths of territory. A major, if not the most important, conquest was East Jerusalem. Besides East Jerusalem and its Old City, Israel took over Jordan's West Bank, the Egyptian Sinai and the Gaza Strip, and Syria's Golan Heights (Shlay and Rosen, 2010).

Following the Six-Day War, as it was to be called, Israel declared that it now had control of all Jerusalem, which it claimed as its political and religious capital (Friedland and Hecht, 2000).

Moving Beyond the Green Line

The Jerusalem that existed before 1967 epitomized the divided city; after the war was over, however, it continued to be divided, despite the rhetoric of unification (Bollens, 2007, 2012). Israel could claim the mainly Jewish West Jerusalem which contained the country's political infrastructures, its Knesset, and other buildings reflecting its sovereignty.

Arab East Jerusalem taken from Jordan was not comparable in political stature or physicality to Jewish West Jerusalem. Its most significant political landmark was the Orient House (see Figure 3.2) – the Husseini family compound that represented what was left of Jerusalem's Palestinian aristocracy (Rosen and Shlay, 2014). No Jews lived in Arab East Jerusalem. The Green Line continued to symbolically separate the east and west of the city, even though they had the same name (Calame and Charlesworth, 2009; Shlay and Rosen, 2010).

A third Jerusalem reentered the Jewish public sphere. This was the Old City, which had been part of Jordan and off limits to the Jews of Israel. Now the Old City was in Israeli hands. Its capture was considered a victory for Jewish nationalism and for Jews all over the world (Friedland and Hecht, 2000).

But there were also two additional Jerusalems, each representing a Jerusalem of memory and dreams, a Jerusalem kept alive in the mind. A Palestinian Jerusalem of memory lived in the minds of

Figure 3.2 The Orient House (© Anne Shlay)

the thousands of Arab refugees with homes and villages that they had lost in 1948 to the Israelis as well as other Palestinians living in East Jerusalem, the West Bank, and in places across the globe. This Jerusalem of memory, to which eventually millions of Palestinians would stake out a claim, was not divided. The Green Line had no relevance for it (Khalidi, 2010).

A Jerusalem of memory also existed for Jews, but this memory was older and much of its historical reference was the Bible. Was this Jerusalem of memory true, that is, empirically verifiable? The work of authenticating the Jewish Jerusalem of memory became the work of Israeli archaeology, a political activity important enough to warrant its own public agency within the Israel government – the Israeli Department of Antiquities and later the Israeli Antiquities Authority (Mizrachi, 2012).

Archaeologists would dig up what some called early Jewish civilizations that would be used to support the claim that the Jewish presence in Jerusalem spanned over three thousand years. This

Jewish Jerusalem of memory would eventually come to compete
with the Palestinian Jerusalem of memory (Brin, 2006).

The 1967 war gave Israel the opportunity to lay claim to a
tangible contemporary Jerusalem upon which it could build apartment buildings, roads, bridges, and to which it could relocate
growing numbers of its citizens. Israel called this process one of
uniting Jerusalem. Palestinians called it occupation. Critical schol-
ars call it colonialism and the Judaization of space (Lustick, 2004;
Amirav, 2009).

Both sides' claims to the Jerusalem of memory would be used
to capture the public imagination and therefore help to establish
the hegemonic presence of "their" Jerusalem. When Palestinians
brought out their keys to their former homes, the world listened
to their pain, particularly as the number of refugees spread across
many refugee camps in Syria, Lebanon, Jordan, the West Bank,
and Gaza (Bowker, 2003).

Israel's Jerusalem of memory was also compelling and captured
the imagination of millions as well. The eventual excavation of
the tunnels beneath the Old City and the archaeological wonders
of the City of David became the evidence that Israel could use to
claim that Jerusalem had been theirs, not for one hundred or two
hundred years, but for several millennia.

These two Jerusalems of memory, one Palestinian and one
Jewish, are political tools in the fight for recognition as the side
that can claim the most correct and legitimate right to its Jerusalem.
Each group works at making its memory more compelling and
true. Each group works at getting followers who believe in its
memory narrative. Inevitably, this also means that one group works
to discredit the memory of the other (Reiter, 2008; Mann, 2011).

The Green Line shifts one way or the other depending on
which memory is triumphal at any point. Palestinian claims are
largely directed at two spatial phenomena: the neighborhoods and
villages left in 1948 and Haram al-Sharif (the Temple Mount) and
the Al-Aqsa Mosque in the Old City (Falah, 1996; Reiter, 2008).
The former legitimates the continuation of a Palestinian presence
in and around the city. The latter is part of the Muslim narrative of
Islam's religious claims to Jerusalem.

The Jewish claims to memories of Jerusalem are recreated and shaped by Israeli government activity. There are two ways to create memories. One way is to create and shape what is: that is, create a present reality that can be remembered later. The second is to create a narrative of the past, the construction of a historical narrative that is believable, verifiable, and, most important, disseminated so that people know about it.

Israel's most prominent method for creating and reinforcing memories of Jerusalem is through its strategic use of power and control over land, housing and communities (Shlay and Rosen, 2010). By creating a neighborhood or a street, it is creating what can and will be remembered. Places can also be claimed as memories de novo through renaming the names of places or streets (Azaryahu, 1996, 1997; Azaryahu and Kellerman-Barrett, 1999; Azaryahu and Golan, 2001; Rose-Redwood et al., 2010; Shoval, 2013). The city of al-Ludd (Arab) became Lod (Israeli). Ramlah (Arab) became Ramla (Israeli). Place making erases memories of Palestinians, Arabs, whoever. The narrative is this: we came, we conquered, they left and it is ours.

In Israel, archaeology is used to create a narrative of a very long-term Jewish presence both in the region and in Jerusalem in particular. This archaeological narrative permits Jews to claim a presence in the region for centuries. Jews are not carpet-baggers to Israel. They belong there just the way they always have. The narrative is this: we came, we left, we came back, we left and now we are back and here to stay.

United Jerusalem

With the capacity to control development after 1967, Israel looked to alter Jerusalem's place as the country's geographical end point (Kotek, 1999). It sought a new united Jerusalem which would transcend the Green Line (see Figure 3.3). Jerusalem, it decreed, would never be divided again. The watchword of the days, weeks, and years that followed was a call for a permanently

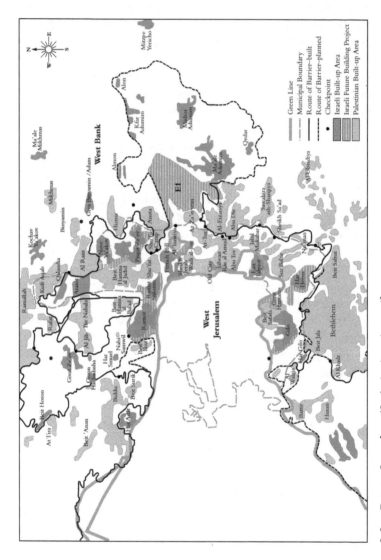

Figure 3.3 Greater Jerusalem (*Ir Amin, ir-amin.org.il*)

united Jerusalem – a Jerusalem whose physical structure, land-use patterns, and demographics worked to protect against any kind of future partition ever again. Israel called for permanent unity in a city that linked urban unification to the politics of its ultimate survival (Friedland and Hecht, 2000).

Israel launched plans to thwart any future partition of Jerusalem. It used its sovereign power to declare itself in charge of almost all of the city. Despite international admonishment and disapproval, Israel annexed East Jerusalem to West Jerusalem. It made East Jerusalem a part of Israel although a mere few countries or governments recognized the legality or legitimacy of this maneuver.

Israel chose development as its tool for conquering East Jerusalem. The plan for unification was to make it an integral part of Israel. Israel took over East Jerusalem by building the physical infrastructure of place – housing, schools, sewers, roads, and more (M. Benvenisti, 1998; Pullan et al., 2007). The strategy was to create "facts on the ground." A Jerusalem planner during that period described the effects of these conquests: "In 1967, Israel was an empire. We threw people out to build Mamilla. We built up Jerusalem all the way to Mount Scopus" (interview, 2007). Scores of "new neighborhoods" were built on these newly annexed territories, removing any spatial divisions between Jerusalem's Mount Scopus (previously spatially isolated) and West Jerusalem. Mount Scopus had originally "belonged" to Israel after the 1948 war but had been an Israeli enclave disconnected from the "main land." Building communities between West Jerusalem and Mount Scopus entailed Israel developing a large swath of East Jerusalem to connect to Mount Scopus.

Within a short amount of time, these newly established communities on previously Jordanian land were indistinguishable from other Jewish neighborhoods (S. Hasson, 2002; Shoval, 2007). According to an Israeli Housing Ministry planner, "This development was designed to connect Jerusalem to Mount Scopus. Then they created satellite neighborhoods. Municipal boundaries were extended to maximize the amount of land in Jerusalem while minimizing the amount of Arabs included within Jerusalem boundaries" (interview, 2007). The new neighborhoods on the

annexed land within East Jerusalem represented the concretiza-
tion of Israel's claim on the territory with the goal of rendering it
permanently part of Israel.

Popular perceptions of these developments were polarized.
Israel was euphoric. It proclaimed Yom Yerushalayim or Jerusalem
Day as a public holiday to celebrate Israel's liberation of East
Jerusalem and Jerusalem's "reunification" within Israel (Lustick,
2008). In 1980, Israel proclaimed the "united" Jerusalem as its
capital, legitimated through national legislation. From now on,
changing the city's municipal boundaries would require additional
law making.

Palestinians were distraught and utterly emphatic that Israel's
conquest of East Jerusalem was unjust. According to a Palestinian
activist working with a major organization, "Israel declared
Jerusalem as its own capital without any consultation with the original people. It installed a regime in Jerusalem to kick out people.
It set up laws so the Palestinians could be kicked out by revok-
ing their citizenship" (interview, 2008). Palestinians had already
marked Israel's Independence Day as the Nakba, a day of tragedy
and disaster (Sa'di and Abu-Lughod, 2007). They now marked
Israel's Jerusalem Day as one of mourning and developed their
own "Quds Day," a day of international protest against Zionism.
Palestinians continued to see themselves as refugees in their "own
land." And this identity as refugees, kept alive the narrative that
they would return to their homes because "refugees retain the idea
of collective memories of land and community" (interview, 2008).

The United Nations and the international community dispar-
aged Israel's claim that it had united Jerusalem. One European
Union official was clear that despite the new neighborhoods, East
Jerusalem belonged to the Palestinians: "East Jerusalem is part of the
occupied territory which is supposed to become part of Palestine.
Israel may not agree that East Jerusalem will be part of Palestine.
Israel is doing what it can to make East Jerusalem part of Israel"
(interview, 2008). The United Nations viewed the annexation
of East Jerusalem within Israel as illegal. From an international
perspective, East Jerusalem was (and is) occupied territory and
Jerusalem's new Jewish neighborhoods are (and were) settlements.

Israel, however, persisted with its development activities, using them to solidify its conquest of Arab Jerusalem (previously under Jordanian control).

Continued high levels of immigration fueled the seeming insatiable demand for housing in Jerusalem (Cohen, 2002). Israel has given automatic citizenship to any Jew who wants to move to Israel. Jewish immigrants come from all over the world, from Africa, Asia, Europe, and North and South America. The new neighborhoods of Jerusalem satisfied an enormous pent-up demand for more housing. Residential construction in East Jerusalem relieved pressure on the overbuilt West Jerusalem, whose Jewish residents had already populated the many vacant homes of former Arab residents.

The Israeli government used new neighborhoods as a way to expand Jerusalem and to remove threats of further division. Israel viewed its planning to unify Jerusalem as the logical expression of Zionism and doggedly continued. Israeli officials did not care that these new neighborhoods were viewed by others as nothing less than imperialism.

Israel had conquered East Jerusalem in the 1967 war. But conquests of war are, by international law, temporary (E. Benvenisti, 2012). Although the housing developments in Jerusalem were called new neighborhoods by Israel, they were called settlements by the rest of the world. Yet Israel's unification of Jerusalem was appealing to the international Jewish community. Jerusalem was the holy city for all Jews, implying the religious and ideological claims that supported Jerusalem's unification. Jews raised in the Diaspora, the community outside of Israel, were directed in their temples and synagogues to sit in those places closest to Jerusalem and its Western or Wailing Wall. The conquest of Jerusalem was not simply a military victory. The unification of Jerusalem was viewed as destiny for Jewish people everywhere.

But what did it materially and physically mean to unite what was considered Jewish (West) and Arab (East) Jerusalem? It meant populating Arab Jerusalem with Jewish Israeli neighborhoods, not uniting Jewish and Arab communities with each other. Although the term "unification" was used to describe the post-1967 housing developments in East Jerusalem, the goal was in essence to take over. Israel intended to make Arab Jerusalem Israeli.

And Palestinians accurately understood the difference. As noted by one major Israeli planner involved in building the new neighborhoods, "I called the new communities neighborhoods. But my Palestinian friends called them settlements" (interview, 2007). The building of Jewish neighborhoods in East Jerusalem was called by one Palestinian advocate a "Jewish settlement program" (interview, 2008).

For Jews, new neighborhoods blurred the Green Line, the cease-fire border from the 1948 war. They had built new neighborhoods "beyond the Green Line," a phrase that came to stand for any form of perceived illegitimate Israeli development. For Israel, building beyond the Green Line was erasing a border that kept them from their most treasured places: the Kotel, the Temple Mount, and the Old City. Building beyond the Green Line was also building settlements outside of Jerusalem.

For Palestinians, the situation was entirely different. Building "beyond the Green Line" did not erase or blur the boundary. On the contrary, it sharpened the boundary and heightened its visibility. Israel's disregard for the Green Line created the impetus for Arab Jerusalem to claim foul.

West Bank Israel Settlements and Metropolitan Jerusalem

One of the major ironies of the Israeli–Palestinian situation is the overwhelming confusion over the geography of the conflict. Israel annexes East Jerusalem to West Jerusalem but the rest of the world does not recognize East Jerusalem as a part of either Jerusalem or Israel. People identified as Israeli citizens populate East Jerusalem but the world does not recognize where they live as Israel, even though the children who are born there are called Israelis. The places where Palestinians live are considered by Israel to be part of the country but they have trouble being recognized as legal residents, let alone citizens. Palestinian children born in East Jerusalem, in what is considered Israel, are citizens neither of Israel nor of anywhere else. Palestinians are given Palestinian passports: that is, passports for a sovereign country that effectively does not exist. As one Palestinian advocate put it, "Israel annexed the place but not the people" (interview, 2008).

Jerusalem's political geography is confusing in part because its territory is disputed. Oddly, this may be the clearest and most definitive statement that can be made about the Jerusalem situation. Maps do not clarify who owns what because it is precisely the ownership of territory over which people disagree – maps argue one side or the other. Maps therefore physically represent these political realities or unrealities (Wallach, 2011). Knowing which group or organization produced a map is essential to understanding why their Jerusalem is represented in this or that way. But in many respects, one must have a detailed understanding of Jerusalem's spatial politics before a map can be understood and intelligible.

The obfuscation and de-obfuscation of Jerusalem requires work. Moreover, as it is a disputed territory, different sides have a supreme interest in seeing their representation of Jerusalem vindicated and accepted. The battle over what is Jerusalem is fought everywhere by anyone and everyone connected with the city, however construed.

This battle over what is Jerusalem and its hinterland is not fought simply with bombs, bullets, and threats of coercion (although that happens too), but also with other, less violent but perhaps more potent paraphernalia: the "facts on the ground."

Taking over territory is a process. It may start with the positioning of a trailer, more commonly known as a caravan. A generator provides electricity. Water is piped in. A road gets built as well as a police station. More caravans and more people come. What was an "illegal" outpost gets legalized. And sooner or later, a "tender" is issued, a request for proposals from developers to build permanent housing.

The creation of greater metropolitan Jerusalem is also part of the ongoing ideological work of Jerusalem's political representation – its representation to school children, immigrants, politicians, the

police, the military, heads of state, and more. What is considered to
be "metropolitan Jerusalem" is an enigma for some, a travesty for
others, and wishful thinking for the rest. "There is no metropolitan Jerusalem," one of our Palestinian interviewees said. "There is
only occupied territory. I am against the concept of metropolitan
Jerusalem" (interview, 2007).

Through Israeli West Bank development, Jerusalem has become
the metropolitan hub and ground zero for Israeli settlement construction. What are these settlements? The most general definition
is that settlements are spatial communities. More specifically in
this case, Israel's settlements are spatial communities established on
its occupied territories, that is, lands it took in the 1967 war. Any
physical developments on land, including the new neighborhoods
of East Jerusalem and part of the West Bank, are deemed settlements (Zertal and Eldar, 2007).

The settlements use housing development and the ensuing residential mobility and relocation of Israelis to permanently settle the
new population (Thawaba and Al-Rimmawi, 2012). While most
of the world views Israel's settlements to be illegal, settlements
have continued to be built.

How international law is perceived, litigated, and applied to
Israeli settlements is both simple and complex. The simple side
is the position that countries take on the legality of Israeli settlements. For the international community, Israel's settlements are
illegal. For Israel, its settlements are not. For the international community, Israel's settlements are being built and exist on occupied
territory. For Israel, settlement land is not occupied territory.

There are fundamental disagreements on the interpretation
of international law. For most of the international community,
Israel's post-1967 developments over the Green Line are viewed as
illegal based on its interpretations of a major international law – the
Fourth Geneva Convention. This addresses the use of land and the
protection of civilians during times of war. It stipulates that war-
time occupiers may not transfer their own populations into these
areas because control is temporary. War-time occupiers may not
treat land and their residing communities as their own because they
are not sovereign over either the land or the communities living

on it. According to the international community, Israel is a war-time occupier and its settlements represent illegal development and property transfers.

Israel's contention is that the Fourth Geneva Convention is not applicable because it believes that the West Bank has no recognized sovereignty. West Bank sovereignty is legally complicated. After the 1948 war, Jordan controlled the West Bank, annexed it, and gave West Bank residents Jordanian citizenship. Although at this time, it would appear that Jordan was sovereign over the West Bank, its sovereignty was, however, contested by most of the international community and it was viewed by most of the world as an occupying power. But when in 1967 the West Bank was then taken over by Israel, it was Jordan that was viewed by Britain and to some extent the United States to be the sovereign country over the West Bank with the recognition that West Bank residents were Jordanian citizens. Yet most of the world viewed Jordan as an occupier. Therefore, from an Israeli point of view, taking control of the West Bank (including East Jerusalem) was not an occupation because there was no reigning sovereignty in place.

Whether Jordan was ever or never legally sovereign over the West Bank will be debated for some time. In 1988, it gave up on its claims to the West Bank, indicating that until that point, it viewed itself as the reigning power there. But when it gave up its claims to the West Bank, Jordan's *de jure* status became irrelevant because it gave up on its *de facto* right to the territory.

If the West Bank has no sovereign power over it, what, then, is Israel's status as the builder of settlements? Even within Israel itself, the legal status of its settlements is contested between different branches of government (M. Benvenisti, 1998). In addition, various Israeli government reports have taken disparate positions on their precise legality.

The Sasson Report (2005) stipulated the illegality of Israeli settlement activity, focusing on government support for illegal outposts that were used to initiate new settlements and to expand existing ones. But the Sasson Report did not challenge Israeli settlements from the perspective of international law. Its charge of illegality was based on the Israeli practice of building settlements in ways that ignored and deviated from Israeli laws and regulations. A good portion of Israeli settlement construction, the report said, violated Israeli law, and the Israeli government funded these illegal activities despite their illegal nature.

The Levy Report (2012) took on the issue of international law. Over-ruling the Sasson Report and the international community, it stipulated that Israeli settlements were legal based on the lack of applicability of the Fourth Geneva Convention. Its conclusions are as follows:

> Our basic conclusion is that from the point of view of international law, the classical laws of "occupation" as set out in the relevant international conventions cannot be considered applicable to the unique and *sui generis* historic and legal circumstances of Israel's presence in Judea and Samaria spanning over decades. In addition, the provisions of the 1949 Fourth Geneva Convention regarding transfer of populations cannot be considered to be applicable and was never intended to apply to the type of settlement activity carried out by Israel in Judea and Samaria. Therefore, according to international law, Israelis have the legal right to settle in Judea and Samaria and the establishment of settlements cannot, in and of itself, be considered to be illegal. (Levy Report, 2012)

The Levy Report said that the West Bank was not occupied and therefore Israeli settlements were not illegal. The report deemed settlement construction in the West Bank to be legal, but it did not necessarily make the case for Israeli sovereignty over the area. Another perspective offered up from the report is that it also makes the case for Palestinian sovereignty (Tobin, 2014). If no country is sovereign in the West Bank, then it legally could be up for grabs. To be sure, the report calls the West Bank its biblical name of Judea and Samaria, suggesting that this area is Jewish and "belongs" to Israel, but this may largely be rhetorical.

The international community maintains that settlements are illegal. The Israeli government maintains that they are legal. International law is used to justify these diametrically opposed positions.

The political use of international law around settlements and occupation is another form of place making, one that makes the place-making process visible to everyone. One group or another may deem the legality or otherwise of the "ownership" of the West Bank, but what is really at stake is what is believed and what is done with these beliefs.

In the absence of any authoritative enforcement, perceptions matter. They matter, in part, because they fuel sentiment for and against settlements, and, for that matter, for and against Israel. Palestinians' belief that Israel is in violation of international law provides legitimacy and energy for their struggle to end occupation. The international community's emphatic stance on the illegality of the settlements provides further energy and impetus to the cause to end settlements. Meanwhile, the United States' seeming ambivalence about settlement legality splits the difference, providing it some credibility in its long-standing role as peace negotiator. But US political ambiguity may have its limitations.

United Nations resolutions against settlements appear to play a similar role, as ideological props for political positions. Only one of our interview respondents thought that United Nations resolutions were important to the growth and metropolitan development of Jerusalem, indicating that, at least on paper, these resolutions' practical effects in stopping the settlements have been minimal. But they may be useful rhetorically. For Palestinians, they provide international condemnation of Israel, bolstering their contentions. For Israelis, they provide continual documentation that (except in 1947) the United Nations has been consistently anti-Israel. Israeli rationalization for settlements is based on four concepts: Jerusalem's unification, Israeli security, religious Zionism, and affordable housing. From Israel's perspective, some of these settlements are on land that Israel has annexed to Jerusalem. They view this land as a permanent part of Jerusalem and therefore part of Israel. According to Israel, settlements built on occupied lands that are politically annexed to it encompass the "new" neighborhoods that connect East and West Jerusalem.

A second group of settlements are those Israel considered necessary to meet its security needs. These include all of the Israeli cities built over the Green Line as suburbs of Jerusalem. According to a mayor of one of the largest settlements, Israeli security has been a central focus for the location of what became satellite cities to Jerusalem.

> In 1975, Israel decided to build Ma'ale Adumim. This was decided by Rabin [then Israel's Prime Minister]. What was desired was a security ring around Jerusalem. This security ring ended up consisting of several cities, Gush Etzion [a regional council], Efrat [an urban municipality], Betar Illit [a city], Givat Ze'ev [a city], and Ma'ale Adumim [a city]. . . . The goal of Ma'ale Adumim was to protect Jerusalem from Arabs. Strategically, it was to protect and keep open the road from the Jordan Valley to Jerusalem. Ma'ale Adumim was built on a hill overlooking the road. Israel wanted and needed a safe and open road to the Jordan Valley. (Interview, 2008)

The third group represents those settlements developed by religious settlers as part of messianic prophecy and said to be biblically promised by God to the Jewish people. This third group of religious settlements is based on the ideology of a right-wing religious movement called Gush Emunim that calls for Jews to settle and develop what it calls Biblical Israel (Zertal and Eldar, 2007). Gush Emunim links locations in the West Bank to writings in the Old Testament. These religious settlers have settled portions of the West Bank called Judea and Samaria in the Bible. These religious settlements are considered part of the "Land of Israel," a religious idea distinct from the "State of Israel," a sovereign nation.

Religious settlers conforming to the messianic ideology of Gush Emunim are different from other settlers, either religious or secular (Reuveny, 2003; Zertal and Eldar, 2007). Many settlers are religious, but their settlement activity is not driven or informed by religion. Settlers who choose to move to religious settlements based on messianic prophecy are a settlement movement unto themselves that is distinct from settlement activity moved by the pull of cheap housing or geopolitical issues.

The fourth group of settlements has been built to house the Haredim – the ultra-Orthodox. The Haredim who live in Israel see themselves as waiting for the Messiah, but do not believe in any connection between Israel as a political entity and the coming of the Messiah. Therefore, they are not considered Israeli Zionists, but a religious Jewish group who lives in Israel.

The Haredim's birth rate is very high, making it the fastest-growing group of Jews in Israel. Many are concentrated in Jerusalem, where housing costs are very high. Therefore the government has built some large settlements (e.g. Betar Illit) to house them.

Nonetheless, most of the largest settlements continue to be rationalized in the name of Israeli security (Thawaba and Al-Rimmawi, 2012). Built at three points of a triangle surrounding Jerusalem, these settlements have grown into huge Jewish cities that house religious and secular Jews alike. These include Ma'ale Adumim (east of Jerusalem), Givat Ze'ev (north of Jerusalem), and Gush Etzion – a block of settlements including the town of Efrat and the City of Betar Illit (south of Jerusalem). These are considered by most Israelis to be non-ideological settlements because their existence is not tied to any particular ideology, only to securing a strategic location for Israel.

According to one public official,

> People who move to Ma'ale Adumim are not ideological settlers. Many are young couples that want a new place to live. They are interested in a better quality of life. They want "green and clean." The Ma'ale Adumim education system is of better quality than the one in Jerusalem. And people pay fewer [municipal] taxes than in Jerusalem. (Interview, 2008)

From a Palestinian perspective, the concept of "metropolitan Jerusalem" has been a cloak to disguise Israeli occupation (Thawaba and Al-Rimmawi, 2012). According to a Palestinian leader employed by a non-profit working on problems of Palestinian refugees, "greater metropolitan Jerusalem is a colonization plan" (interview, 2008). One left-wing Knesset member agreed: "Greater Jerusalem is a metaphor for avoiding the Palestinian state" (interview, 2007). A Palestinian leader and researcher put it even more harshly: "There is no metropolitan Jerusalem. There is only occupied territory. The term 'metropolitan' is not a neutral term. It is harsh policy. It is a loaded term designed to make Jewish Jerusalem more Jewish and to get rid of more Arabs" (interview, 2008). Palestinians considered Jerusalem's unity and integration as either a city or metropolitan area to be a mirage – an illusion of unity.

The Palestinian demystification of Jerusalem's unity came in the form of an explosion of violence, the First Intifada. This began in late 1987 as a response to Israel's development activities and associated behaviors with the Israeli occupation (Friedland and Hecht, 2000). It was also a statement by a younger generation of Palestinians that enough was enough. Palestinian violence and Israeli settler vigilantism worked in tandem with a cascade of hostility and brutality on both sides. To halt the aggression, a secret set of diplomatic activities took place in far-flung Oslo, Norway. The clandestine talks were intended to end the conflict between Israel and other Arab nations. They culminated in an agreement that was intended to, at least on paper, reduce uncontrolled Israeli development, provide legitimacy to Palestinian political activities, and guarantee a future for the Palestinians and Israel, respectively.

This was the Oslo Agreement of 1993, which was intended to curb the violence and eventually create a Palestinian state. Although no agreement was reached on either the status or division of Jerusalem, the plan was to discuss Jerusalem once trust was established on both sides, Israeli and Palestinian.

The Oslo Agreement, Jerusalem, and the Shifting Green Line

The significance of the Oslo Agreement was threefold. First, it created a Palestinian Authority that would become the official Palestinian government. Palestinians were recognized as a legitimate group with claims on land and the political authority to negotiate for a now recognized Palestinian people. Second, land

was officially ceded over to the Palestinian Authority for governance. Third, the Palestinian Authority officially recognized the
State of Israel. These were huge concessions on both sides.

The West Bank was divided into areas defined by who controlled them. Area A constituted those places that were controlled
solely by the Palestinian Authority. These were largely already-
existing Palestinian cities. Area B areas were those controlled
jointly by Israel and the Palestinian Authority – with Israeli
military control and Palestinian civil control. Area C areas were
those controlled by Israel alone. Area C areas (full Israeli control)
comprised almost three-quarters of the West Bank (see Figure 3.4).

Therefore, Israel retained full control over various parts of
the West Bank. Much of the West Bank was deemed for joint
Palestinian Authority and Israeli control, meaning that Israel
could legally control both Palestinian land use and its population
mobility. Ultimately, joint Israeli–Palestinian control resulted in
checkpoints and restrictions on Palestinian mobility. Palestinians
in the West Bank were less free after the passing of the Oslo
Agreement (Shlay and Rosen, 2010).

Although required by the agreements, no post-Oslo talks
emerged on either Jerusalem or a future Palestine state. Instead the
Oslo Agreement enlarged expectations on both sides but failed to
deliver. Increasing levels of mistrust, violent clashes, and frequent
suicide terror attacks on Israeli civilians set the stage for a new fierce
and intense clash between Israel and the Palestinians. Ultimately,
however, failure to advance a peace agreement or launch an alternative non-violent route for promoting peaceful coexistence led
to the outbreak of the Second Palestinian Intifada (also known as
the Al-Aqsa Intifada) in 2000. This time threats were backed not
by stones and knives but by the use of bombs in Israeli restaurants,
hotels, and buses. Palestinian terrorism was met by Israeli repres-
sion. Hundreds of people were killed or maimed on both sides.
Israel jailed thousands of violent dissidents and cracked down even
further on Palestinian mobility.

The Oslo Agreement explicitly deferred negotiations around
settlements until a later point. It did not contain a settlement freeze.
Settlements that were built after the signing of the Agreement

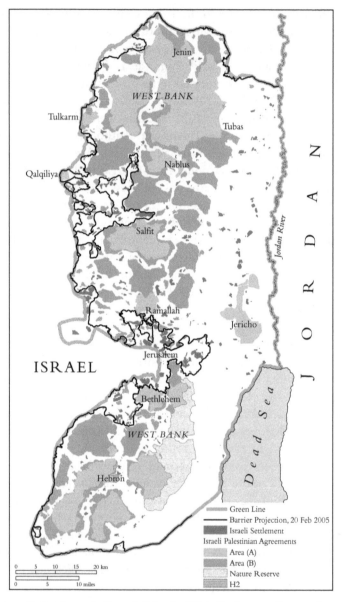

Figure 3.4   Areas A, B, and C in the West Bank according to the
Oslo Agreement (The United Nations Office for the Coordination of
Humanitarian Affairs)

within the municipal boundaries of Jerusalem were considered less legitimate than their pre-Oslo counterparts. Settlements essentially violated the spirit of the Oslo Agreement, which was to indicate transfer of land and power to Palestinian control, and adoption of political negotiations rather than violence or unilateral steps as an accepted formula for conflict management. The intensified development of two settlement neighborhoods in particular was strongly denounced as impeding the meeting of important demands by Palestinians (Thawaba and Al-Rimmawi, 2012). The two settlements/neighborhoods were Har Homa and Gilo (see Figure 3.5). In addition one other potential settlement location was cause for alarm by the Palestinians, their allies, and those engaged in the peace process. This additional West Bank area was called E1, its name in Israeli planning documents (Shlay and Rosen, 2010).

There were two major issues with these settlements from the perspective of Palestinians. First, Har Homa and E1 were located

Figure 3.5   Har Homa (© Anne Shlay)

on land Palestinians viewed as destined to be part of the future capital of their state – essentially Arab Jerusalem. This land was already disputed by international law. Har Homa and E1 tipped the ownership of Arab Jerusalem in Israel's favor. Israel's response was unsympathetic. It was adamant that this area was now part of Israel and that as a sovereign country, it would build wherever and however it wanted. The second issue was that these settlements blocked off or threatened to block off physical continuity between areas expected to be part of a future Palestinian state as outlined by the Oslo Agreement. In particular, Har Homa could break off physical continuity between the Palestinian city of Bethlehem, Palestine's future capital East Jerusalem, and the rest of the West Bank.

The area E1 was also located in what was believed to be the path of a future Palestinian state and would create physical continuity problems. E1 is located between Israel's largest settlement, Ma'ale Adumim, and the city of Jerusalem. The development of E1 by Israel would physically connect Ma'ale Adumim with Jerusalem. Connecting Ma'ale Adumim and Jerusalem through E1, however, would cut off East Jerusalem (the hoped-for Palestinian capital) from the rest of the West Bank. In other words, developing E1 might be a barrier to a two-state solution.

A right-wing Knesset member acknowledges that E1 would increase a disconnection between Ramallah and Bethlehem, saying that "I want a new neighborhood in E1 to separate the chain of growth between Ramallah and Bethlehem" (interview, 2007). The same anti-West Bank advocate goes directly to the political implications: "The argument is that if E1 is built, it will render a genuine Palestinian state impossible." Development of E1 has been halted, at least temporarily, largely owing to diplomatic intervention by the United States.

Whether the Israeli development would ultimately be a barrier to a two-state solution is subject to a debate, although recently Israel issued a proposal to continue its development of this area. Nonetheless, international arbiters have continued to block E1's development, at least for now.

Center of Life

Complementing Israel's attempts to facilitate expansion have been ongoing attempts to contain Palestinian growth and alter the social composition of East Jerusalem. Forces that move Palestinians around East Jerusalem, either from one neighborhood to another or out of East Jerusalem altogether, include: land expropriation; discriminatory zoning regulations; intentional absence of plans for Palestinian areas; obstructing development; rules governing residency requirements and the acquisition and attainment of identity cards; demolition; and transfer of property from Palestinians to Israelis (Kaminker, 1997; Bollens, 1998; Chesin et al., 1999; Klein, 2008).

To legally reside in Jerusalem, Palestinians are required to have Jerusalem identity cards. Therefore, Palestinians' loss of their Jerusalem identity cards has been a major source of concern. Israel now requires Palestinian Jerusalemites who are not Israeli citizens (which constitutes the majority of Palestinians in Jerusalem) to establish Jerusalem as their "center of life" before being eligible for benefits such as health care. Palestinians must be able to show evidence that they have lived in Jerusalem within a seven-year period or they will lose their Jerusalem identification card (Stein, 1998; Jefferis, 2012). Note that Palestinians are required to prove Jerusalem residency for seven consecutive years, making it essential that they retain some type of permanent residency within the city. A Palestinian lawyer working with Palestinians who have lost their residency status explains the power dynamics involved:

> Jerusalem is disempowering the Palestinian community through the threat of loss of the residency identification card. Jerusalem Palestinians have a special status but are not citizens. They have special social rights. But the status is conditional. Palestinians can only stay inside the city if they have an ID card. If they move outside the city, they lose their ID card. They have to provide documentation that they are legal and living in Jerusalem. It is very expensive if one loses their ID card. It can cost $10,000 for legal fees. (Interview, 2008)

This policy is criticized as an effort by Israel's government to reduce the number of Palestinians within its border. Since most Palestinians in Jerusalem were effectively annexed to Jerusalem but not given citizenship, they are at risk of being penalized by this policy. It is estimated that thousands of Palestinian Jerusalemites have lost access to their Israeli benefits through its arbitrary enforcement.

The Israeli Security Barrier/Fence/Apartheid Wall: A New Green Line?

In the wake of waves of suicide bombings and other forms of terrorism emerging from the Second Intifada, the idea of a physical barrier to terrorism was born. In 2002, the Israeli Knesset approved the construction of what Israeli advocates call a "security fence." A towering cement wall in some places and a chain-link fence in others, the security barrier was coined the apartheid wall by some. Designed to fence in almost all of Israel, and fence out the Palestinians, the security barrier/fence/wall represented a new form of technological sophistication combined with brute force.

Israel emphasizes that the goal of the security barrier/fence/wall is to protect Israel from terrorism (Kliot and Charney, 2006; Gelbman and Keinan, 2007). The barrier, they say, would be eliminated once it was no longer needed (Israel Defense Forces, 2003).

From the perspective of negotiations for a future Palestinian state, Palestinians saw the wall as a maneuver by Israel to dodge negotiations and to determine the boundaries of the future Israel. According to a lawyer and participant in a left-wing Israeli peace organization, "[Ariel] Sharon determined the security fence border with the goal of influencing a greater Israeli sphere over Jerusalem. Sharon's goal was to seal Jerusalem, create buffers, and dismember the Palestinian State" (interview, 2007). Although the explicitly stated goal of the barrier/fence/wall was to prevent terrorists from traveling into Israel, it ultimately had a myriad of effects, including physically separating Palestinians and Israelis (Klein, 2005, 2008).

The barrier/fence/wall is the penultimate work at boundary construction that provides concrete expression (literally) of what Israel's policy desires – in the name of security. The barrier/fence/wall established what the Sharon government hoped would "delineate the optimal borders" in the event of a two-state political solution (interview, 2007).

But the impact of the barrier/fence/wall is broader than safety alone (Brooks et al., 2009). Its effects have been social, economic, and, of course, geopolitical (Alatout, 2009; Allegra, 2013; Chiodelli, 2013; Handel, 2013). The largest effects have been felt in Jerusalem. A *Jerusalem Post* reporter said that a popular left-wing idea was to have the "separation barrier go through Jerusalem and have East Jerusalem on the other side to hasten the two-state solution" (interview, 2007). But that was not the route chosen and instead, according to one Palestinian researcher, "they put the wall inside the municipal boundaries of East Jerusalem because this was a way [for Israel] to get rid of eighty thousand Arabs" (interview, 2007). The barrier/fence/wall did not appear to facilitate a separation of Jerusalem. Rather, it seemed to be intended to prevent any form of meaningful Jerusalem separation altogether.

The tallest part of the barrier/fence/wall goes through Jerusalem. It ultimately was built through the heart of East Jerusalem, leaving Al Quds University, the neighborhood of Abu Dis, and the Jerusalem Palestinian Parliament on the other side of the wall. Most of the Jerusalem satellite settlements, all Jerusalem's new neighborhoods built on former West Bank land, and much of East Jerusalem adjacent to the Old City remain inside this new tangible boundary.

The barrier/fence/wall has excluded areas of East Jerusalem that were formally annexed to Jerusalem, and therefore Israel, immediately after the 1967 war (see Figure 3.6). These areas were to be part of the new unified Jerusalem. With the barrier/fence/wall physically expelling these East Jerusalem areas from the city, they have lost access to most municipal services. These fenced-out areas are neither part of the Palestinian Authority nor part of Israel (Owais, 2008), displaying a condition of hybrid sovereignties (Fregonese, 2012).

Figure 3.6   The separation barrier/fence/wall that runs through East Jerusalem (© Anne Shlay)

The barrier/fence/wall also creates enclaves within the West Bank, enclosing and isolating many Palestinians. Its construction severely restricts Palestinian freedom of movement, separating villages from their agricultural land and fundamentally reshaping people's everyday lives (Bimkom, 2006; Handel, 2013).

Like settlements more generally, the barrier/fence/wall is viewed by Palestinian activists as another Israeli land grab, one that will be used to promote the "demographic balance" of Israel – namely reduce the number of Palestinians. According to one activist living in the walled-in city of Bethlehem: "The wall is portrayed as a barrier for terrorism but it is another fact on the ground. It is a tool for stealing more Palestinian land. The wall is taking a chunk of the West Bank with minimal Palestinian residents" (interview, 2008). The wall, he says, "also redefines the boundaries of Jerusalem."

For much of Israel, the barrier conforms to the Green Line. But the Jerusalem barrier deviates heavily from the Green Line where decisions were made over what was fenced in (as part of the Jerusalem region) and what was fenced out (removed from Jerusalem). Fenced in with Jerusalem were portions of the West Bank that are not annexed to Jerusalem as well as portions that are. In East Jerusalem, however, the borders did not conform to the municipal boundaries of Jerusalem with the post-1967 annexation of East Jerusalem. Rather, portions of East Jerusalem were fenced out. This process was described by a high-level planner in the Ministry of Interior:

> The barrier is not exactly on the Green Line. Parts of the Jerusalem municipality are beyond the wall. The Ministry of Interior has planning authority on both sides of the wall. But the planning authorities had no part in drawing the line of the barrier. The wall was entirely a military operation. It was by the Prime Minister [Ariel Sharon] and the Army. There were no real planning considerations involved. There was no planning, but now planners have to deal with the consequences. (Interview, 2007)

The barrier/fence/wall has had many consequences for East Jerusalem. First, it eliminated from the Jerusalem municipality a significant portion of the Palestinian population. Second, it attracted more Palestinians to live in East Jerusalem and the Old City. According to a major Palestinian peace activist, "the separation wall has encouraged Palestinians to move back to Jerusalem to keep their Israeli identification cards" (interview, 2007). Palestinians moved inside the barrier/fence/wall to continue to receive educational services for their children, services unavailable once they were fenced out of Jerusalem.

Third, the barrier/fence/wall has brought about shifts in population in suburban satellites to East Jerusalem. In the words of one Palestinian activist, it has created a situation where the "areas outside East Jerusalem are dying" (interview, 2008). The barrier/fence/wall's impact on local economic development and housing markets was large. According to one researcher:

The Israeli government's decision to construct the Separation Wall and the commencement of its construction in 2002 led to the spatial amputation of these suburbs from East Jerusalem. It rendered them residential ghettos and pockets disconnected from East Jerusalem, except via a handful of crossings and numerous checkpoints completely controlled by the Israeli military. (Owais, 2008: 55)

In an article published at the end of 2010, we concluded that the barrier/fence/wall represented the nail in the coffin for East Jerusalem ever becoming the capital of a future Palestinian state. The barrier/fence/wall, we believed, would severely impede any meaningful division of Jerusalem that would provide a Palestinian state with a reasonable land base for governance. In other words, we thought that the barrier/fence/wall, coupled with the long-term effects of both the Oslo Agreement and Israeli policy, eliminated East Jerusalem as a future site for the Palestinian capital. We stated the following:

The maintenance of this fence/wall speaks volumes of the extensive disparities between what Israel and a possible future Palestinian state view as "their" Jerusalem. The fence/wall going through Jerusalem with its Palestinian Parliament and its premier university walled out of the city potentially destroys the possibility of Jerusalem as the capital of a future Palestinian state. This marking of territory by Israelis coupled with the gradual dissolution of important Palestinian Jerusalem civic and political institutions makes it difficult to conceive a Palestinian Jerusalem capital without serious compromises. (Shlay and Rosen, 2010: 374)

We now feel that this conclusion was premature and largely incorrect. The barrier/fence/wall, while an impediment, is not a fatal flaw. We believe that walls can easily be demolished. Although the East Jerusalem that is currently in the hands of the Palestinians has been compromised, its social and physical infrastructure can be rebuilt. In fact, walling out such a crucial portion of East Jerusalem from the rest of the city may underscore more that its status as a future capital of Palestine has instead been preserved. East

Jerusalem's future as a capital of Palestine has not been preempted by a barrier/fence/wall. More control over the growth of settlements and a timely negotiation of borders may ultimately provide what is necessary for a Palestinian capital in East Jerusalem.

The Old City, Silwan, and the City of David: Spotlight on the Green Line

If only one place could be called Jerusalem, where would it be? For those already initiated into one of the oldest cities on earth, close your eyes and think of it. What comes to mind? Jerusalem is chock-full of rich and exciting images that speak to its longevity across millennia, not mere decades or centuries like either the State of Israel or the United States. Jerusalem's staying power is the stuff of legends – of the comings and goings of peoples and empires. So what is left standing that speaks to Jerusalem's long life on this earth?

The Old City is in the heart of what is called the Holy Basin, a valley of churches, mosques, and cemeteries adjacent to it. Next to the Old City is Silwan, a large Palestinian village (neighborhood/ town) of fifty-five thousand people. Silwan is now officially part of the Jerusalem municipality, although, like other parts of East Jerusalem, it is considered to be occupied territory. Located in Silwan is the City of David or Ir David. This is a large archaeological site in an area believed to be the ancient city over which King David ruled (see Figure 3.7). It is a site of archaeological excavations run by the Israeli Antiquities Authority and funded by the Ir David Foundation known as El'ad.

The Old City, the City of David, and parts of the village of Silwan are located in the City of David/Jerusalem Walls National Park. The designation of the area as an Israeli national park, the excavation and expansion of the City of David site, and the movement of Israeli Jews into houses located in Silwan have set the stage for major conflict between Jews and Palestinians. This is a concrete expression of the battle for the Jerusalem of memory, a battle that

Figure 3.7   City of David excavations (© Anne Shlay)

is funded by El'ad, a private entity with enormous power over development in one of the most controversial and contested parts of the city.

The Old City

Jerusalem's Old City is not simply a museum or historic artifact that showcases life as it once was. The Old City is as much about the present as about the past – particularly about contemporary Judaism, Christianity, and Islam. While the meanings of places in the Old City are derived from the past, their relevance for the present is what excites people. Particularly for religious practice, the Old City's relevance competes with any religious historical landmark on the planet.

The Old City may be old, but as a city, it is very much alive. Until 1860, Jerusalem's Old City was, in fact, the city of Jerusalem.

Jerusalem's newer frontier is really quite recent. The Old City only became "the Old City" when the new one began to expand outside of the Old City walls.

The Old City contains four quarters of unequal sizes, all with a religious and ethnic identity characteristic of how people congregated in times of yore. One is Muslim, another is Christian, a third is Armenian, and the fourth is Jewish. All contain important religious artifacts that speak to the origins of the three monotheistic religions. Much that is religious in the modern age and across the globe originated with what happened within this small place. The Old City is also about the people who currently live there. Current estimations put the Muslim population at thirty thousand and about four and a half thousand Jews (Slae, 2013).

The Old City is very much alive in terms of actual people who live there and how they and others choose to sanctify and practice religion within these hallowed walls. The Old City contains all kinds of schools and in the afternoon its walkways are filled with students coming home. There are shops of all kinds – hardware stores, grocers, meat markets, dress shops, and more. Offices abound with doctors, lawyers, and social service personnel. Visitors experience an Old City that caters to tourists, selling meals and souvenirs. But tourists coexist with Old City regulars and residents whose lives are very much contained within these walls.

Most of the Old City's residents are Palestinians and less than 10 percent of its population is Jewish (International Peace and Cooperation Center, 2007: 15). The Palestinian population has increased in recent years. Palestinians have moved into the Old City for three major reasons. The first reason is to gain access to East and West Jerusalem. Second, by living in the Old City, legally or illegally, they avoid the myriad of checkpoints required to get into Jerusalem for Palestinians who live outside of the city. The third reason is that Palestinians living outside the barrier/ fence/wall fear losing their Jerusalem residency identification card owing to the more recent enforcement of the "center of life" requirement.

The Old City has been a ping-pong ball in the Palestinian– Israeli conflict. Recognizing the universal importance of Jerusalem's Old

City's, the 1947 United Nations partition plan prescribed that it would not politically or legally reside in either Israel or Palestine. The Old City was intended to be an international city, one not owned by any particular country or religion.

But this was short lived when the Old City went to Jordan as one of the spoils of the 1948 war. When Israel conquered the Old City in 1967, it set about recreating Jewish memory and rebuilding and preserving the Jewish historical legacy. This was accomplished by demolishing Palestinian homes, and immediately incurring wrath toward the new Jewish governance within the Old City.

Group relations in the Old City largely mirror the political tensions existing at different times in the region. During both intifadas, Israeli Jews experienced routine stabbings while in the Old City. These threats of violence caused many Israeli Jews to avoid the Old City altogether. Today, many Israeli Jews come to the Old City, some to pray at the Kotel, the Western Wall.

The religious settlement movement that has encouraged religious people to take over portions of the West Bank has also supported the residential relocation of Jewish religious right-wing activists to move within Palestinian communities in the Old City as well as to Palestinian neighborhoods nearby. Extreme right-wing foundations such as Ateret Cohanim provide money and support to buy homes for "settlers" (Sherwood, 2013). Jewish settlers are accused of Judaizing the Muslim Quarter of the Old City. In recent years, it has been estimated that over a thousand Jews now live outside of the Jewish Quarter in the Old City.

Young secular Jewish Israelis tend to stay away from the Old City. The conflict over the permissibility of women to pray like men at the Kotel has renewed secular interest in the Old City, or at least in its Western Wall. Led by the Women of the Wall, this conflict is not new and is in fact almost thirty years old. The struggle received recent international attention when a female rabbi who is sister to the American comedian Sarah Silverman was arrested for wearing a *tallit* (prayer shawl) on the women's side of the Kotel. The struggle for female inclusivity has become an international movement that has also been taken up by reform and conservative congregations in the United States and Europe whose practices of gender inclusivity effectively ban them from prayer at the gender-segregated Kotel. Although tensions remain, the dictatorial Kotel governance has been forced to compromise and it is anticipated that at some point a satisfactory resolution to the gender conflict may occur (Rosen and Shlay, 2014).

Silwan and the City of David

Wars are fought over places. While countries often wage war to acquire places, their use of coercion and violence is not the best method for holding on to them. In the long run, coercion has proven to be an unstable method for political dominance. Max Weber argued that maintaining stable political leadership requires that the dominant power structure be recognized as legitimate. Governing inevitably requires the consent of the governed. For most kinds of prolonged leadership, the leaders must win the hearts and minds of those being led (Weber, 2009).

Israel has managed to maintain political dominance over Jerusalem for almost fifty years. While it acquired East Jerusalem in war, its ability to keep Jerusalem is not just a contest of force but also one of ideas. Israel wants the world to appreciate, understand, and accept that Israeli Jerusalem is the rightful Jerusalem and is therefore here to stay.

The City of David archaeological excavation is one tool in Israel's arsenal for showing the world that the Jewish Jerusalem of memory preempts any claim by Palestinians that Jerusalem is theirs. This excavation provides evidence of the existence of a civilization consistent with what has been written about in the Bible. Note the phrasing of this sentence – that it provides evidence of a civilization consistent with what has been written about in the Bible. It does not prove either that David existed or even that the city is Jewish (Mizrachi, 2012).

Questioning the truth value of archaeological findings from the City of David excavation has been the domain of Emek Shaveh, a non-profit organization of Jerusalem-based archaeologists and activists that focuses on the role of archaeology in the Palestinian-Israeli conflict, particularly in Jerusalem. It has developed a partnership with the village of Silwan to offer competing ideas over what comprises the facts associated with the El'ad project. Emek Shaveh educates the public over biases and political agendas associated with El'ad and exposes flaws in the story being told about the different civilizations and peoples that have comprised the long history of the Old City and the Holy Basin.

Working with the Silwan Palestinian village (town/suburb/neighborhood), it stresses the presence of the village coupled with the claim that the physical area of the Old City and its surroundings represent a diversity of religious, ethnic, and nationalistic interests – not simply Jewish or Israeli ones. The claim that Jews were part of the ancient history of Jerusalem ignores the presence of other groups that are also part of the history and topography of the area. Emek Shaveh's perspective is that since Jews have historically shared the area with Arabs in the past, they should continue to share it now (Mizrachi, 2012). Archaeological evidence of the presence of Jews is used as a political tool for Israel to claim the space as theirs. But why, asks Emek Shaveh, is the mere historical presence of Jews a reason for others to have to leave?

The City of David has succeeded in convincing many Israelis that their Jerusalem of memory has a firm historical basis. By comparison, the Jewish Jerusalem of memory is much longer than the couple of hundred years claimed by the Palestinians of Silwan. El'ad has upped the ante on the question of who belongs in Silwan. It has been purchasing Palestinian homes, restoring them, and renting them to Jews as "settlers" of this community. Jewish homes are guarded by El'ad-funded guards who have the job of protecting Jewish families from dangerous Palestinians. El'ad has also been changing street names from Arab-sounding ones to Israeli ones (Pullan et al., 2013).

Israel, through El'ad, is working at creating a credible archaeological picture. But the portrayal of the work of the City of David is profoundly ideological, almost nonsensical in its glorification of a Jewish presence in this particular location. In its desire to project and convince others of the legitimacy of their project, Israel and

El'ad have turned this archaeological site into a quasi-Disneyland experience. Israel's refusal to allow any kind of improvements to the housing of the residents of Silwan provides the image of a dirty and decaying community next to the sparkling clean City of David infrastructure along with its newly refurbished (once Arab now Jewish) homes.

The Jerusalem Light Rail

After years of planning and infrastructure development as well as billions of shekels spent, in 2010 Jerusalem opened a new light rail line that connected East and West Jerusalem with plans for more construction of what is considered by Israelis to be a "fully integrated" public transportation system (Cohen-Blankshtain and Feitelson, 2011). The initial route of the Jerusalem Light Rail (JLR) is a journey through time, space, as well as social and political worlds. Future plans for the JLR will further jolt much of Jerusalem to the twenty-first century.

By increasing accessibility to different parts of the Jerusalem area, the JLR is intended to integrate areas of the city in ways that until now have been unimaginable. It is a form of "unification" of Jerusalem that surpasses previous efforts because it connects diverse social and spatial worlds. And it is precisely this integration that has put the JLR in the political hot seat because it works to specifically connect portions of East Jerusalem to the rest of the city.

The initial JLR route moves from West Jerusalem (Mount Herzel) to Pisgat Ze'ev, one of the new neighborhoods pioneered in the 1970s. Its route travels along the Jerusalem seam line that used to divide East from West Jerusalem. Its route moves deliberately through neighborhoods and communities that were developed as part of the unification plan in the 1970s. Stops have also been built in Palestinian towns, including Beit Hanina and Shuafat.

The route of the JLR essentially appears to treat Jerusalem as a more conventional city, one without walls, that has universally

recognized municipal boundaries, and that is not subject to political conflicts and challenges on a routine basis. Building a mass
transit system under these political and social constraints is bold.
Most transit systems are concerned with getting people from here
to there and back again. Jerusalem's Light Rail is concerned with
much more, including routine threats of terrorism.

The JLR has been the target of international challenges that
have altered its funding structures and sought to block its development. The charge has been that Israel continues to treat East
Jerusalem as a part of the city of Jerusalem as well as Israel. It is
considered a "voracious colonization project in the occupied West
Bank" (Barghouti, 2009: 51).

In other words, the JLR further extends a long-standing political goal in Jerusalem to unify various parts of East Jerusalem with
the rest of the city despite political opposition. Several years into its
operation, it may be one of the few places in Jerusalem other than
its major shopping mall and zoo in which Palestinians and religious
and secular Israelis coexist, even if only for twenty minutes or less
a day.

The Shifting Green Line

Jerusalem is a place infused with two kinds of memories. One
kind calls up the warmth and security of close family, community,
and a reigning deity. This Jerusalem of memory is a nurturing
one, providing emotional, physical, and psychic sustenance to its
people over time. This Jerusalem anchors people in material and
social space, reminding them of who they are by virtue of where
they came from. They are from Jerusalem. This is a critically
cultivated identity which has been part of this place over many
centuries.

People claim Jerusalem as a part of who they are. Jerusalem has
a very long history with a rich legacy of survival. Other cities are
bigger and may seem to be more important. But the Jerusalem of
memory, of family and community, provides a solid place-based

attachment that is stronger than the glitz and glitter of other metropolitan areas.

The Jerusalem of memory is also one of conflict, struggle, conquest, and rejection. Being of Jerusalem is not being part of a place that lets one relax, take it easy, and smell the flowers. To be of Jerusalem and to stay in Jerusalem requires a fight. The story of Jerusalem is one of belonging but it is also a history of fighting to belong. For thousands of years, people have come and gone with supreme regularity. Jerusalem is not an easy place to cultivate as home, particularly if predictability and long-term stability are primary needs.

The Jerusalem that has been the focus of so much strife in the conflict between Palestinians and Israelis has been both a targeted political object to be fought for and acquired as well as a tool to be used to further conquest. The fight over Jerusalem causes people to become extreme and to do extreme things. Jerusalem is not and may never be a normal city.

Since 1947, Jerusalem has been carved up, chewed, and spat out on a regular basis. What has emerged to date is a place where every location is meaningful and nothing can be taken for granted. Every place in Jerusalem is tied to some kind of strategy. Jerusalem does not have mellow moments. People cannot relax about it. There is too much at stake and too much to lose.

The activities around Jerusalem are a conscious attempt to create and reinforce social and political ownership through place making. Place-based activities are directed at furthering its conquest of the urban hinterland. It cannot do conventional suburbs because there is no authentic urban fringe. So instead it builds settlements. Jerusalem's growth and legitimacy as an urban place are linked to its physical expansion and its ability to socially cultivate more and more land that is no longer under the control of the Palestinians. Israel has a grab-bag of motivators for people to move to these settlements – religion, homeownership, price, housing affordability, and more. Jerusalem's growth machine builds up its frontier because Israel does not want to share the city with the Palestinians. All the Palestinians can really do is resist. But they resist very well and have remained an obstacle to Israel's metropolitan ambitions.

Israel's development activities have shifted perceptions of boundaries and changed what people call Jerusalem. In just a few short years, Palestinian land has come under Israeli control, to the point where the ownership and control of this space by Israel are literally taken for granted. Israel has built housing, roads, tunnels, bridges, police stations, synagogues, schools, and community centers. Israel projects its memories onto the present and, as a result, seems to have developed physical and hegemonic control over the region. People outside of Israel debate what is or is not Jerusalem. But in Israel and among Israeli Jews, that debate is largely moot, particularly when it comes to the annexed territories viewed by the international community as occupied East Jerusalem.

Israel, however, has not completed assimilating its Jerusalem places into its political regime because Palestinians have remained part of the Jerusalem scene. Rather than leave Jerusalem, Palestinians have been increasing in population. They have a Jerusalem that they remember too, and their Jerusalem of memory has staying power. Israel has the power to build many things, but the Palestinians of Jerusalem have the power to resist. And they have mobilized and globalized this resistance so that it seems to echo around the world. But opening up East Jerusalem for consideration in any negotiated settlement will face obstacles because of the physical and social realities of Jerusalem today.

Jerusalem is a place infused with meaning – really a set of different meanings emanating from the disparate groups that have come into contact with it. Some groups claim their relationship to Jerusalem encompasses thousands of years, while others have more recent histories. It is these groups with their varied identities – be these political, spiritual, ethnic, or whatever – that shape this ever-changing place called Jerusalem, Al Quds, and Yerushalayim.

4

Who Is Jerusalem?

Introduction

It was October 7, 2013. I (Shlay) was hanging out in the halls of
Hebrew University, located on Mount Scopus in Jerusalem, when
a graduate student bolted out of his office and said, "The rabbi
died. They are going to close the roads. I have to go. I just wanted
to let you know." Like many things that happen in Jerusalem, I did
not put two and two together. The newspapers had been talking
about some rabbi being near death for the last couple of weeks. I
thought that, well, he finally died and that was that. I decided to
go for a workout at the gym and head home later on.

Post-workout, I trudged to the Jerusalem Light Rail station
at Ammunition Hill to go home. I could tell right away that
something was wrong. I saw men with yellow vests, indicating
some kind of emergency. People were crowding around them,
muttering and disgruntled. I went up to one of the yellow-vested
guys and asked, "What's up?" He told me that the trains were not
running. "Not running," I said, "why not?" He shrugged. I persisted in my questioning. It was not a holiday, there was no snow,

and I could see no evidence of a nuclear or any other type of disaster. A man came up to me, white shirt and black hat. He said to
me very nicely, "You see, this rabbi died."

Huh? This rabbi died and there is no train service. I was flum-
moxed. What did a dead rabbi have to do with no trains? Question:
Why no trains? Answer: You see, this rabbi died. Even now, in
writing this, I can feel the irritation return as I ponder what I
thought was a totally ridiculous answer to my question about the
lack of public transportation during rush hour in the largest city in
Israel. They shut down the trains because a rabbi died? You have
got to be kidding.

But this was not a ruse. There were no trains. And so the carless
masses and I joined the long line of people walking down the
highway. Mothers pushing their kids in strollers, a few men in
wheelchairs, and just regular able-bodied people like me traversed
along the seam line that divides East and West Jerusalem. Traffic
was unreal. We walkers were going faster than the cars, which
appeared stuck in some kind of nightmarish limbo. Just over an
hour later, I got to my room in Tabiya and turned on the television
to see what was happening. I knew that there had to be more to
this urban crisis than the death of a mere rabbi. Jerusalem is filled
with rabbis.

The television provided a few answers. Yes, a rabbi had died.
But this was no ordinary rabbi. It was Ovadia Yosef, the rabbi
who, as leader of the ultra-Orthodox Shas party, had altered the
political, social, and economic landscape not only of Jerusalem but
of all of Israel. He was a leader of the Mizrahim, the Sephardic
Jews who originated from the Arab countries of the Middle East
and North Africa. He was a rabbi who interpreted and pronounced
more Jewish rules and regulations than anyone else in the country,
maybe in the entire world; a rabbi who had more followers than
any politician; a rabbi who was not God per se, but pretty darn
close.

You see, this rabbi died and the religious turned out en masse
to go to his funeral. Reports are that eight hundred thousand
people showed up for the funeral procession. To put this in
some perspective, the number of people coming to the funeral

was comparable to the population size of the entire city of Jerusalem.

The next day I pestered my geography colleagues with questions. "The city knew that this guy was dying" I pontificated, "If they knew this, why not plan for the crowds?," I asked. In response, I was told that the city did plan, that what I had witnessed was the best planning possible. The rabbi died that morning, and the funeral had to be held that day. As it was, the city had closed down all of the major highways going into the city to keep more people out. In other words, it could have been a lot worse.

You see, this rabbi died. This gentle explanation for the generation of seeming mass chaos within a not so small urban area provided a window into the social world of this place. Jerusalem is not a worldly city where anything goes. To the contrary, it gained its reputation and standing as an other-worldly city. It is a place where deities have walked the streets. It is a place where messiahs have come and gone and may come again. The intensity around Jerusalem is not because of hype or hustle like in New York or Miami. Jerusalem's intensity derives from a set of beliefs that are supremely strong and compelling. You see, this rabbi died and at that moment there was nothing more important than paying respect and being part of the community.

I am a sociologist. How could I not see that?

This chapter is about the people of Jerusalem. Although some will talk about Jerusalem in broad strokes, many find their experience of it to be very particularistic and personal. It is based as much on what people bring of themselves to the city as it is on the city itself.

Jerusalem is characterized by its diversity. It is the spatial aggregation of a multitude of people who differ from each other in many extraordinary ways. Its residents vary by religion, religiosity, ethnicity, nationality, and race. But Jerusalem is not a multicultural city. Identities are gripped tightly. Jerusalem is a city built more on social antagonisms than on spiritual continuity and cohesion. Although Jerusalem is the official capital of a Jewish state, being Jewish is not as unifying as one might think. In Jerusalem, everyone is a minority in his or her own way. While among Jews, most are religious, the religious differ in terms of how they are religious. Secular Jews are Jewish, of course, but these Jews often take on the role of the stranger in a strange land.

The experience of Jerusalem compels intense reactions and feelings. People may hate it or love it. But the experience of the city rarely engenders indifference. Jerusalem is not a feelgood place. But Jerusalem makes people feel things most of the time.

This chapter is about the social groups that make up and shape Jerusalem. It looks at the characteristics that define these groups of people and explores how these characteristics affect Jerusalem's spatial patterns and development. In the language of the Chicago School of urban sociology, this chapter examines Jerusalem as a mosaic of social worlds.

These groups are part of Jerusalem's political environment. Group characteristics are intimately connected to the power to shape the space of Jerusalem. Jerusalem's urban political economy is one that uses the social characteristics of different groups to expand the city. And in the process, these resulting social spatial forces also become the mechanisms by which Jerusalem continues to be divided. Growth and division in Jerusalem go hand in hand.

The first part of this chapter describes Jerusalem's importance as a religious center. The second part provides an overview of the demography of Jerusalem. The third part describes the key variables that differentiate Jerusalem's population. The fourth part examines the role of different social groups in shaping the city. The final part raises the central question of to whom Jerusalem belongs. To its different conflict-ridden ethno-national and religious groups? To its rich foreign residents and the Jewish Diaspora? Or to its most dominant group, the poor?

Holy Jerusalem

Jerusalem is central for the three major religions: Judaism, Christianity, and Islam. For each religion, Jerusalem is sacred, although to varying degrees. All three regard Jerusalem as a place containing geographical layers of holiness based on the locations of events from days long past.

In 1928, an international Christian organization, the YMCA (Young Men's Christian Association), bought a plot of land from the Greek Orthodox Church in central Jerusalem. During this period, known as the British Mandate (1917–47), desires for pluralism and religious harmony appeared to prevail. The YMCA was intended to serve as a bridge between the religions, giving deference and offering respect to each. Although in Jerusalem religious differences were prevalent throughout the twentieth century and remain so today, the YMCA continues to be Jerusalem's symbol of spiritual unity, not division.[1]

The sites of some sacred places are shared among all three religions because one religion's sacred activity is reported to have occurred in exactly the same place as another's. Places that share sacredness across religions are intensely holy – in part because of the competition for religious place-based domination. Yet each religion has its own place-based story to tell.

Jerusalem is translated for some as the city of peace (Hebrew) and for others as the holy city (Greek). Each religion has its own name for Jerusalem. For Christianity, it is Jerusalem. For Islam, the name is Al Quds (the Sacred City). For Judaism, it is Yerushalayim.

For Christianity, the city is sacred because, while Jesus was born in Bethlehem, according to the New Testament it was in Jerusalem that he walked as an adult, performed miracles, ate his Last Supper, was crucified, buried and, ultimately, raised from the dead. Jerusalem is the location for the miracles surrounding Jesus. His brief but wondrous life was spent in the city, and it was there that the historical basis for the belief system underlying Christianity largely took shape. Indeed, the place and the people are invariably linked with Christianity. It is no accident that Jesus ended up in Jerusalem, not Rome or Athens. As the professed son of God, Jesus, and therefore God, chose Jerusalem as Christianity's spiritual foundation. Jesus-linked earth-based activities infused a multitude of locations with sacredness, as memorialized in the Church of the Holy Sepulchre, the Via Dolorosa, and the Mount of Olives. Jerusalem is very central to Christianity.

Islam's connection to Jerusalem originates with a dreamed bodily journey of its founder, the Prophet Muhammad. Muhammad traveled one night from Mecca to Al-Aqsa, Islam's name for what became an intensely holy place for Muslims. As a bodily journey, getting from Mecca to Al Quds (Jerusalem) would have been almost physically impossible in a single night. Therefore, this excursion itself is regarded as a miracle and a spiritual and holy event. Muhammad's night journey took him to the Temple Mount (in Arabic, Haram al-Sharif) in Al Quds (now part of the Old City). From the Temple Mount (itself already a holy place for Jews called Har Habayit), he ascended to heaven. In heaven, Muhammad met with some of the founding fathers of Judaism and Christianity, now in their afterlife. This magical and spiritual journey rendered the Jewish Temple Mount a sacred place for Islam, forever linking Jerusalem to this religion's origin. Muhammad's journey inspired the construction of the Islamic Dome of the Rock on top of the Temple Mount. For Islam, Jerusalem represents the third holiest place in the world after Mecca and Medina.

Judaism's attachment to Jerusalem is derived from a host of foundational moments chronicled in the Old Testament. The origin of the Jewish covenant with God was established with Abraham's binding of his son Isaac on Jerusalem's Mount Moriah. The Jewish King David built his city in Jerusalem and his son King Solomon built the First Temple. A Second Jewish Temple is famous for Herod's expansions, and was ultimately destroyed by the Romans, leaving the Western Wall as a physical memory of these ancient formative times. Judaism views its origins and religious infrastructure as indelibly linked to Jerusalem. Each year at the Passover seder dinner, which celebrates the Jewish escape from Egyptian slavery, the refrain "next year in Jerusalem" is repeated, further reinforcing the memory of Jerusalem for present-day Jews. Jews all over the world pray in the direction of Jerusalem. In Jerusalem itself, they face the Temple Mount when they do so.

For all three religions, the connection between Jerusalem as a place and what happened in Jerusalem thousands of years ago is intense and powerful. Of course, religious beliefs among the most faithful are typically passionate irrespective of location per se. But the link between Jerusalem as the historical venue for the transmission of holiness and the beginning of each religion intensifies religious beliefs. A place is holy only to the extent that the religious believe it is holy. It is the ensemble of religious beliefs about a space that makes it holy, not any kind of intrinsic holiness attached to the space itself. Nonetheless, beliefs are concentrated in space, making it difficult, if not impossible, to separate the religion(s) from the place itself. Jerusalem as a place is a blend of these religious beliefs and identities.

The historical accuracy of what occurred and when in Jerusalem is a source of political conflict, particularly between Jews and Muslims, who insist that particular spaces belong more to one of them than another (Reiter, 2013). But fighting in this world about visions, dreams, and wonders has its limitations. Proving miracles is not the stuff of science. Moreover, empirical verification of what happened where may largely be pointless. What people believe about Jerusalem may be far more important than what is empirically accurate or verifiable. Since the veracity of beliefs cannot be proven, neither Christianity, Judaism, nor Islam relies on the truth value of its beliefs. Fighting over whose truth is more true is largely irrelevant. One conclusion may be drawn with some definitiveness, however. Jerusalem will never be one place for just one people. Rather, it is a place where several groups legitimately claim ownership. Each religion may compete to get top billing. But as a holy city, Jerusalem is an important place-based center for all three religions.

Owing to its concentrated religious intensity, as well as the divisions between religions and within them, Jerusalem presents a kaleidoscope of images that are constantly shifting so that one is not entirely clear at any given point what one is seeing. Jerusalem is a place where perspectives, cleavages, world views, religious cultures, ethnicity, historical experience, people, and ideas continally collide and rebound.

The Demography of the Israeli Municipality of Jerusalem[2]

For many, an accounting of the demography of a place is soporific stuff. How many people are young? How many people are old? Is the place growing? Are people having lots of children? Are people moving or leaving this place? Demography counts people in places. Even the word "demography" invites the reader to snooze. Demography may be destiny but it can be deadly dull.

The demographics of Jerusalem, however, are more interesting than in other places because here demography is political. The basic facts about Jerusalem are regarded neither as basic nor as facts. The demography of the city provides ammunition for challenging its social and political ownership. In most cities, population growth is important to local economies and is used for promoting the economic development of places. In Jerusalem, population growth and its connection to economic development is secondary to its role in solidifying or dissipating claims over political ownership. Facts and figures about the city are mobilized in the war over who will ultimately call Jerusalem its capital – their nation's (Israel or Palestine's) political flagship.

Jerusalem's demography is a central component within the geopolitical struggle between Palestinians and Israelis over who owns Jerusalem. Other geopolitical weapons include archaeology ("proving" Jews or Palestinians to be part of Jerusalem's historical foundation), community development (providing "facts on the ground" that establish ownership), the barrier/fence/wall (preventing Palestinian residential and spatial mobility), and housing development (facilitating and encouraging the residential inclusion and exclusion of different groups). Demography, archaeology, housing, and community development are soft yet powerful tools that can be used to legitimate Jerusalem's ownership by either Palestinians or Israelis.

But the ability to use these tools is dependent on already-existing power relationships. Israel controls almost all development within Jerusalem. Almost all new Jerusalem developments are built for Israeli and foreign Jews, not for Palestinians. Most developments built by Palestinians are considered illegal, and are routinely subject to threats of demolition (Jabareen, 2010; Chiodelli, 2012; Braier, 2013; Dumper, 2014). Palestinians, like other socially and economically marginalized groups, have more control over their demography than over land and housing. They may not legally build homes to enlarge their communities but they can have more children. While they often are unable to legally move to Jerusalem, many are able to enter the city illegally and become part of the city's growing informal economy. As discussed in Chapter 3, their ability to affect the demography of the city is an effective weapon in their control for eventually and perhaps inevitably claiming Jerusalem. Their everyday practices, essentially living on and in Jerusalem, are a form of asserting their right to Jerusalem.

What Is Jerusalem?

Although the world defines its Jerusalem as the spatial area contained by the Green Line (what is known as West Jerusalem), the State of Israel does not. Israel collects and assembles Jerusalem data for an area that includes East and West Jerusalem, essentially the Jerusalem that Israel says is within the now established Israeli-defined municipal boundaries. Therefore, for our purposes here we rely on the Israeli officially sanctioned public data for the defined municipality combining East and West Jerusalem as of 1980.

How Big Is Jerusalem?

Jerusalem is the largest city in Israel. But the city of Jerusalem is not big according to conventional standards of city size. As of 2012, it contained 815,300 people. At that time, its population size was comparable to Columbus (809,798) and Indianapolis (834,852), two moderately sized cities in the United States.

The Jerusalem metropolitan region is much larger. But like everything concerning the spatial area defining Jerusalem, its definition is subject to debate because most of the city's "suburbs" are settlements located in the West Bank and are not officially located in Israel. The municipality of Jerusalem combined with its suburbs (including settlements) is over a million people (Shlay and Rosen, 2010; Allegra, 2013). The number of people living in settlements continues to grow at a faster rate than the municipality.

Nonetheless, Jerusalem's population size is not big even when taking into account its suburbs and contiguous settlements. In fact, it only begins to approximate the size of a significant metropolitan area when Ramallah and Bethlehem, two Palestinian cities currently on the other side of the barrier/fence/wall, are included as part of what could be called the Jerusalem–Ramallah–Bethlehem greater metro-region. It is when artificial spatial barriers like checkpoints and the barrier/fence/wall are removed from the equation that the metropolitan area can begin to be considered large.

Jerusalem's Population Groups

What gets counted by government statistics reflects the importance of particular social groups. The US Census counts race, ethnicity, whether one is foreign born or of Hispanic origin. In the United States, race is distinct from ethnicity. The United Kingdom focuses on "identity," whether this is religious, sexual, national, or ethnic. In the United Kingdom, race is an ethnic identity. In Canada, people are counted according to ethnic origins and whether they are "visible minorities," meaning whether their minority status can be visually identified. In all of these countries, difference is measured, although in very different ways.

Israel is also characterized by enormous racial and ethnic diversity. But its counting of its social make-up is parsimonious. Although in everyday life it matters if one is Mizrahi or Ashkenazi or Ethiopian or Russian, for the Israeli government these differences appear less important. The Israeli Census counts only two groups: Jews and Arabs. Anyone else is classified as other. Note that the Israeli Census counts Arabs, not Palestinians.

Arabs include all Muslims, Christians, and those with no

religion. Others are Christians who are not Arabs, other religious groups, and those not classified by religion (who are not Jews and not Arabs). Although information on different groups (e.g. Ethiopians) may be available, official census counts are of Israel's specific "population groups."

Ethnic Identification

Jerusalem contains more Jews than Palestinians within its municipal limits, but not a lot more, and the percentage of Palestinians is gaining on the Jews. The numbers of Palestinians living in Jerusalem continued to grow at a much faster rate than the numbers of Jews. In 1967, the Jerusalem breakdown was 74 percent Jewish and 26 percent Palestinian. By 2011, this breakdown was 63 percent Jewish and 37 percent Palestinian. Each year, the percentage of Palestinians has gotten incrementally higher. Note that these counts do not include the large number of "illegal" Palestinian residents known to increasingly live in the city, particularly with the construction of the barrier/fence/wall.

Socioeconomic Characteristics

Jerusalem contains a large number of poor families. In 2011, over one-third of all Jerusalem families were poor. Poverty was disproportionately concentrated among Jerusalem's Palestinian families (approx. 73 percent), but it was also high among Jewish families (approx. 24 percent). Moreover, poverty among Jerusalem's Jewish families was concentrated among the ultra-Orthodox.

In most places, poverty is typically concentrated among single-parent households because female-headed single-family households with children do not have access to the same types of employment and monetary resources as married-couple families or men in general. But Jerusalem has defied this trend, not because single-parent households are not poor, but because so many married-couple families are. Family structure is one predictor of poverty among Jerusalemites. But a dominant one is religiosity. Among Jews, poverty was heavily concentrated among ultra-Orthodox families (64 percent). Among Jerusalem's Palestinians, it is almost universal (73 percent).

Poverty in Jerusalem is not simply a function of family composition and gender economic discrepancies, but is tied to religiosity as well as to ethnicity. Wealth is overrepresented among the city's secular population. Poverty is overrepresented among the city's most religious population and its Palestinian population.

Age Distribution and Natural Growth

Jerusalem has a relatively young population compared to other Israeli cities (median age in Jerusalem = 24). But like other demographic characteristics, Jerusalem's age distribution is related to religiosity and ethnicity. Jerusalem's ultra-Orthodox and Palestinian populations have higher reproductive rates than its other religious and more secular populations, therefore accounting for a greater share of the younger population.

While the Palestinian reproductive rate in Jerusalem remains high, it has been steadily decreasing (2011 = 3.6). The Jewish reproductive rate in Jerusalem has been steadily increasing, largely owing to the increasing numbers of high birth-rate, ultra-Orthodox, and other religious families within Jerusalem (2011 = 4.2). The high fertility rates of both religious Jewish families and Palestinian families is the largest source of population growth for Jerusalem.

In- and Out-Migration

The number of Jews immigrating to Israel has been steadily declining over the last decade. But the number of Jews who have immigrated to Israel and then chosen to live in Jerusalem has been increasing relative to other Israeli cities. Proportionately more of Israel's new immigrants are moving to Jerusalem compared to

Haifa or Tel Aviv. These new Jewish immigrants have tended to move to some of Jerusalem's wealthiest neighborhoods.

People also have been moving out of Jerusalem to other places in Israel. A significant number are moving to what is considered part of the greater metropolitan Jerusalem area, including Jerusalem's conventional suburbs and the settlements surrounding it in the West Bank.

The Growth of Jerusalem

Is Jerusalem growing? Yes and no. After the 1967 war, Jerusalem more than doubled its size, dramatically increasing its land mass with the annexation of East Jerusalem. Many people moved to Jerusalem and resided in the housing built in its new neighborhoods in the 1970s. Today, Jerusalem's growth rate has slowed. Although foreign-born Jewish immigrants are moving more to Jerusalem than to other Israeli cities, their numbers are not large. The municipality of Jerusalem is maintaining its size, largely through high reproductive rates of its poorest populations, the ultra-Orthodox and Palestinians. The wealthy immigrants coming from around the world to Jerusalem cannot cancel out the growing numbers of increasingly impoverished families, both Jewish and Palestinian.

Jerusalem, Tel Aviv, and Haifa

The Israel that is experienced by its three largest cities varies considerably. Tel Aviv (population = 411,500) is about half the size of Jerusalem (population = 815,400). Haifa (population = 272,200) is about one-third the size of Jerusalem.

Although bigger, Jerusalem's social world is light years from the ones lived by its urban sisters. Both Tel Aviv and Haifa contain far fewer Palestinian citizens; in Tel Aviv and Haifa, Palestinian Israeli citizens comprised 4.2 percent and 10.5 percent, respectively, of each city's population in 2013. Jerusalem's Palestinian residents

(not citizens) comprised more than one-third of the city's residents
(36.8 percent in 2013). The difference in the legal status and visibility of Palestinians in these urban settings is large and could affect
the ways in which each urban population experiences the tensions
associated with the inequities that govern the Israeli Palestinian
experience.

But Jerusalem is also economically different. It is poorer (47
percent poor) compared to either Tel Aviv (14 percent) or Haifa
(21 percent). For working people, Jerusalem's average monthly
salaries are NIS 3,400 and NIS 2,400 lower than the average salaries of those in either Tel Aviv or Haifa (about $700–$1,000 lower
per month).

Jerusalem's age structure is much younger than those associated
with either Tel Aviv or Haifa. The majority of Jerusalem's families
(62%) are married, many with very young children. In Haifa, 56
percent are married. In Tel Aviv, only 46 percent are married. Tel
Aviv contains many more people in their mid to late twenties and
thirties, who are younger and single.

Jerusalem: An Amalgamation of Difference

For many American baby boomers, their first experience with
Israel was the 1960 blockbuster *Exodus*. The first Zionist they got
to see in the flesh was not Theodore Herzel but the blond-haired,
blue-eyed Paul Newman, who successfully woos Eva Marie Saint
(another blonde, although not Jewish) with Israel's violent creation
in the background. At the end, one anticipates the fair-haired and
pale offspring to come from this union, leaping out of the womb
singing and dancing to "Hava Nagila."

How astonishing it is to visit Israel and to find out that not only
are there very few Paul Newmans to be found but also that Jews
come in a variety of colors and speak many different languages,
only a few with a New York accent. The Jews of Israel vary in
almost any way that people can, making for endless permutations
of physical Jewish characteristics.

Like "Jewish," the term "Palestinian" is an ethnic identity defined by a common culture and history, not by physical characteristics. How someone looks Jewish, Palestinian, or any other amalgam type of identity is the stuff of stereotyping bordering on racism. With the formation of the State of Israel, the idea of looking Israeli Jewish has never been so utterly and completely laughable.

The ensemble of defining social characteristics in Jerusalem is large. The major social attributes are shown in Table 4.1. These characteristics represent the major ways in which people in Jerusalem are classified and stratified (S. Hasson, 1996, 2001). These identifying features represent those that are most commonly used to define who is what and who gets what in Jerusalem. Not surprisingly, the Israeli reward structure is tied to race, religion, ethnicity, and religiosity.

Table 4.1 Defining social characteristics of people living in Jerusalem

Faith and religion	Religion: Major religions (Judaism, Islam, and Christianity)
	Religiosity: Scope of religious observance, e.g. ultra-Orthodox (Haredi)
Geography	Ethno-national identity: Israeli Jews and Palestinians Country of origin
	Jewish tribal/regional identity: Ashkenazim (European identity), Mizrahim (Middle Eastern and North African origin), Russian (former Soviet Union), Ethiopians
	Jerusalem residential location: Arab Jerusalem/East Jerusalem, Israeli Jerusalem/West
	Barrier/fence/wall location: Inside the barrier/fence/wall, outside the barrier/fence/wall
Socioeconomic	Income
	Education
	Race
	Gender
Political	Citzenship/residence
	Political ideology/political party
	Zionist/non-Zionist

Religion and Ethno-Nationality

Israeli Jews are united by virtue of being Jewish. But in many ways, Israeli solidarity exists in spite of the resounding differences among the Jews of Israel. Two primary characteristics that distinguish Jerusalemites are religion and national identity.

As a nation, Israel defines itself as a Jewish state. The laws of the land are self-consciously informed by Jewish religious customs and traditions as well as by Jewish definitions of life-cycle events and the yearly calendar. For example, many countries in the world have established Sunday as a day off and Monday as the beginning of the work week, reflecting governmental adherence to a Christian calendar. In Israel, Sunday is the beginning of the work week and Christian holidays are not nationally observed. Instead, Jewish holidays are national holidays in Israel. School holidays conform to Jewish holidays, for example Rosh Hashana, Yom Kippur, and Passover, not Christmas and Easter. Israel employs the Jewish calendar because it is a nation of Jews, a Jewish state.

Adherence to the Jewish calendar and rejection of a Christian one is one of the clearest statements Israel has made proclaiming itself as a Jewish state. The Jewish calendar is organized around Jewish religious holidays. But for the many secular Israelis, these holidays are not claimed as religious holidays per se but as national holidays that celebrate and commemorate their lives as Jews in Israel. A Jewish holiday in Israel is both religious and secular at the same time.

This distinction between Jewish as a religion and Jewish as a nation is not easy to grasp from an American perspective, where national identity is intended to embrace all cultures, religions, and identities. Being American is celebrating the Fourth of July, eating turkey on Thanksgiving, and having a barbeque on Memorial Day. Being Jewish in the United States is a religious identity tacked on in addition to a nationalist identity. For many Jews in Israel, Judaism as a religion is secondary to its role as a nationality.

Being Jewish, Christian, Muslim, Buddhist, or whatever religion is in addition to being an American. Being American in the United States is a secular experience. Being Jewish in Israel is also a secular experience. It is the religious Jews who tack on the religious experience to being Jewish in Israel. Being a religiously observant Jew in Israel is an extra identity to being a Jew there, just as being a religiously observant Jew in the United States is an extra identity to being an American there.

In Israel, being identified as a Jew can be either a religious or national identity or it can be both. The availability of a choice in Israel over how to be Jewish is what is fundamentally different about Israel as a Jewish state. Israeli Jews are not required to go to synagogue on Shabbat or to eat matzah during Passover because they are first and foremost Jews from the get-go. At the same time, either being religious or observing some Jewish holidays does not make Israeli Jews more Jewish. As Israeli citizens, they live and breathe being Jewish just as American citizens live and breathe being American. The idea of Jews as a people or nation is that they share a common historical and cultural identity, like Italians or Australians. As a national identity, Jews share a common identity whether they are religious or not. According to Israeli law, Jews have the right of return to Israel because, by tradition, they are linked to Israel as an originating place for Jews as a people.

Palestinians are also connected to an ethno-national identity as well as a religious one. But the Palestinian identity is not a religious identity. Palestinians may belong to any number of faiths, although most are identified as Muslim, while a significant number are Christian.

Being Jewish in Israel creates multiple identities. A secular Jew may be more strongly identified as being part of Israel as a Jewish nation than as being part of the Jewish faith/religion. An ultra-Orthodox Jew may be more strongly identified as being part of the Jewish faith than with belonging to Judaism as a national identity. Other Israeli Jews, like the National Religious, combine Jewish nationalism with religion.

How Americans and Israelis choose to express their Jewishness is different. Until quite recently, being Jewish anywhere in the world was largely not a choice or an identity per se. People were born Jewish as an ascribed characteristic, not as something one could choose to be.

But with the decline of anti-Semitism, one may choose to be Jewish, that is, to express one's Jewishness or not. American Jews make a choice to *be Jewish* by joining a synagogue or having their children attend a religious school. And if they choose not to act on their Judaism – to be Jewish – they may get swallowed up by the secular Christian traditions that are part of everyday life. Not choosing to be Jewish in countries other than Israel often means choosing not to be Jewish by default or effectively having no Jewish identity at all. Israeli Jews can be Jews without being religious. In other countries not being a religious Jew often means not being Jewish at all.

Zionism

In Israel, religious and national identities are also related to political identities, particularly whether one identifies as a Zionist. Zionism represents a longstanding movement to establish a national homeland for the Jewish people. People who are Zionists support Israel's standing and identification as a Jewish state, as a homeland for the Jewish people.

In Israel, people's religious, ethno-national, and Zionist identities vary considerably. Some ultra-Orthodox Jews are religious Jews but are not Zionists. Secular Jews may not self-identify as religious Jews but they are likely to be Zionists. There is no uniformity in Jewish or Zionist identities across Jews. People may identify as Jews but not as religious. People may identify as religious but not as Zionists. People may see themselves connected to a nation of Jews but not connected to the idea of a national state for Jews (Zionism). Not all Israelis are Zionists. This can be very confusing.

In March 2014, the Israeli government reversed its policy and ruled that ultra-Orthodox men are required to enlist for service in the Israeli military like non-Haredi Israelis. This was met with complete and total outrage and contempt by Haredi authorities. Protest ensued throughout the country, with the largest demonstration in Jerusalem. The city was shut down as hundreds of

Figure 4.1 Haredi demonstration against their people being drafted (© Anne Shlay)

thousands of Haredi men, women, and children came to Jerusalem to express their view that by mandating conscription the government of Israel was anti-religion (see Figure 4.1).

Country of Origin and Regional Identity

Israeli Jews have originated and continue to originate from a variety of countries. Some Jews migrated to Israel before the 1948 war that established the State of Israel. But most Jewish immigrants came to Israel afterward. They did so from all over Europe, particularly Eastern Europe. Jews also came from North Africa (Morocco and Tunisia, Algeria and Libya) and the Middle East (Turkey, Iraq, Iran, Syria, Egypt, and Yemen). Jewish immigrants continue to come from all over the world, from the United States and Canada, from Zimbabwe and South Africa, and even from

Ethiopia and India. After the breakup of the Soviet Union in the 1990s, Israel received one million immigrants from former Soviet Union states (mainly Russia and Ukraine).

Israelis' countries of origin contained and continue to contain the predictable connections of class to race and ethnicity. The lighter-skinned Europeans, the speakers of Yiddish, were known as the Ashkenazim. Jews expelled from Spain and Portugal were called Sephardim. But it was with the growing number of Jews from the Middle East and North Africa that a clear racial and ethnic distinction from the Ashkenazim (light skin) was made. These Middle Eastern and North African Jews became known as Mizrahim (a term for describing Sephardic Jews of Middle Eastern and North African origins).

Ashkenazim and Mizrahim emerged as the initial, more or less tribal characteristics by which Israeli Jews were stratified. Ashkenazim were regarded as the superior ethnic group, with lighter skin, more education, and more money. The darker Mizrahim were perceived as inferior to the Ashkenazim. These markers became incorporated within the Israeli reward structure (Horowitz and Lissak, 1989).

With the migration of Ethiopians and Russians to Israel, further ethnic distinctions were made. Ethiopians are neither European nor Middle Eastern. As black Sub-Saharan Africans, not like the much smaller number of white South African Jewish immigrants, Ethiopians were regarded as lower in status than the Mizrahim. The Russians who came to Israel after the breakup of the former Soviet Union have also become an ethnic group unto themselves. These later European migrants were not Ashkenazim, that is, the higher-status ethnic identity of Jews who had immigrated earlier from Europe. Although welcomed to Israel as Jews, they knew little about Jewish customs or traditions. The Russians and Ethiopians are similarly positioned Jewish tribal groups that appear distinct from the tribes of the Ashkenazim and the Mizrahim.

With intermarriage, class mobility, and the eventual emergence of an Israeli identity that is a blend of the originating cultures, the distinctions between the Ashkenazim and the Mizrahim are slowly diminishing. Nonetheless, one's country of origin, tied to race and ethnicity, remains an important mechanism for stratification within Israel. Ethiopians and Russians, the most recent group of immigrants, continue to be socially unique subgroups distinct from either the Ashkenazim or the Mizrahim.

Political Ideology/Political Party

The political and economic inequalities between these groups fostered organizing around different political parties. The Ashkenazim were initially represented by Israel's leading political parties affiliated with the Labor movement. The coming of age for the Mizrahim was to organize themselves into political parties that would challenge the hegemonic political elites. First, the Likud party took power in 1977. This had symbolized a new age in Israeli politics: power alignments were significantly changed, and welfare state ideology was replaced with principles like neoliberalism and privatization. This change also strengthened nationalism and religion as core values of the State of Israel. Then, in 1984, Shas, a Mizrahi Orthodox religious party, was established. Shas has attempted to promote the Mizrahi-Jewish heritage and adopt an ultra-Orthodox lifestyle. Eventually the Russians followed suit with the parties Yisrael BaAliyah and Yisrael Beiteinu. Different parties continue to proliferate. These parties are as much about ethnic identity as they are about politics.

Israeli political parties, like political parties everywhere, are organized around different groups competing for resources within the public realm. But the defining characteristics of Israeli political parties represent two very different and fundamental political cleavages.

The first political cleavage is Jewish religiosity, a variable also tied to class. Secular and religious Jews are represented by different political parties. In particular, the political parties of the poorer religious Jews are organized to deliver material economic assistance to these ultra-Orthodox constituencies. These religious political parties also create allegiances and loyalty among their members through their ability to deliver resources to their constituents.

Party members typically vote as instructed by their rabbis and
turnout is often close to 100 percent. Political party and level of
religiosity go hand in hand.

The second political cleavage is somewhat less instrumental in
terms of delivering material benefits to political supporters and is
more ideological. Parties are organized around different positions
on the Palestinian–Israeli conflict. Should Israel be working to
compromise and generate a peace agreement with the Palestinians?
Should Palestinians be given their own state? Should Israel help
to further the self-determination of the Palestinian people? Those
who answer the questions in the affirmative are considered left-
wing on the political spectrum. Those who answer negatively are
considered right-wing.

The political positions of these parties also reflect different
stances on the role and importance of settlements. Right-wing
parties are pro-settlement. At one extreme they believe that Israel
is not occupying the West Bank per se but is taking up residence
in the "Land of Israel," the biblical lands of Judea and Samaria that
they believe belong to Israel by right. According to people at this
end of the political spectrum, God promised this land to the Jews.
It is neither occupied territory nor illegal. For right-wing settlers,
any peace agreement that does not cede this land to Israel is for
heathens, not real Jews. Right-wing parties are similar to ultra-
Orthodox parties in using their political clout to leverage resources
for the settlement movement and have been able to yield huge
amounts of money for housing, infrastructure, and security over
the Green Line and in the West Bank (Zertal and Eldar, 2007).
And like the ultra-Orthodox, these parties tend to have political
clarity; they know what they want and do not compromise.

Left and more centrist parties have more ambiguous belief
systems and are fuzzier on what they want. They tend to be more
overtly pro-peace and tend to be more anti-settlement (depending on the definition of what settlements are and where they are
established). The pro-peace movement is more subdued than it
was prior to the Second Intifada with the ensuing conflicts that
emerged out of the carnage. Nonetheless, parties that are more
on the left remain committed to negotiating some kind of peace

resolution. Most believe that peace with the Palestinians is possible. They largely believe that constructing settlements is bad politics (although building housing in Jerusalem is considered by most parties as legitimate), and they believe, more or less, in the rights of the Palestinian people to self-determination and their own state.

Jerusalem Residential Location and Citizenship

Post-1967, Jerusalem planners and politicians alike have worked feverishly to "unite" the city. But implementing the concept of a united Jerusalem has meant attempting to make it indivisible. A united Jerusalem has become a symbol for a Jerusalem that cannot be divided in the event of a peace agreement. Building the new neighborhoods was intended to prevent any future attempt to divide East and West Jerusalem. By building Jewish neighborhoods in areas that once were Arab, Israeli planners and politicians hoped to prevent East Jerusalem, and, in particular, the Old City, from being initially returned to Jordan or becoming part of a Palestinian state.

With the continual building of housing in and around Jerusalem by Jews and Palestinians alike, the terms East and West Jerusalem have lost some of their precise meaning in respect of who lives there – Palestinians or Israelis. In discussing a future peace agreement, people still refer to East Jerusalem as a possible location for a Palestinian capital. However, much of what was once Arab East Jerusalem is now firmly integrated as part of Israeli Jerusalem. The world refers to these areas as settlements, but in terms of everyday life they are Jerusalem.

Yet whatever one calls those parts of Jerusalem that are more Palestinian/Arab or more Israeli/Jewish, these largely ethnically homogeneous neighborhoods continue to divide the city according to ethno-national and religious lines. Jerusalem is a divided city, not a Jewish one. It is a Jewish and Palestinian city. On Jerusalem Day, Yom Yerushalayim, the government hosts parades and proclaims the unity of the city, but if the city were truly unified, there would be no need for such a proclamation.

With these spatial divisions comes an incredible amount of

inequality. Palestinian neighborhoods have lower-quality ser-
vices, including schools and recreational and sanitation facilities.
There are separate bus systems for Palestinians and Jews and the
Palestinian system has less funding and is inferior to the Jewish one
(Kaminiker, 1997; Jabareen, 2010).

Jerusalem remains divided. Arab/Palestinian and Jewish/Israeli
neighborhoods are not equal. And no one pretends that they are.

Citizenship or the lack thereof explains some of this discrepancy. Most Palestinian Jerusalemites are not citizens of Israel
(S. Hasson, 1996). The post-1967 Palestinian Jerusalem residents
whose neighborhoods were annexed to Jerusalem have been
given legal residency, that is, the right to live legally in Jerusalem
and to receive some of the services provided to citizens. But they
have not been given citizenship. Legal residents may apply for citizenship, but acquiring it is rare (Klein, 2004). Arab Jerusalemite
citizens of Israel largely live in Palestinian neighborhoods that
became part of Israel immediately after the 1948 war, such as
Beit Safafa, or in neighborhoods considered as frontier areas near
Palestinian areas, such as the French Hill (Masry-Herzalla and
Razin, 2014).

The building of the security barrier/fence/wall through
Jerusalem has challenged and largely confounded what it means to
be a legal or illegal resident. Portions of Arab/East Jerusalem have
been walled out of the city. Whether these residents are legal or
not, they are spatially cut off from the city and country in which
they allegedly live (Nasrallah, 2007; Owais, 2008).

Socioeconomic Characteristics

Usually the best predictor of people's social and economic outcomes is the social and economic environment in which they were
born. It is through the confluence of class/income, educational
attainment, ethnicity, and gender to shape people's social and economic outcomes that social scientists talk about how inequality is
reproduced over time. These characteristics are termed predictors
of socioeconomic achievement because the economic situations of

people in these groups tend to persist over time. Israel and, in particular, Jerusalem are not exceptions to this general social mobility rule.

But the typical stratification variables of race, class, education, and gender are tied to other critical social dimensions in Jerusalem that heighten the varied effects (negative and positive) of these factors. It is the other social characteristics that stand in for the effects of class and education.

Ethno-national characteristics act as a proxy for class and education. Almost all Palestinian neighborhoods in Jerusalem are poor. Being a Palestinian living in Jerusalem may be socioeconomically better than being a Palestinian living outside of Jerusalem.

Religiosity also functions as a proxy for class and education. Ultra-Orthodox families are typically poor with less education, although many, particularly the men, may be well schooled in Jewish law, philosophy, and practice. Secular and more Orthodox Jewish families are more educated with more wealth and have occupational and therefore social mobility.

The role of gender in Israeli society as a predictor of life chances is complex and challenging to understand (Greenberg and Shoval, 2013; Masry-Herzalla and Razin, 2014; Singer and Bickel, 2014). Women in the ultra-Orthodox and Palestinian communities are circumscribed into traditional gender roles, with major household and child-care responsibilities. In addition, because ultra-Orthodox men eschew employment for Torah study, ultra-Orthodox women bear the responsibility for economically supporting their families. To be sure, the Israeli government provides income to ultra-Orthodox families in the form of child allowances and other subsidies. But these families, while able to make ends meet, remain poor.

The poverty of ultra-Orthodox families seems from the outside to be more voluntary than structural. Ultra-Orthodox families could change their economic situations by making different choices – by acquiring more education, by going to university, and by having fewer children. Being Haredi, or ultra-Orthodox, is ultimately a life-style, not a structural liability per se. Becoming and remaining Haredi is not equivalent to being Palestinian.

The Role of Social Groups in the Shaping of Jerusalem

International politics, the media, and leaders from across the globe focus on Jerusalem as the ultimate contested space between two sides: the Israelis and the Palestinians. Both want Jerusalem as their capital. Both make effective arguments for their longevity and religious credibility in the region. Both have amassed considerable amounts of support for their case, although Israel has reigned supreme over Jerusalem since 1967.

Internal to Jerusalem's municipal borders are a set of societal and spatial issues that divide the city. Arab–Jewish cleavages are viewed as being dichotomous but vary along major dimensions of religion, class, and ideology (Horowitz and Lissak, 1989). Since 1967, Jerusalem has increasingly been characterized by a hierarchy of political power, social and spatial segregation, and political exclusion. These segregative and exclusionary processes have worked to alter the spatial distribution of different groups. Spatial dominance and political dominance have gone hand in hand with the social and spatial separation of religious, less religious, non-religious, and foreign Jews and Palestinians. This part of this chapter provides a synopsis of the different groups of Jerusalem and examines how their presence, political activities, and defining characteristics shape Jerusalem.

The first part examines the Jews of Jerusalem and looks at their divisions by levels of religiosity (or secularity), by whether they are Zionists or anti-Zionist, or whether they are part of the Jewish Diaspora. The second part examines the Palestinians of Jerusalem and looks at their differences by whether they are Israeli citizens, Jerusalem residents and non-Israeli citizens, live in Jerusalem inside the barrier/fence/wall, or live in Jerusalem outside the barrier/fence/wall.

Difference defines Jerusalem. A well-known Jerusalem advocate wished out loud that the city's differences could be managed in another way like the Jerusalem Biblical Zoo (officially known as the Tisch Family Zoological Gardens). For her, the zoo was a model of how everyone could get along. Her words:

The zoo is self-sufficient and gets no financial aid from the state. Sex is taught freely. The visitors are mixtures of all kinds of Jews and Arab. It is friendly. On Saturday, the zoo is open. Women teach about sex. There are countless volunteers. There is a peccary that looks like a pig and a sign that says that it is not a pig. It is a zoo with humor. The zoo is clean ecologically. It saves animals from other countries. It has two eagles that appear to be gay. They were given an incubated egg to sit on which they did and they raised together the baby eagle, who now has her own family. (Interview, 2010)

She wished out loud that Jerusalem could become like its own zoo: welcoming, friendly, multicultural, and with a sense of humor, a place of tolerance that enthusiastically embraces difference.

Jerusalem Jews, Religiosity, and Zionism

The prominence of Jewish religiosity in Israeli as well as Jerusalem politics is relatively recent – a product of post-1967 spatial, ideological, and demographic changes. In the aftermath of the 1967 war, the unification of Jerusalem, and Israeli occupation of the West Bank, new ideological ideas and values have worked to reshape the Zionism that was previously largely associated with Jewish secularism (Mayer, 2008). With its perceived loss of the Old City in the 1948 war, Israel declared West Jerusalem its capital and crafted nationally integrative symbols that were largely political and non-religious. Being Israeli was primarily about living as a Jew in Israel: that is, surviving as a nation in its violent struggle for independence. According to historian Menachem Klein,

Until 1967, the symbols and culture of Zionism and the desire to establish a state overcame the Jewish symbols in Jerusalem. . . . In West Jerusalem, Israel created an alternative symbolic space to what had been left behind in the Old City. (Klein, 2004: 179)

Secular Jerusalem Jews

Secular Jerusalemites tend to be modern, educated, and have higher incomes than either Palestinians or ultra-Orthodox Jews. Their wealth provides them with choices over residential locations not available to the lower-income groups such as higher-priced suburbs (not settlements). Many secular Jews have left or abandoned religiously changing neighborhoods for other in-town secular communities or have moved out of Jerusalem altogether.

Israeli planners and policy makers describe neighborhood changes from secular to Haredi using Chicago School sociological terms like invasion and succession. In this now scientifically outdated vernacular, Israeli ultra-Orthodox Jews are cast in the role of "invaders" who move into secular neighborhoods and by default take over, residentially and socially. It is also a truism in Israeli planning circles as well as the general public that there is a fundamental incompatibility between secular Jews (as well as traditional Jews) and the religious ultra-Orthodox population that prevents them from coexisting in the same residential space. The deliberate segregation of ultra-Orthodox from secular Jews is not considered to be discrimination. Rather, it is viewed as normal as well as practically necessary. Segregation by religiosity is built into ongoing housing development and planning schemes.

Policy makers fear that secular Jews with resources will leave Jerusalem just as white middle-class people left central US cities in the 1960s and 1970s, with similar devastating political, economic, and social consequences.

According to one prominent national government planning official, "The Haredim are increasing. They are largely low income. This hurts the tax base, continues a cycle of decline in neighborhoods, precipitates neighborhood change largely based on invasion and success, and the Haredim are always looking to other sites" (interview, 2006). Another Jerusalem scholar and former local government official stated boldly that "people don't want to live in a city strangled by the ultra-Orthodox" (interview, 2007). Even the leader of a major advocacy organization for West Bank settlements argued that having secular people within Jerusalem is a vital issue, stating that "it is important that Jerusalem has a diverse population. Otherwise all of the secular Jews will leave Jerusalem" (interview, 2008).

However, building new neighborhoods for young families in Jerusalem involves a spectrum of interwoven considerations (demographic, environmental, class, and political). Most affordable housing is offered beyond the Green Line, either in the new neighborhoods built to unify Jerusalem after 1967 or in large settlements adjacent to its municipal boundaries. Political considerations deter some left-wing secular families from living beyond the Green Line. Increasingly, secular families are faced with either suburbanization to non-settlement suburbs or settlements or moving out of the Jerusalem metropolitan area. The housing options of secular young Jewish families in Jerusalem are constrained.

Environmental considerations are also important to secular Jewish groups. They typically withhold support for plans for affordable housing inside Jerusalem in order to avoid urban environmental degradation. They will then support building these developments beyond the Green Line, essentially trading off political politics for environmental ones. According to an environmental reporter for the *Haaretz* newspaper,

> The Greens [environmentalists] are not involved in what is happening beyond the Green Line. On this issue they gave up. Beyond the Green Line, it is much easier to get development approved. This reflects the power of the army and the civil administration. The Defense Department has the power to wield anything anywhere. (Interview, 2007)

As a peace advocate and NGO executive director explained, it is better to build in East Jerusalem areas "that are environmentally already destroyed or built beyond the Green Line in desert areas than to build in West Jerusalem green hills" (interview, 2007).

Among Jerusalem's residential Jewish populations, there are clear divisions over their vision for Jerusalem. Secular Jews with their state-forming Zionist roots believe in Jerusalem as a capital of the Jewish state that provides sanctuary, safety, and a homeland for Jews. Secular Jews readily support efforts to develop the City of David because it highlights a three-thousand-year heritage that substantiates a Jewish presence in Jerusalem and their claim to Israel as their homeland community.

For secular Jews, Jerusalem provides them with status, pride, and protection in a world that historically promised Jews none of these things. But Jerusalem's importance does not rest with its religious significance as much as with its historical significance, with Israel's position as a nation state not as a religious icon – and Jerusalem as a capital city of the nation (not religion) of Jews.

National Religious Jews

National Religious Jews are religious Zionists. They view their religious and political orientation to be compatible as a form of biblical Zionism. They believe in "*Haaretz*" – Hebrew for "the land," which is a shorthand way of referring to the geographical areas known biblically as Judea and Samaria, which encompass much of the land that makes up the West Bank. For National Religious Jews, Israel's conquest of the Old City, East Jerusalem, and the West Bank is not a geopolitical strategy. Rather, it is a national destiny tied to religious providence. For the National Religious, Jews are part of the Land of Israel because it is meant to be.

The National Religious, however, are not fatalistic but are passionate believers in shaping their religious destiny. In 2005, this commitment was tested with the evacuation of settlers out of Gush Katif, a block of settlements developed in the Gaza Strip. The National Religious vehemently protested this evacuation with tremendous fervor and met other evacuations and closings of settlements and outposts on the West Bank with the same passion.

National Religious Jews find it difficult to find a place for political compromise about what constitutes Jerusalem or Israel post-1967. Their vision for Jerusalem encompasses a broad unity of faith, ideology, and unfailing commitment to ensuring that their sense of the will of God is achieved. For them, Jerusalem is not only a secular capital city per se, but also a holy capital city. For the National Religious, Jewish people are the holy people of God.

National Religious people blend their religiosity with their Zionism. They do not see a conflict between being a Zionist and being religious, and the two meld together as one religious and political ideology. Many of the settlers who "pioneer" by moving to Palestinian neighborhoods – to Silwan, to the Arab Quarter of the Old City, and to the West Bank – are National Religious people.

Ultra-Orthodox: The Haredim

Ultra-Orthodox Jews' political orientation is also guided by their religious orientation, but for many of them it is not Zionist. Many Haredim live in Jerusalem. Their politics toward Israel and Jerusalem are pragmatic and in some cases instrumental – geared toward using government to obtain the requisite housing, services, and money that will permit the survival and expansion of their communities. Their religious beliefs are to live as religious Jews and to obey Jewish law. With the goal of recreating Jewish life as it existed in Eastern Europe prior to the Holocaust, ultra-Orthodox Jews await the Messiah, who they believe will restore the Temple (the Jewish Temple) in the Old City. The ultra-Orthodox believe that Jerusalem is holy and therefore should exhibit its holiness, for example by observing Shabbat.

By being who they are and through demanding respect for their adherence to their way of life, the Haredim have had enormous and long-lasting effects on Jerusalem and ultimately on Israel itself. Their population size, life style, economic position, and beliefs are the most important factors affecting Jerusalem. This community is central to how the city develops spatially.

The Haredim are not a uniform group, although they may look that way because the men typically wear some form of black hat and black suit (Gonen, 1995). Nonetheless, differences in Haredim attire can still be distinguished, with variations in hat, haircut, and clothing acting as insignia denoting membership of a club. Haredi groups are different from each other, and these differences have political consequences, particularly for forming a ruling coalition in the Israeli government. The cleavages are along lines of ethnicity and country of origin. There are the Ashkenazim versus the Sephardim, the Hassidic versus the Lithuanians, and the Chabad versus everybody else. The Haredim also speak a variety of different languages, including Hebrew, Yiddish, French, and English (Alfasi et al., 2013; Flint et al., 2013). Some Haredi Israelis will only speak Yiddish, reserving Hebrew for religious activities.

A significant variation is how different Haredi Jews view the State of Israel. At one extreme is Naturei Karta, a group of religious ultra-Orthodox who routinely protest any and every form of Zionism. They vehemently do not believe in the Jewish State and are classic anti-Zionists. The group Agudat Yisrael, an original Haredi Jewish political party, is not anti-Zionist but rather non-Zionist, allowing its members political flexibility on the issue of Israel. Shas, a political party formed by Israel's formerly downtrodden minority groups of Mizrahi Jews originating from the Middle East and North Africa, is both Zionist and Haredi. Thus, while Haredi Jews are uniformly religious, their politics vis-à-vis Israel vary considerably.

The role of the size of the Haredim population is critical to Jerusalem for two main reasons. First it is large and continues to grow. The Haredim mandate procreation as part of their fundamental belief structure, so their rate of growth is higher than either secular, National Religious, or Palestinian families. Given the Israeli concern with maintaining Jewish numerical dominance in Jerusalem, the Haredim are viewed as doing their part for Israel by literally producing the numbers of Jewish people which allow the government to call Jerusalem Jewish. There is political appreciation for Haredi growth, particularly since this is taking place in Jerusalem.

Second, the Haredim use their size in electoral politics. Their political endorsement and votes are important sources of political leverage that provide them with a huge amount of political capital. The ultra-Orthodox are well organized politically, with large voting turnouts that can dictate the size of public expenditures for education, subsidies, family allowances, and housing for Haredi communities.

The ultra-Orthodox community in Jerusalem makes frequent use of violence, rioting, and intimidation as political tactics for ensuring that its point of view on conduct in its neighborhoods and on Shabbat is understood (Friedland and Hecht, 2000). With no tolerance for driving or any commercial activity on Shabbat, the Haredim barricade their streets off from Friday afternoon through Saturday night so that no cars enter their neighborhoods. The segregation of Haredi neighborhoods on Shabbat, however, is a compromise for the ultra-Orthodox, who would like to see no one in Jerusalem driving at all on Shabbat. The political pressure from the Haredi community for religious conformity by the secular population is severe (Rosen and Shlay, 2014; see Figure 4.2).

Secular neighborhoods seek protection from the residential mobility of Haredi families to their communities in anticipation that they will be forced out. Although not absolute, the housing

Figure 4.2   Signage in ultra-Orthodox neighborhoods enforcing dress codes (sign says "Private Yard: Please do not pass through our neighborhood dressed immodestly") (© Anne Shlay)

market is segmented by religiosity, resulting in two markets, one for Haredi people and one for others. There can be a falloff in demand for housing by secular households once neighborhoods become "mixed." Therefore, secular people fear the entrance of Haredi households to their communities and organize to prevent it. But with the enormous growth rates and demand for housing on the part of the Haredi communities, the residential spread of such households in Jerusalem is inevitable. The key to neighborhood stabilization is tolerance and openness to diversity, but the ultra-Orthodox by definition are not tolerant. In this kind of social contest over space, many secular people choose to leave the religious "craziness" of Jerusalem altogether.

The Haredim are messianic but are not intentional religious settlers. Many Haredi live in settlement housing prepared specifically for them. They moved there not to settle the land and not to be "political" but simply to live as Jews. What is important to them are Jerusalem's holy places, in particular the Kotel in the Old City.

The Haredim's influence on the Old City is large. The Kotel's chief rabbi is Haredi, as is much of the staff of the Western Wall Heritage Foundation, the group that manages the Kotel. Following Haredi religious precepts, the Western Wall staff have managed the Kotel in a manner identical to an Orthodox synagogue. Men and women are required to pray separately and differently according to what has been prescribed by the Orthodox establishment. As we saw in the previous chapter, this type of gender difference has been the target of protest by the Women of the Wall for almost the past thirty years, resulting in a degree of compromise.

The Jews of Jerusalem

The religious politics of the Haredim are different from those of the National Religious and secular Zionists. Secular Zionists fuse their nationalism and their Judaism as one ideology – to support and be part of a Jewish state, and as a consequence are not viewed as religious. Although they may believe in God, their belief structure focuses on the State of Israel, not on God per se.

The National Religious also combine religion and nationalism and use their religion to inform their nationalism. But their nationalism is not tied to any particular government. It is tied to the Land of Israel. National Religious people equate God and the Land of Israel. The Land of Israel and its place with the people of Israel are just as important to them as the State of Israel.

The Haredim largely do not want land. Neither the Land of Israel nor the State of Israel holds tremendous importance to them. Their focus is predominantly on the people of Israel. They want to be part of an observant Jewish community wherever it is. In Jerusalem, they wait for the Messiah, who they believe will eventually come if they are reverent, patient, and obey the rules.

The Jewish Diaspora

The Jewish Diaspora represents an amorphous group of Jews, namely all Jews who live outside of Israel. It is believed that the original Jewish Diaspora was created with the fall of the First Temple, but today all Jews living outside of Palestine (pre-1948) or outside of Israel (post-1948) are considered by most to be living outside of their designated homeland. Israeli law gives automatic citizenship to any Jew who desires to live in Israel. This "law of return" privileges Jews as potential citizens of Israel with rights equivalent to any other Israeli.

The Jewish Diaspora makes its claims on Jerusalem in six major ways: (1) through purchasing housing and property in Jerusalem; (2) though regular travel to Israel and Jerusalem in particular; (3) though influencing foreign policy toward Israel in their respective host countries; (4) through educating and socializing future generations of Jews about the importance of Israel (e.g. religious education, Hillel, Birthright); (5) through giving money to Israel; and (6) through the support of organizational dissemination of public information about Israeli political and cultural issues. All these activities have considerable effects on Jerusalem.

Diaspora Jews often visit Israel, and when they are not in Israel, many raise money for it. Diaspora Jews are energetic fund raisers and view raising money for Israel as part of their Jewish identity.

But raising money for Israel and living in Israel, particularly living in Jerusalem, are not equivalent, because Jews in the Diaspora have competing as well as different loyalties and identities. Outside Israel, being Jewish is not a full-time identity.

Diaspora Jews are active participants in Jerusalem place making as well. Their political voice is largely expressed through money. In addition to buying Jerusalem vacation homes for themselves, some also support the purchase of property for Jews in Palestinian neighborhoods and suburbs, a form of geopolitical support for claiming Palestinian neighborhoods for Israel. At the other end of the political spectrum, Diaspora Jews support religious alternatives to Jewish Orthodox hegemony through their involvement in Reform and Conservative Israeli movements that organize around religious pluralism such as the Women of the Wall and the Israel Religious Action Center (Rosen and Shlay, 2014).

Palestinians

In Israel, Jews and Arabs mostly live apart at both the city and neighborhood level (Gonen 1995; Falah, 1996; Yiftachel and Yacobi, 2003; Klein, 2004). Despite differences within these broad social groups, the Palestinian–Jewish division is primary. According to Dan Horowitz and Moshe Lissak (1989: 31), "The Arab–Jewish cleavage differs from all the other cleavages in that it is strictly dichotomous, in the sense that an individual belongs to either one group or the other."

As one Jerusalem-based scholar noted: "Israel has a bi-national condition. . . . It is permanently controlled by one ethnic group over the other" (interview, 2007). This is described as "ethnic democracy" (Peled, 1992; Smooha, 1997) and "ethnocracy" (Yiftachel, 1991). Inequality and ongoing discrimination are systematically exclusionary. Palestinian access to political remedies is idiosyncratic and results in uneven development and massive disparities in opportunities and resources across Israel and its occupied territories (Falah, 1990; Yiftachel, 1991; Tzfadia, 2005).

In Jerusalem, however, the allegedly clear-cut Jewish/Palestinian hierarchy becomes more complex. One organizational leader called Jerusalem "a mosaic of communities" (interview, 2007). Another advocate who focuses on halting West Bank expansion believes that Jerusalem is "more complex than any ideology that purports to explain it. Is Jerusalem two cities? Yes, but it is also one city and three cities. And it is really two metropolitan areas" (interview, 2007).

Yet Palestinians as a people bridge many worlds. They are situated in a nexus between religion, ethnicity, and nationalism. Palestinians are part of religious communities, including Islam and Christianity, that span the globe. They are part of the Arab civilization, an ethnic identity found in several continents and regions. Palestinian nationalism is the identity that is focused on place – on the place of the Palestinian people historically and socially within the Middle East. Being religious provides Palestinians with their claim to God. Being Palestinian is their claim to place and space. In relationship to Israel and particularly to Jerusalem, several other variables and characteristics are central as well. These are citizenship, residency status, and whether they reside inside or outside the barrier/fence/wall.

Emphasizing these important social and spatial differences, we look at major subgroups of Palestinians and their relationship to Jerusalem: (1) Israeli Palestinians/Israeli Arabs (Palestinians living in Jerusalem who are Israeli citizens); (2) East Jerusalem Palestinians (Palestinians living in Jerusalem who are not Israeli citizens); and (3) Jerusalem satellite Palestinians (Palestinians living outside of Jerusalem but in places they would consider part of the Jerusalem metropolitan region); and (4) the Palestinian Diaspora. For East Jerusalem Palestinians, we focus on differences between those living in Jerusalem on either side of the barrier/fence/wall.

Israeli Arabs

Prior to the 1948 war, Palestine was home for large numbers of both Arabs and Jews. Following the war, many Arab residents were either forced out of their homes or exhorted to leave. The result was mass immigration out of their communities (Falah, 1996;

Krystall, 1998; Shavitt, 2013). Many of the departed Arabs became the initial refugees that now populate the many refugee camps that dot the Middle East. Over five hundred thousand Arabs left Palestine because of the war.

Arabs who remained in what became Israel after 1948 were granted citizenship. They were provided with voting rights identical to Jewish Israeli citizens. Their rights to participate politically and to partake of the public basket of social services remained identical to Jewish Israelis. A major difference between Jewish and Israeli Arab citizens has been their military conscription status (Horowitz and Lissak, 1989). Military service became and remains compulsory for most Jews. With the exception of several Arab communities (e.g. the Druze, Bedouins, and Circassians), Muslim Arabs are exempt from military service. They can alternatively volunteer for another form of civil service, known as National Service, in hospitals, schools, and other areas of society. But most choose not to take part. This situation excludes most Israeli Arabs from a vital sector of participation and belonging in Israeli society as well as a key Israeli source for the acquisition of social capital.

The mass relocation of many Arabs from Palestine in 1948 meant that initially there were a small number of Israeli Arabs – Palestinians living under the Israelis. But despite their small size, these Israeli Arab citizens did not and could not assimilate because they were not Jewish.

Assimilation for Israeli Arabs is even more difficult than it has been for African Americans in the United States. The early history of the United States is about breaking down barriers to assimilation through easing the entrance of new European immigrant groups (e.g. Russians, Italians, Irish) into the dominant culture by eventually becoming white (Lieberson, 1981). At the outset, African American people could not assimilate in the same way as Europeans because of their defining racial characteristics which made them not white. But African Americans were not confronted with an official white state but with a racist state that could be changed. Unlike African Americans, Israeli Arabs are confronted with a state that builds difference into its governance. Israeli Arabs are citizens of a Jewish state and Israeli Arabs cannot become Jews.

Israeli Arabs are politically isolated within Israel. They can neither advocate for Israel (because of the need to support Palestinians' self-determination) nor advocate for a greater Palestinian state (because they are citizens of Israel). This dilemma is portrayed routinely by the *Haaretz* columnist Sayed Kashua, who writes about being an Israeli Arab living in Jerusalem. Kashua has produced books, movies, television shows, and has a regular newspaper column, yet faces a multitude of challenges living as a Palestinian Israeli Arab.

Arab Israeli citizens are in a precarious and largely unenviable position. They are discouraged from involving themselves in, if not required to remove themselves from, the historical events that have so radically shaped their status and community. They cannot realistically reinvent themselves in what has become a nation that largely does not want them there. But their physical location remains one of continuity. Many have been in Jerusalem for generations. The Arab Israeli situation is characterized by intense social and political dislocation.

Israeli Arabs have the right to participate in local and national elections. At the national level, they are represented by several different political parties that typically obtain a few seats in the Knesset. At this writing, 36 per cent of Jerusalem's population is Palestinian, compared to 20 percent of the entire country of Israel.

East Jerusalem Palestinians

The physical, social, and economic conditions of East Jerusalem have declined over time with Israeli housing demolitions, development and exclusionary housing policies, the closing of Palestinian political and economic institutions, and the development of the barrier/fence/wall (Kaminker, 1997; Bollens, 1998; Chesin et al., 1999, Klein, 2008). The rights of East Jerusalemite Arabs to the city have been severally and systematically compromised (Weizman, 2007; Jabareen, 2010; Wari, 2011; Rosen and Shlay, 2014).

The progressive isolation of Palestinian East Jerusalemites from the rest of the Palestinian community has weakened it because it has rendered these Palestinians an oppressed minority with limited rights in Israel, not part of a Palestinian nation or community. The importance of identity as a people or nation state to the Palestinian community cannot be overstated. According to an advocate for a Palestinian refugee community, "Palestinian means being part of a nation, not a minority" (interview, 2008).

A combination of policies has worked to intensify the marginalization of East Jerusalemite Palestinians. A major influence was the Oslo Agreement, which gave East Jerusalem, by virtue of its annexation to Israel, a different set of rules than those established for the West Bank. The Palestinian Authority was forbidden to operate in East Jerusalem; all political activity for East Jerusalem Palestinians was disallowed except voting in Jerusalem's municipal elections – a political activity rejected by most Palestinian East Jerusalemites because they believe it legitimizes Israeli governance of the area.

The Oslo Agreement also created a legal political separation between East Jerusalem and the rest of the West Bank. This spatial isolation of East Jerusalem from the West Bank was described by a leading Palestinian researcher: "In May 1993 the closing off of the West Bank into Jerusalem effectively cut off East Jerusalem from the West Bank. Israel blocked the regional roads. Now the roads leading from East Jerusalem to the West Bank became dead-end roads" (interview, 2007).

The aftermath of Oslo was the closing of East Jerusalem political and economic institutions and the removal of vital social infrastructure from East Jerusalem to Ramallah. This was, according to a Palestinian leader in health care and community development, a change in the "sphere of influence in East Jerusalem" as organizations increasingly moved to Ramallah (interview, 2008). There was a serious class dimension to this shift, he said, because "petty bourgeois people are leaving East Jerusalem. They need a cultured life, a liberal life. They can obtain this life in Ramallah." Leaving East Jerusalem for Ramallah meant leaving "the harshness of Israel and avoiding the high taxation" (interview, 2007). According to a prominent Israeli researcher, "There was a clear policy to move the centrality of East Jerusalem to Ramallah and to move institutions from East Jerusalem. The government closed the Orient House. It moved the judicial system to Ramallah" (interview, 2007). Political life for Palestinians in East Jerusalem was institutionally erased. According to a well-known writer, "Israel has destroyed all political aspects of Arab Jerusalem. It has pushed out to a substitute community" (interview, 2007).

This political disinvestment from East Jerusalem has been replicated with economic disinvestment. According to a Ramallah businessman and political activist, Oslo halted investments by West Bank investors where financial capital was concentrated because "banks in occupied territories cannot make loans in East Jerusalem. There is financial investment in the West Bank but no collateral is in East Jerusalem" (interview, 2008). Moreover, Palestinian banks were not allowed to operate in East Jerusalem.

The remaining legitimate source of investment, particularly for housing, was by default Israel. But Israel did not invest and at the same time placed heavy restrictions on Palestinian housing development, including home remodeling and additions. Israel restricts the issuing of building permits to East Jerusalem Palestinians. The Palestinian status quo is for Israel to deny building applications. So Palestinians build illegally. As a consequence, there is always the threat, and often the reality, of housing demolitions. As reported by a Palestinian researcher, "Since 1967, Israel has demolished over two thousand houses in East Jerusalem. More than seven thousand homes are under a demolition threat" (interview, 2008).

Israelis have also been developing Jewish settlements inside of East Jerusalem. Jews are essentially moving into Palestinian communities and taking housing away from Palestinians. A *Haaretz* newspaper reporter explained how this often works.

> Jews are trying to have property in these areas. They find old Jewish property and challenge the ownership. They prove that the property is Jewish and take it from the Arabs. This is a terrible process. It gives legitimacy to racist and apartheid impulses. And it is a one-way street. Jewish property is never revealed to be Arab after property is auctioned to the Jews. So when Israel occupied East Jerusalem, Israel became the custodian of the property in East Jerusalem. (Interview, 2007)

When Palestinians build their homes without building permits, they risk having these homes demolished. At the same time, investment activity is being directed at transferring housing from Palestinians in East Jerusalem to Jewish residents. This is a major expression of Israeli dominance over everyday life in East Jerusalem.

Israel has also introduced changes in residency requirements that require that East Jerusalem is the "center of life" for its Palestinian inhabitants or they risk losing their identity cards. Proving this residency status is often arduous, bureaucratic, and political. According to the Palestinian social worker who assists Palestinians retain their residency cards, "It is a power game. Jerusalem is disempowering the Palestinian community though the threat of loss of the residence identification card. They have to provide documentation that they are legal and living in Jerusalem" (interview, 2008).[3]

Israeli development of settlements on the West Bank near Jerusalem has had the effect of further isolating East Jerusalem from other West Bank communities. As noted by one Palestinian researcher, "Israel has been leading a demographic war since 1967. But it really shaped up in 1990. Settlements were built to isolate East Jerusalem" (interview, 2008).

The barrier/fence/wall represents the exacerbation of the social and political isolation already experienced by East Jerusalem since the implementation of the Oslo Agreement. Here are some of the ways this isolation is manifested: "Now with the wall, Palestinians cannot come to East Jerusalem for errands and daily life" (interview, 2007); "Now it is impossible to deliver services since the barrier was constructed (interview, 2007); "Metropolitan Jerusalem for Palestinians is fragmented. The West Bank is cut off from Jerusalem by the Jewish settlements. It is cut off by the wall" (interview, 2007).

Palestinians living inside and outside of the barrier/fence/wall are marginalized in different ways. Those fenced in may have access to Jerusalem services and employment markets, although the poverty and unemployment rates in East Jerusalem are very high (Brooks, 2007). But they incur major problems in attempting to travel outside of Jerusalem: family, friends, and communities are spatially cut off from those fenced-in Palestinians. Palestinians who are fenced out are less restricted from traveling in the West

Bank but they too have lost friends, family, community, and jobs.

Two important institutions have been fenced out of East Jerusalem. These are the Palestinian Parliament and Al Quds University. Fencing in the Palestinian Parliament would obviously restrict access to this political institution for most of its Palestinian base. Notably, however, the barrier/fence/wall has been located immediately next to the Parliament building.

Since 1967, Palestinians living in East Jerusalem have become socially, politically, and economically isolated. Israeli policy has directly fostered this isolation, leading some to suggest that Israel is attempting to sabotage East Jerusalem's future as the capital of a would-be Palestinian state (Klein, 2003; Khalidi, 2007; Nasrallah, 2007). East Jerusalem has incurred severe problems with the building of settlements and the barrier/fence/wall, residency requirements, road blocks and barriers, housing restrictions and demolitions, and the depletion of social and political vitality from the city overall. The question remains, according to a Palestinian peace activist, whether "time is running out for a two-state solution" (interview, 2008).

A Palestinian Jerusalem Metropolitan Area Free of Geopolitics

Most metropolitan regions in the world are shaped by growth that is typically a product of different kinds of economic activity. Urban growth is a function of investment and disinvestment activity. As a consequence, metropolitan areas are characterized by outward expansion (economic investment) as well as uneven development (economic disinvestment). Although cities vary considerably, their development patterns are largely a result of economic factors within varying social and political contexts. Politics matter but they are overtly tied to economic development.

Jerusalem radically defies this trend. Jerusalem is what it is because of geopolitics. Geopolitics shape the types of development that occur and where they occur. In the language of research, Jerusalem is an urban outlier. Its metropolitan growth is a world unto its own, guided by government decisions over how to capture and maintain a Jerusalem that Israel can call its own. Jerusalem is a metropolitan region that is shaped by political power over land, development, and the people it chooses or does not choose to retain within its boundaries.

In most developed countries, major cities are spatially integrated and connected through heightened urbanization. Cities are now linked together as giant metropolitan regions rather than evaluated as individual cities. Likewise, Jerusalem will inevitably be linked to nearby Tel Aviv because of urban growth. But what about Palestinian cities and towns that are also proximate to Jerusalem? Ramallah and Bethlehem are both twenty minutes away. Yet they might as well be in Shangri-La. An authentic region with ties to economic growth and advancement would not be either a Jewish metropolitan area or a Palestinian metropolitan area. It would transcend politics and become one region based on a shared economy. This is how normal metropolitan regions operate.

In the mid-1990s, Mahdi Abdul Hadi described his vision of a Palestinian metropolitan Jerusalem that would be much larger than the constrained Jewish one that assiduously avoids its Palestinian towns and villages:

> The Jerusalem I am talking about is not the Jerusalem with its current 1995 boundaries, nor is it the Jerusalem that excludes either the western or eastern parts of the city. I am speaking of Jerusalem in 1947, together with the neighboring towns and villages which [were] included within the municipal boundaries in 1948. There were 32 villages and towns, most of which have subsequently been demolished. The boundaries of this city ran from the village of Abu Dis in the east to the city of Ain Karim in the west, and from the city of Bethlehem in the south to Shu'fat in the north. (Hadi, 1996: 67)

This Palestinian Jerusalem metropolitan area is based on connections upon which a typical or normal metropolis thrives. The Jerusalem of Israel is an antithesis of the Palestinian historic one, a metropolis that is based on maintaining divisions and separateness rather than connections and relationships.

The Palestinian Diaspora

Since 1948, the Palestinian Diaspora has played a crucial role in the formation of a Palestinian identity. The Palestinian Diaspora has been developing a politics around Palestinian issues and has been instrumental in the formation of a pro-Palestinian international advocacy community, in maintaining a memory of Palestinian attachment to the lands that they left, in investing money in Palestinian business and real estate activities, and in organizing international resistance to Israel and Zionism.

Organized Palestinian resistance to Israel in exile was originally centered in Tunisia but spread to other countries in the Middle East. The Palestine Liberation Organization (PLO) was created in exile in 1964 and was led for many years by the political party of Fattah. The PLO was largely made irrelevant with the creation of a Palestinian governing body, the Palestinian Authority, after the signing of the Oslo Agreement in 1993.

Palestinian politics has a broad presence in its Diaspora. A sophisticated Palestinian intelligentsia consistently makes the case for Palestinian place attachment, the community's right of return, and Israel's role in fomenting disruption in the Palestinian community and undermining its efforts at self-determination. The most well-known intellectuals are the late Edward Said, former Professor of English and Comparative Literature, Rashid Khladi, Professor of Arab Studies at Columbia University, and Sari Nusseibeh, Professor of Philosophy and President of the Al Quds University.

The Palestinian Diaspora has a network that is central to organizing opposition to Israel. These efforts are directed at supporting Palestinians on three issues: (1) the Israeli occupation; (2) Palestinian refugees; and (3) Israeli Palestinians. Palestinians both at home and in the Diaspora have organized a very large international effort around education on the conflict with Apartheid Week and have exerted economic pressure with the Boycott, Disinvestment and Sanctions (BDS) campaign. These efforts have given the Palestinian platform an international base similar to the one that Israel has with its Jewish Diaspora.

Unlike Jewish refugees who left their home countries and

immigrated to Israel and other countries, many displaced Palestinians continue to live in refugee camps in the Gaza Strip and the West Bank, Syria, Lebanon, and Jordan. To be sure, both immigrants and refugees are people who have left their home countries. But immigrants have made the decision (freely or not so freely) to live somewhere else; immigrants are migrating to a place.

Refugees also have left their homes but the focus is not on where they are going but on what they have left behind. Refugees are in limbo. The Palestinians living in refugee camps since the 1948 and 1967 wars remain in this refugee limbo because they are not immigrating but rather holding on to what they have left. The Palestinian refugee community represents an important part of the Palestinian Diaspora that maintains a memory of its place-based heritage and holds on to the idea of returning. The Palestinian refugee part of the Palestinian Diaspora is a most significant physical and human component of the conflict. The Palestinian refugees are the heart of the Palestinian Diaspora's organization around its claims of its right to return to its former homes.

Often in partnership with other Middle Eastern countries like Qatar and Saudi Arabia, the Palestinian Diaspora invests in the Palestinian community. It helps to build the educational, economic, and physical infrastructure of a current Palestinian territory that is hoped to be central to a future Palestinian state. A major material example of a possible Palestinian future is Rawabi, a completely new privately developed master-plan community built north of Ramallah. It will eventually provide new state-of-the-art housing for forty thousand people.

Jerusalem for Whom?

Jerusalem is a showcase of ethnic diversity (S. Hasson, 1996; Bollens, 1998; Friedland and Hecht, 2000). The first layer of difference in Jerusalem is between its two largely antagonistic groups: Israelis and Palestinians. The second layer of difference is within these groups.

Countries typically work to integrate and assimilate their immigrant newcomers. But what that means and how it is put into play in Jerusalem may not be as assimilative as in other places. Jews fleeing or surviving from the Holocaust wanted to shed their country of origin just like the Russians and Eastern Europeans who fled from the pogroms to the United States at the turn of the twentieth century. But unlike the United States, Israel is intended as a nation of and for Jews. Holocaust survivors did not come to Israel to shed being Jews. They came to Israel so that they would not be persecuted and annihilated for being Jews. They came to be what they already were, not to add on another identity or affiliation. At a basic level, by becoming Israelis they were permitted to be who and what they were in the first place.

Simply based on the composition of Jews, Jerusalem is a powder keg of diversity as well as conflicting and sometimes contradictory views of the world. It is not a city where people politely disagree. It is a city where people think that other people are simply wrong. You may know the joke – two Jews and three opinions. In Jerusalem's Jewish communities, those differences and disagreements are intensely magnified. Two Jews and three opinions is an understatement.

Jerusalem is home to a diversity of Palestinians. Political distinctions are in the realm of citizenship, residency status, and national identification. Jerusalem is the home of Arab Israeli citizens who self-identify as Palestinians, a national identity that may be considered a contradiction to their membership as Israeli citizens. These seemingly contradictory and perhaps ironic political classifications and identities fuel the flames of burning questions about the future of the Israeli and Palestinian people.

But even larger numbers of Palestinians who live in Jerusalem are not citizens but legal residents. These Palestinians are constantly at war with the municipal authorities to avoid being stripped of their residency status and either banished from the city or forced to take on the precarious life of an illegal Palestinian Jerusalemite. Around one-third or more of Jerusalem's population, a number which can wildly fluctuate depending on the boundaries used, are Palestinian residents. Palestinian residents, who are viewed by

Israel to be illegal, are not included in these counts and their exact
numbers are unknown.

Jerusalem's problems, however, transcend the conflict between
Israelis and Palestinians. It is a hugely diverse city with various
antagonistic populations that do not always get along and have
different identities – within both its Jewish and non-Jewish communities. Moreover, besides its diversity and religious significance,
Jerusalem is characterized by its poverty. It has a limited economic
development base with huge amounts of deprivation concentrated
in its Palestinian and ultra-Orthodox populations. This trend of
increased poverty in the city is exacerbated by the continued
construction of affordable housing in settlements at its fringe.
Israel's geopolitics seem to undermine the economic foundation
of its most important city. While Jerusalem's neighborhoods of
rich foreign Jews are conspicuously visible because they are in the
center of the city, they are not large enough to make a significant
economic dent in the poverty rate. Jerusalem's poverty rate is
higher than those of Detroit and New Orleans, two central US
cities notorious for their impoverished status. Even were the conflict between Israelis and Palestinians to be solved in the future, this
would only lay bare these seemingly hidden urban problems, for
which there is no easy solution.

5

The Palestinian Challenge and Resistance in Arab Jerusalem

Introduction

East Jerusalem is the most critical and irresolvable part of any potential peace agreement between Israelis and Palestinians. It is the spatial part of the conflict that appears to be devoid of elements for compromise, the consummate zero-sum game. Israel says that East Jerusalem is part of a unified Jerusalem and claims that it is Israel. Palestinians say that East Jerusalem is the future capital of a Palestinian state separate from Israel and claims that it remains part of the West Bank.

These claims beg for legal and political solutions. But as students of the right to the city know well, claims of place ownership rest with everyday life – how people use the city (Purcell, 2002, 2003). Abstract claims are well and good, but the right to the city also rests with how people vote with their feet. And it is in the use of East Jerusalem by Palestinians and Israelis, respectively, that there is an absence of absolute clarity.

While Israel has physically, legally, and politically taken over huge portions of East Jerusalem, much of East Jerusalem resides with Palestinians. It is not the case that Palestinians totally live in segregated communities, separate from Jews. Palestinians leave their neighborhoods and move around Israeli Jewish communities (Greenberg Raanan and Shoval, 2014). Rather it is Jews who do not traverse Palestinian communities. Particularly with the violence associated with the 2014 Palestinian and Israeli murders and the Gaza War, the amount of Jewish movement in Palestinian neighborhoods, such as it is, has diminished even more. If everyday life is the measure of ownership, East Jerusalem is as much part of Israel as Ramallah or Bethlehem or even Nablus. They are completely different social worlds.

This chapter focuses on what we call Arab Jerusalem. It is an Arab and Palestinian world inside of an Israeli one. It is partially defined by social segregation and land use. But most important, it is that part of Jerusalem that is defined by ideas – by the memories and history of the Jerusalem owned by generations of Arab families. Arab Jerusalem is the Jerusalem of memory for Palestinians. This chapter is about the Jerusalem owned by the Palestinian residents and Israeli Arabs of East Jerusalem, how its memories are honored and kept alive, and how Israeli ownership and control of Arab Jerusalem are resisted. This chapter is about the overt resistance of Palestinians through armed struggle, violence, and intifadas and covert resistance ranging from the refusal of legitimate aspects of Israeli authority to simply staying put – by remaining and living in their Jerusalem communities, raising their families, and being part of Arab Jerusalem.

Arab Jerusalem and East Jerusalem

Although claims to East Jerusalem are made in the present, the legitimacy of each side's claims is authenticated through its constructed proof of historical ownership over an extended amount of time, literally hundreds if not thousands of years. Each side says Jerusalem is theirs.

For Palestinians, the claim to East Jerusalem is based on family lineage and longevity. Palestinian family ties to Jerusalem are akin to what might pass for royal blood in countries like England or Sweden.

In the case of Israelis, the claim to East Jerusalem is biblical in source, authenticated ostensibly through archaeological evidence. But Israel also has power and military might that constitute overt political control over East Jerusalem. Israel calls East Jerusalem its own, and though most of the world denies this, it has been under its control since it was captured in 1967.

No peace negotiation, not the Oslo Agreement, not Camp David, nor any other forum, has attempted to negotiate the fate of East Jerusalem. Although the status quo cedes control to Israel, the battle for Jerusalem continues. In the end, it may be won by the side that remains standing in the ancient rubble. The world should not kid itself. No one, particularly its Palestinian inhabitants, is backing down from claims to East Jerusalem. East Jerusalem's centrality to the entire conflict cannot be overstated. Its historical and symbolic significance may ultimately decide the fate of the Arab–Israeli conflict.

East Jerusalem is part of the Jerusalem metro-region acquired by Jordan in 1948 and then conquered by Israel in 1967. Its status as the central element in the fight for Jerusalem makes it important to understand what it means to people and why they so desperately want it.

But East Jerusalem's political identity and position within the conflict have been constructed by Israelis, not Palestinians. East Jerusalem became a political pariah within Palestinian politics as designed by the Oslo Agreement, which ceded political control of the area's Arab residents to Israel. Politically isolated from its Palestinian West Bank community, it has also become spatially isolated by the separation barrier/fence/wall that has cut off Arab Jerusalem from the rest of the West Bank.

East Jerusalem is an Israeli construction; it is an artifact of Israeli power and political domination. East Jerusalem is juxtaposed against Arab Jerusalem, a Jerusalem based on memory. Palestinians in East Jerusalem fight for Arab Jerusalem, not for East Jerusalem.

Arab Jerusalem is an idea of a physical place that predates the

1948 war. As an idea, Arab Jerusalem collides so violently with Israeli/Jewish Jerusalem because a place of memory does not recede in the face of oppression.

The Arab Jerusalem of memory is pre-1948. It is no wonder that Israel has feared and tried to outlaw the conception of 1948 as the Nakba, a disaster and tragedy for the Palestinian people and the original source of their first loss of Jerusalem as a place. Israel controls East Jerusalem but not Arab Jerusalem, because it is much easier to take hold of a piece of land than it is to control people's ideas about land, community, and ownership (Mann, 2011). Ultimately, this means that the ownership of Jerusalem, despite what Israel says and does, is unstable.

The fight for Jerusalem is over a physical place. But physicality is only part of what a place contains. A place is a state of mind, a memory, an idea. For Palestinians their Jerusalem of memory – what we call Arab Jerusalem – does not coincide with the Jerusalem that is politically dominated by Israel (H. Cohen, 2007). But Arab Jerusalem is only partially realized or relatable because Arab Jerusalem has only existed under someone else's control and has never been controlled by Palestinians. The list of controllers of Arab Jerusalem is long: the Ottomans, the British, the Jordanians, and now Israel.

Arab Jerusalem does not conform to the boundaries of East Jerusalem, although it certainly includes it. Arab Jerusalem is the Jerusalem that Palestinians claim despite the military might of the Israeli government. Arab Jerusalem is an idea of an imagined place that transcends today's political boundaries. The Jerusalem of memory is of lost Palestinian communities, heritage, and villages that were once located in an Arab-controlled space but are now in a place called Israel.

According to Sari Nusseibeh, President of Al Quds University in East Jerusalem, a Palestinian Jerusalemite, and with family ties to Jerusalem that go back for generations, Jerusalem may be more closely identified with Palestinians than being Palestinian altogether. Being of Jerusalem is central to many Palestinians' identity, more so than being either Palestinian, Jewish, or whatever. He writes,

Arab families – and certainly some of the Jewish families as well – belong to the city far more than they belong either to an Israeli nation or a Palestinian nation. These are people who belong to the actual city and for whom it is extremely difficult to exist without thinking of themselves as belonging to Jerusalem. (Nusseibeh, 2008: 200)

Despite the stresses of daily life that emerge from the ongoing struggle and conflict, the fight over Jerusalem is much more than a battle over whose Jerusalem is their home. Arab Jerusalem has come to represent a symbolic and concrete battlefield between rival communities and nations.

This chapter is about the paths of Palestinian resistance to the Israeli regime in East Jerusalem. The focus is not on who is winning or losing the fight for Jerusalem or who should win or lose. Rather, it is on the everyday life dynamics that reveal the continuous violent and peaceful Palestinian struggle to live in East Jerusalem. Israel has the power to demolish housing, expel Palestinian residents, and create instability and stress for Palestinian Jerusalemites. But Palestinians have not been passive or without influence. In East Jerusalem, the Palestinian response to Israel's domination is to systematically deny the legitimacy of its right to rule in ways that challenge its idea of a unified city. For Arab Jerusalem, by default, there is no one Jerusalem, nor is there an Israeli Jerusalem.

The quest to unify Jerusalem has been the hallmark of Israeli development policy since 1967. Moshe Amirav notes that the funds spent on housing development that would cement East and West Jerusalem are extraordinary. He writes,

In order to further the territorial objective, billions of dollars were spent in settling about 200,000 Jews in the eastern part of the city. The scope of the infrastructure that was built in the eastern neighborhoods and surrounding settlements was greater than the infrastructure of all the development towns in Israel. (Amirav, 2007: 9)

Under the guise of housing policy, Jerusalem's new neighborhoods were built and continue to be built in the name of Jerusalem's unification (Amirav, 2007: 10).

The political dominance by Israel of Arab Jerusalem depends on the acceptance of two big ideas: (1) there is and can be only one Jerusalem and (2) Jerusalem is Israeli. Both ideas of Jerusalem potentially unite secular and religious Jews in a common cause. It is the seeming ideological universality of a united Jerusalem that connects Jews everywhere to it, even those Israelis who are loath to visit the city because it is too religious. This is how Israel dominates Jerusalem, politically and ideologically, as well as how it legitimates the use of force in everyday life.

But the everyday life of the people who claim Arab Jerusalem is one that is counter-hegemonic and that challenges these ideas. Arab Jerusalem challenges what the rest of Israel and, frankly, the rest of the world seems to have conceded – that East Jerusalem is now firmly spatially entrenched within Israel. Common sense says that, of course, East Jerusalem is Jerusalem and Jerusalem is Israel.

Palestinians of Arab Jerusalem challenge this idea of a unified Jewish Jerusalem in every aspect of their being. During times of overt conflict, they use the force they have at their disposal. They throw rocks and vandalize property.

But most of the time, counter-hegemonic activities appear more passive and indirect, although stubbornly in the face of the ruling regime. The Palestinians of Arab Jerusalem challenge Israeli hegemonic dominance by being present and absent at the same time. They remain in the city, build homes, and raise their families. The Palestinians of Arab Jerusalem are present and are not going anywhere. While adhering to Israeli rules and regulations governing taxes and public services, they shun the Israeli political structure, reminding everyone that they are not Israeli political subjects.

Is Jerusalem One Israeli City?

Israel rules East Jerusalem. Yet Israel's dominance is not a clear-cut victory. The fate of East Jerusalem has not been sealed.

Israel's position is that Jerusalem will for ever remain its political capital city. Contemporary Jerusalem is not formally divided between East or West Jerusalem; there is only one "united" city under Israeli rule. As explained in Chapter 3, Israel has been extremely successful in strengthening its control and applying its sovereignty over East Jerusalem through redrawing Jerusalem's political boundaries, annexing new lands, and establishing new neighborhoods and settlements (Friedland and Hecht, 2000; Klein, 2008; Shlay and Rosen, 2010; Allegra, 2013; Chiodelli, 2013).

Equally successful has been Israel's ability to recreate powerful images and myths, ultimately attempting to project a new understanding that redefines what Jerusalem is to Israelis (Said, 1995; M. Benvenisti, 1998). In this "new" Jerusalem, there are no barricades dividing the city, there is no barbed wire and no struggle over Jerusalem. In the words of Palestinian scholar Edward Said, Israel has worked to "project an idea of Jerusalem that contradicted not only its history but its very lived actuality, turning it from a multicultural and multi-religious city into an 'eternally' unified principally Jewish city under exclusive Israeli sovereignty" (Said, 1995: 7).

There is a huge disjuncture between what people see and call Jerusalem and what they know as Jerusalem. The world labels all of the Israeli Jewish neighborhoods of East Jerusalem settlements but few Israelis are aware of this. Many Jews of East Jerusalem would be surprised to learn that they are living in what the rest of the world calls settlements or even that the land on which they live was once part of Jordan. For them, all of what exists in the municipality of Jerusalem is, in a word, Jerusalem.

To be sure, Jerusalem's alleged unity is challenged in Israel not only by either political pronouncements or the counter-hegemonic activities of Palestinians. The idea of a unified Jerusalem is challenged by the actual behavior and everyday activities of Israeli Jews who live and work in Jerusalem.

It works like this: Israeli Jews perceive any Jerusalem neighborhood populated by Jews to be Jerusalem. But this is far less true of neighborhoods populated by Palestinians. For Israeli Jews, Palestinian East Jerusalem neighborhoods are the equivalent of the dark side of the moon. Arab Jerusalem, those parts of East Jerusalem home to Palestinians, is a place largely out of sight and reach. The idea of a united Jerusalem as experienced by Israel is a monumental achievement of a once scattered and almost annihilated Jewish people. The Israelis' narrative is that in 1948, Israel "lost" that Jerusalem. But by their own hands, they got it back with no help from anyone. In 1967, Israel claimed the rest of Jerusalem and conquered the idea of a united Jerusalem. It is that idea of a united Jerusalem that is precious, regardless of who mingles with whom.

But in reality, a united Jerusalem is a utopian and romantic aspiration, a desire to reclaim the core area of the historic homeland of the biblical Hebrew people – a desire that appears almost hard-wired into the psyche of the Jewish community both in Israel and in the Diaspora. The problem is that a united Jerusalem is not a gift from a deity or a holy entitlement but an ideological and political construct.

Of course, Jerusalem is not simply an abstract idea or ideological construct. It is a physical place. It is real, concrete, and home to people with different desires, dreams, and needs – Jews and Palestinians.

The battle between the idea of a united Jerusalem and its physical reality has come to a head with Jerusalem's most recent transportation initiative – the Jerusalem Light Rail (JLR). As noted in Chapter 3, the JLR line moves from West Jerusalem through East Jerusalem with stations in several Palestinian neighborhoods. Israel represents the JLR as a good-faith effort to provide valuable infrastructure to both Jewish and Palestinian residents and to treat Jerusalem as a normal city that needs to build its central place and local economy. From this perspective, the JLR is for everyone and benefits everybody, Palestinian and Israelis.

But by treating East Jerusalem as normal and working to integrate East and West Jerusalem, the JLR is seen as a disguise for another form of Israeli imperialism designed to solidify its hold on East Jerusalem and to deny Arab Jerusalem. To be sure, the use of the JLR as a tool for the political domination of East Jerusalem was noted early in the planning process by activists who viewed it as a more insidious version of another Israeli settlement (Barghouti, 2007). By the summer of 2014, with the Jerusalem murders and

Gaza War, this animosity erupted as the JLR became the physical target for vandals and demonstrators who destroyed stations and tore up the rail lines from the very streets in which they were embedded. The JLR was seen as another weapon with which to conquer East Jerusalem, much like the new neighborhoods, the Jerusalem provisions of the Oslo Agreement, the demolition of Palestinian housing, and Palestinian deportations from Jerusalem.

Although many saw the JLR destruction simply as malicious vandalism, it can also be viewed as an act of protest. Destroying the JLR was also a form of resisting Israeli domination operating through its goal of Jerusalem unification. Moreover, Jerusalem's Palestinians could not have picked a more potent (and expensive) target, their actions wreaking havoc with the notion of an Israeli Jerusalem. The destruction of JLR infrastructure and the continued danger posed by rock-throwing Palestinians has led to calls to move the JLR lines away from Palestinian neighborhoods (Beaumont, 2014).

Although Israel arrested Palestinian perpetrators, the long-term effects of the violence on Jerusalem place making remains to be seen. At the same time, the rhetoric of a "happily ever-united city" is seen by some to be a highly problematic myth (M. Benvenisti, 1998; Lustick, 2004). In Jerusalem, if the past is a prediction of the future, Israel's goal is not to bring the Palestinians into the social and economic mainstream but to maintain a separate sphere for Palestinians while extending Israeli Jewish dominance over Arab Jerusalem (Bollens, 2000; Kallus, 2004; Pullan et al., 2007). This appears to be Israel's unfinished business to unite its Jerusalem.

Socio-spatial separations and growing dissatisfaction already test Jerusalem's fragile social urban fabric. This is compounded by overt acts of hatred that come from both sides. Rock throwing and property destruction are clear signs of unrest. But other quieter frustrations within the Palestinian community are also apparent. Unequal power relationships are displayed and felt on a daily basis.

Israel has invested huge amounts of resources to build the physical infrastructure it deems necessary to unify East and West

Jerusalem. It has built new Jerusalem neighborhoods that the world calls settlements. Despite these vast investments and efforts, it has failed to generate the conditions for a true unification because these neighborhoods are for Jews, not Palestinians. An Arab and Jewish Jerusalem, two parts of the same city, are segregated, easily distinguishable, and display very unequal urban realities (S. Hasson, 1996; Bollens, 1998, 2012; Klein, 2004, 2005; Yiftachel, 2006; Clarno, 2008).

In many ways, this separation between Jewish and Arab Jerusalem is not surprising. Politically, Palestinian/Arab East Jerusalemites are largely neither Israeli citizens nor formally integrated into the democratic Israeli polity. They hold a conditional residency which creates daily problems and massive social, spatial, and economic inequalities. They may travel within the West Bank and Israel but only with great difficulties. They receive municipal services from the City of Jerusalem, but their volume and quality are much less than what Jerusalem's Jews receive.

As residents of Jerusalem, East Jerusalemites may vote in local municipal elections. But they are not Israeli citizens and cannot vote in Israel's national elections. This limited franchise may therefore be regarded as a pseudo-democratic illusion and as a condition of oppression and exclusion (Young, 2004).

Palestinians describe their political situation in Jerusalem as occupation. For them, East Jerusalem is not united with West Jerusalem. It is not even part of Israel. East Jerusalem is land occupied by Israel dating from its conquest by Israel in 1967. Palestinians view East Jerusalem's political status as identical to the West Bank. The land was captured and then occupied. For Palestinians, the sole difference between East Jerusalem and the West Bank is that Israel officially calls East Jerusalem part of Jerusalem and part of Israel, which is a false and illegal claim. Israel says that Palestinians have political rights to participate in local elections. Palestinians call this a sham.

The power inequalities between Israelis and East Jerusalemites are massive. The Palestinians of East Jerusalem are victims of discrimination and exclusion of all sorts. Although some suggest that being in Israel is preferable for Palestinians than living in the West

Bank, few would argue that East Jerusalemites are treated either as well as or equitable to Israeli citizens (Yiftachel, 1991, 2006; Yiftachel and Yacobi, 2002).

Yet Israel's power over Jerusalem's resident Palestinians is not absolute. Within Jerusalem there is Palestinian resistance to Israel and a battle over the nature of development in East Jerusalem. The battle is neither dormant nor silent. But it is also not overt and direct because Palestinians have limited political resources for the struggle. In Jerusalem, Israelis know Jerusalem as theirs. The fight for Arab Jerusalem is far less contested than the one in the West Bank.

The East Jerusalem Palestinian struggle assumes many forms of resistance in daily life. It is sometimes active and sometimes passive. It can be violent but is sometimes peaceful and subversive (see Figure 5.1). Palestinians routinely challenge Israeli legitimacy and sovereignty over Arab Jerusalem.

Figure 5.1   Subversive Palestinian graffiti on the separation barrier/ fence/wall (© Anne Shlay)

The Paradox of Municipal Elections and East Jerusalemite (Non-)Participation Practice

The absence of participation by the Palestinian residents of East Jerusalem in municipal elections may appear perplexing. Given their legal residency status, a clear and specific right to participate, and the potential to have a direct effect on the outcomes of local municipal elections in Jerusalem, the obvious questions that comes to mind is – why not vote?

In particular, Palestinian non-participation in local Jerusalem elections is an important issue because Palestinians could influence local political outcomes. Jerusalem Palestinians represent almost 40 percent of the local Jerusalem population. If the Palestinian community voted with large turnouts, its voice theoretically could be heard. Why not take advantage of its size as a potential voting bloc to alter the balance of power, just as is done by the ultra-Orthodox, who have consistently voted as a bloc.

If Palestinians participated, their voice would be heard because they have a lot of voices. If organized and strategic, they could change the political power alignment in City Hall and take control of anywhere from one-fourth to a one-third of Jerusalem's city council. They could thereby potentially reverse all sorts of problems that they face in Jerusalem, including the unequal and discriminatory allocation of resources. They might be able to compel much-needed investment in the physical infrastructure of Arab Jerusalem.

Given Palestinians' numbers and the ballot box options, some shifting in political power might ultimately be actualized. Of course the history of civil and political right acquisition is not always this straightforward, but a more typical situation is to fight for these voting rights, not seemingly ignore them altogether.

Moreover, students of the American Revolution are enthusiastically taught that the American uprising hinged on "no taxation without representation." As one local East Jerusalem Palestinian leader explained, "We pay taxes. We have to pay taxes. Otherwise we lose our rights" (interview, 2008). Palestinians are well aware of this tax obligation, which often does not accrue much in the way of return. And they have something that other minorities in other places do not have along the continuum of variables that make up the right to the city. In Jerusalem, Palestinians have the right to participate in politics and presumably take part in resource allocation (Lefebvre, 1991, 1996).

Since they became residents of Jerusalem in 1967, Palestinians living in East Jerusalem have not taken part in local elections, but instead have boycotted them. Voting participation rates have remained extremely low – on average less than 5 percent vote. The influence of Jerusalemite Palestinians on municipal politics has been extremely limited, really nonexistent.

East Jerusalem's Palestinians do not particulate in Israeli elections in the city and do not vote. But this is not an expression of political apathy; it is intentional. When we met Mr Hanna Siniora, a Palestinian journalist and political activist, he explained that Palestinian non-participation does not indicate that Jerusalem Palestinians do not care about their rights. On the contrary, they care so deeply for Arab Jerusalem and for their Palestinian national identity that they choose to forfeit their basic rights and not participate in the local political arena (interview, 2007). Non-participation, in this case, is a tool for the expression of political power.

How is the absence of participation a mechanism for expressing power? For years, East Jerusalem Palestinians have boycotted municipal elections to refuse both to provide legitimacy to Israel as a reigning authority structure and to recognize Israeli control over their city. This refusal to legitimate Israeli rule has strengthened their separate identity as Palestinian Jerusalemites even at the price of losing out in service and infrastructure allocation. Non-participation has been an active choice. East Jerusalem Palestinians acquire the power accrued to the community with their collective identity as Palestinians, not simply spatially dispossessed Arabs. But they suffer the material consequences of having far less access to services than they both desire and deserve.

The Palestinian boycott of Jerusalem's local elections is near unanimous. If they chose to participate, however, a positive outcome would be neither predictable nor inevitable. An East Jerusalemite working as a planner for the Palestinian Authority further explained that had Palestinians simply voted in the municipal elections, their voices would not be heard as one voice because "[they] won't vote as a bloc . . . may not vote for Palestinian lists . . . and it would probably create some kind of backlash" (interview, 2007). The expectation is that if Palestinians were to vote, there would be negative consequences and they would in some way suffer and be punished.

Some Palestinians support taking on a different form of participation, to protest Israeli rule and to cry out that Arab residents of the city are "real people not ghosts" (interview, 2007). Meron Benvenisti, an Israeli former deputy mayor of the city, has argued that Jews do not recognize that Jerusalem is a city of two peoples, not one; that they have "to realize that they are in a bi-national condition. . . . It is control by one ethnic group . . . But they are in denial. They have to think about boundaries and communities. . . . But they hide behind the occupation" (interview, 2007). In other words, Benvenisti argues that the Israelis and Palestinians living in this city can and must share it.

Nonetheless, other Israeli Palestinian supporters would like to see Arab participation in local elections. What would Israel do in the event that Palestinians actually mobilized themselves to vote in large numbers? Would it stand back if and when a Palestinian mayor of Jerusalem is elected? A Palestinian majority city council? Even a balance of Israeli and Palestinian representation on the city council? This kind of political showdown could compel Israel to address its professed allegiance to democracy.

At the same time, most of the Palestinian leadership (local and national) has consistently opposed the idea of Palestinian local political participation. This position is supported by two major arguments. First, they want to withhold any type of symbolic recognition of Israel's rule over the city. By voting, Palestinian Jerusalemites could be viewed as giving implicit consent to Israel as a legitimate government. Second, for most Palestinians, voting in an Israeli election is practically irrelevant. They do not perceive that Israeli political parties have differences on issues associated with a united Jerusalem, so there are limited gains from choosing among these parties (Friedland and Hecht, 2000).

The collective decision to boycott local elections ultimately prevents Palestinians from relinquishing their national identity. Non-participation is not passive but is a conscious non-violent act of opposition that symbolically challenges Israel's control over Arab Jerusalem. Palestinian non-participation is and continues to be a form of active resistance to Israeli domination – a domination by force, not by democratic legitimation and the consent of the governed.

The First Intifada

The First Palestinian Intifada (uprising) abruptly changed Palestinians from being a passive and largely quiescent group to a violent one. This uprising, which began in 1987 and came to conclusion in 1993 with the Oslo Agreement, was a reaction against Israeli occupation of the West Bank, Gaza, and Jerusalem. The Intifada marked Palestinians' successful initiation in their quest for national self-determination, a milestone event intended to lead to an internationally recognized independent Palestinian state.

This rebellion was characterized by both violent and non-violent actions that challenged Israel's sovereignty over the West Bank and Gaza. It included a range of tactics: large-scale general strikes; civil disobedience; economic boycotts in the form of refusal to work in Israeli settlements; barricading roads leading to Palestinian villages and cities; extensive graffiti that symbolically redefined power relations and re-marked territory; widespread throwing of stones and Molotov cocktails (gasoline bombs) at Israeli military and civilians; and suicide attacks targeting Israeli buses and civilians. The First Intifada radically destabilized the day-to-day rhythm of the city and made the case of Arab Jerusalem versus Israel visible and seemingly obvious.

Resistance was no longer restricted to sporadic rallies of Palestinian university students. The rules had clearly changed, with large-scale violent riots and numerous incidences of stones thrown at Israeli civilians, police, and military forces (especially in East Jerusalem neighborhoods). Israeli cars parked in Arab neighborhoods were set on fire; there were stabbings of Israelis, especially in East Jerusalem; and graffiti expressed resistance and challenge to Israeli rule and advocated Palestinian claims over Arab Jerusalem (H. Cohen, 2007). Palestinian claims to territory could not be ignored. The First Intifada marked out what Palestinians called theirs and made it essential to call the question on Palestinian sovereignty. Accustomed to visiting East Jerusalem for shopping and business purposes, Israelis were now violently pushed out. Israeli security forces fought back in an attempt to return order and to increase Israelis' sense of security. At the same time, municipal and private service providers stayed away from these renewed urban frontiers that had become real battle zones.

Ironically, although in hindsight not surprisingly, Israel's denial of place to Palestinians helped to launch independent Palestinian East Jerusalem non-governmental institutions. The most important was the Orient House.

The Orient House was initiated by the late Faisal Husseini, the head of a long standing Jerusalem based Arab family. Based in Jerusalem, it ultimately came to represent Palestinians on a national basis. It remains associated with Husseini's activities as an active PLO leader who became the Palestinian spokesperson representing the East Jerusalem community.

In the 1980s, Husseini created the Arab Studies Center/Society, a non-governmental organization affiliated with the PLO and located at the Orient House. The Arab Studies Center was established as a research institution and archive to record Palestinian historical and cultural data – essentially establishing the intellectual identity of the Palestinian people.[1] Books, newspaper articles, and documents were catalogued and saved, creating the foundations of a national archive and strengthening Palestinian national identity in East Jerusalem. The Orient House soon emerged as an imperative Palestinian institution – the headquarters of the Palestinian negotiating team (Nasrallah, 2005). According to Abed Husseini, Faisal Husseini's son, "It became the PLO headquarters in Jerusalem.

. . . The Palestinian flag was placed there. . . . Husseini [Abed's father] was made the Palestinian representative to negotiate over Jerusalem" (interview, 2008).

The Orient House became the place where Jerusalem's Palestinian leadership, officially representing the Palestinian people, received heads of state. Abed Husseini further explains its importance: "It used to be the house of state for the Palestinian people in the event that there would be Palestinian statehood" (interview, 2010).

Faisal Husseini and Hanan Ashrawi were two of East Jerusalem's most influential local leaders during the First Intifada who advocated for a Palestinian homeland. Their leadership succeeded in placing Arab Jerusalem on the map of both Israeli and Palestinian national politicians. East Jerusalem would no longer go unnoticed, and the Orient House would be considered a national political icon and center – a bridgehead for Palestinian nationalism in Jerusalem, as well as the political center for Arab Jerusalem.

The Oslo Agreement and Its Consequences for Arab Jerusalem

The Oslo Agreement established the Palestinian Authority and gave it jurisdiction over selected areas in the West Bank. The Agreement also contained a resolution on Jerusalem. Any decision about Jerusalem, namely its role in the creation of a Palestinian state, was postponed for five years in anticipation that negotiations over Jerusalem would ensue during this period.

Postponing a decision about Jerusalem was a major Palestinian concession in the Oslo process (Friedland and Hecht, 2000). Most importantly, the Oslo Agreement stipulated that East Jerusalem be treated differently from the rest of the West Bank. East Jerusalem was forbidden from participating in any Palestinian political activities. Palestinians in East Jerusalem were permitted to identify as Palestinians, but they could not organize or politically act as Palestinians other than vote in Palestinian national elections.

Why did Palestinian leaders concede complete control over Arab Jerusalem to Israel? The importance of the Oslo decisions over Jerusalem cannot be overstated. In exchange for Palestinian governance over parts of the West Bank, the Palestinians relinquished control over what they professed to call the future capital of their Palestinian state. We emphasize that the Oslo Agreement gave Israel total control over East Jerusalem. Unlike the agreement made over the West Bank, there were no shared elements and no clear prospects for sharing. Oslo gave Jerusalem to Israel, to be a topic for discussion down the road.

Israel also acquired control over East Jerusalem's political activities. Palestinian East Jerusalemites were forbidden to be part of the official Palestinian governance over the West Bank. East Jerusalem could not run candidates, organize, or campaign: it was politically emasculated.

To be sure, the plan of talks down the road in five years held out the promise that East Jerusalem might have a future as part of a Palestinian state. But promises like these are typically made in situations where there is mutual trust – trust that has been tested and relied on before. Why would the Palestinians concede East Jerusalem so completely?

A benign explanation is that the Palestinians and Israelis operated in a situation of prospective and expected trust and respect. In that context, Oslo was intended to be a temporary agreement, one step in a process that is geared at building this trust between the two people, teaching both sides to coexist and live together in peace. In this new world, negotiations, not violent struggle, would eventually and inevitably lead to a geopolitical compromise where Israelis and Palestinians would share space and rule the city together.

Yet there is no real basis to suggest that this kind of seeming naïveté propelled this element of the agreement. Israel and the Palestinians were coming out of the First Intifada. While the spirit of negotiations was hopeful, they were not surreal.

Another explanation rests with politics, people, and specific individuals – the politics of the PLO in the hands of its leader, Yasser Arafat. Some suggest the Jerusalem agreement may have been the best deal he could reach at this time (Zertal and Eldar, 2007). Arafat and many other Palestinian leaders had been leaders in exile, living and organizing in Tunis. The Oslo Agreement's establishing of a legitimate and recognized Palestinian political authority represented a huge achievement. From being refugees living in exile in Tunis, Arafat and many other Palestinian leaders would return victorious to their homeland and enjoy extensive international acclaim. They would not be a labeled terrorist organization, but an internationally recognized national governmental organization with considerable, although limited, sovereignty.

Still, it is difficult to understand such severe concessions with what was considered the clear place-based price of a future capital Palestinian state. Palestinians retained partial control of Gaza and the West Bank but gave up East Jerusalem. How can the expectations of good will, the pragmatic difficulties of negotiating, or even the sheer thrill of realized power be used to explain why they essentially gave up on East Jerusalem's future as part of a Palestinian state?

What makes the most sense as an explanation is something else, something more dramatic, lurid, highly unflattering to the Palestinians, but understandable in a realm of cut-throat Middle East politics. This explanation rests with internal divisions within the Palestinians themselves, not disagreements between the Palestinians and Israel (H. Cohen, 2007). As a result, the existing Palestinian institutions in Jerusalem and political activities were removed from the spotlight and power was reoriented toward Ramallah and into the hands of the Palestinian Authority's 'national' leadership (Friedland and Hecht, 2000).

In other words, local Jerusalemite leadership was not passive, but was forced to give up power and influence in the name of national interest and unity by comrade Palestinians. At the same time a strong Jewish Israeli mayor, Ehud Olmert – later to become the Prime Minster of Israel – advanced plans to develop the city and strengthen its position as the capital of Israel. Palestinian and

Israeli politics together seemed to doom Arab Jerusalem's political future as Palestinian and Arab.

Oslo hindered for that particular time period the recognition of Arab Jerusalem as the capital of the Palestinian future state. It is possible that these negotiations undermined East Jerusalem's standing so completely that they ultimately have jeopardized its possibility as a Palestinian capital altogether. Excluding Arab Jerusalem from the rest of the Palestinian Authority's formal scope of influence separated East Jerusalem from its political home. Tensions between East Jerusalem and the West Bank had existed before, but the post-Oslo period increased them.

These enormous political difficulties could have wreaked havoc with the identity of East Jerusalemites as Palestinians. East Jerusalem Palestinians were indeed Palestinians. Yet they were essentially discarded as part of the Oslo Agreement. How they retained their Palestinian identity despite these obstacles is an important part of the Jerusalem story. Oslo solidified East Jerusalem's unique position vis-à-vis Israel. But it also transformed East Jerusalemites into "others" among the rest of the Palestinian people. In the face of Israel's political dominance and Palestinian official hands-off policy, the Palestinian population of East Jerusalem was left with the daily challenge of continuing to live in an Israeli city as unwanted Palestinian residents without established political outlets of participation within Palestinian governance.

This challenge has been monumental. East Jerusalemites were not given the choice of assimilating into Israeli society. Ostracized by Palestinians, they have also been politically and socially shunned by Israelis. Moreover, as a Jewish state, Israel holds few options for Palestinians. As non-citizens, they do not even achieve the dubious status in Israel known as a "minority," the term used to describe non-Jewish citizens.

What can the Palestinians of Arab Jerusalem be, that is, politically? Most are not allowed to become Israeli citizens. It is difficult to assess comparable situations of marginal social groups in other democratic states. In the United States, although not required, legal residents can eventually opt for citizenship and become Americans. But in Jerusalem, Palestinians cannot even begin to become fully integrated within Israeli society. Their legal residency status is largely unstable and, for most, citizenship is out of the question.

As Palestinians, East Jerusalem residents may not organize politically or run for office within the Palestinian political establishment, but they may vote in national Palestinian elections. Arab Jerusalem remains very much part of Palestinian politics. It continues to challenge Israel's sovereignty over Jerusalem and Israel's political legitimacy more generally.

Temple Mount/Haram al-Sharif – the Epicenter of Conflict

Among all embattled issues that pit Palestinians against Israelis, there is one where Palestinians seem to hold the upper hand. This is the battle over the Temple Mount/Haram al-Sharif – the holiest place for Judaism and the third holiest site for Islam, after Mecca and Medina. Both are located in Jerusalem's Old City. Both are in precisely the same location. The battle for place does not get bigger than this.

The Temple Mount is the location of the Jewish First and Second Temples. Haram al-Sharif is the location of the Al-Aqsa Mosque and the Dome of the Rock. Both have legions of claims to religious importance. It is not a question of whose holy is more holy. It is only a question of power.

The Temple Mount/Haram al-Sharif was controlled until 1967 by the Jordanians. Since that time, it has been under direct Muslim control and run by the Islamic Waqf of Jerusalem, a trust that is independent of the Israeli government. Jews may visit the site but are not allowed to openly pray, a condition that is periodically challenged. This place is under Islamic religious control.

Israel controls the Old City. Although the operations of the Temple Mount/Haram al-Sharif rest with the Muslim religion, its day-to-day activities are influenced by Israel, which routinely controls Palestinian access to the site. In addition, at times of conflict, particularly when rocks and other items are thrown at people visiting the Kotel, Israeli security forces and police intervene.

Israel routinely prevents Palestinian people from entering Jerusalem and praying in the mosques on Haram al-Sharif based on age, marital status, working permit, and other characteristics. When this happens, Palestinian men gather at checkpoints around the city and pray (H. Cohen, 2007). When Palestinians are seemingly most powerless (denied access to the city) and allegedly silenced, they actively but peacefully take ownership over Israeli checkpoints as a form of protest, a Muslim sit-in or prayer-in of sorts. Mosques are used to house religious/political protest as well. They are used to mobilize and unite people.

Excavation and construction around this area has been extensive and conflict-ridden. The Western Wall Tunnel project has been a long-standing excavation works underneath this location but was intensified in 1988 by the Western Wall Heritage Foundation, a non-profit charged with operating the Western Wall and run by the Israeli government. Israeli Jewish heritage reconstruction was met by Muslim heritage reconstruction. Palestinians set in motion a sizable project of unprecedented scale at the heart of Haram al-Sharif – the (re)construction of the Marwani Mosque, also known as Solomon's Stables.

This project initiated more development that shifted the balance of power at the Temple Mount/Haram al-Sharif. By the mid-1990s, the Waqf began construction in the lower southern platform of Temple Mount. The area was formed as an extension of the original First Temple ramp. In the 1990s the area once again was transformed and converted into a mosque. This marked the successful initiative taken by the Islamic Waqf to strengthen its claim of sovereignty over this area.

The Second Intifada

The intense violence of the Second Intifada (2000–5) became a painful reminder of the dual-city condition, and a violent symbol of Palestinian resistance to Israeli rule (Savitch, 2005; Kliot and Charney, 2006; Benmelech and Berrebi, 2007; Hazam and Felsenstein, 2007). The security breakdown gave rise to a "geography of fear" resulting in the increased fortification of market places and public spaces; the setting up of observation towers, ditches, barriers, gates, road blocks, and checkpoints; and severe enforcement and restrictions on the mobility of Palestinians across Israel and particularly within Jerusalem (Dumper, 2014). The culmination of this fear is concretized in the security barrier and wall that has been set up throughout Israel and around and through Jerusalem.

The barrier/fence/wall makes it difficult to enter Jerusalem. Palestinians who need to be in Jerusalem for work or family reasons have come to stay on a permanent basis because they cannot predictably come and go. The walling out of Palestinians and increased residency requirements have encouraged more Palestinians to move to Jerusalem. Since the construction of the barrier/fence/wall, the "illegal" population of Palestinians is believed to have increased (Nasrallah, 2007; Owais, 2008). This is a political irony for the government of Israel, which has a long-standing desire to maintain a significant Jewish majority in Jerusalem. Instead, the demographic balance is shifting in the opposite direction in favor of Jerusalem's Palestinians.

Increased numbers of Palestinians in Jerusalem have become forces for neighborhood change. Palestinians are moving in greater numbers to Jewish neighborhoods, particularly those adjacent to Palestinian neighborhoods. Jewish residents protest vigorously, citing that they are being "invaded" by Palestinians. This language mimics the early Chicago School of urban sociology, which employed this (racist) terminology to describe neighborhood racial change from White to African American. Yet this visible movement of Palestinian people into Jewish neighborhoods has invisible structural causes.

Estimates are that as many as eighty thousand East Jerusalemite Palestinians (around 10 percent of the city's population) have been forced to move into Jerusalem. These Palestinians have relocated and migrated from neighboring Palestinian villages and suburbs back to various neighborhoods (including post-1967 Israeli neighborhoods/ suburbs/settlements of East Jerusalem) in an attempt to retain their residency status and accompanying rights. By doing so they choose to fight over their identity and status as residents of Jerusalem, initiating residential control over Jewish neighborhoods in the city.

Planning Arab Jerusalem and the Battle over Collective Memory

Since the beginning of the twenty-first century, non-profit organizations have become important to Israeli society. They establish political agendas and promote issues of environmental and social justice. Some of these groups promote their values and aims through the planning arena; they assist impoverished communities and provide them with information, guidance, advice, work with them to draft alternative plans, and represent them in legal battles through the planning and court systems (Yacobi, 2007; Rosen and Razin, 2008; Ron and Cohen-Blankshtain, 2011; Shmueli and Khamaisi, 2011).

In Jerusalem, Bimkom – Planners for Planning Rights – is one of these non-profits that aim to strengthen democracy and advance human rights in the field of planning. Bimkom has been invested in assisting the Palestinian communities of Arab Jerusalem. In one case, an (alternative) master plan for the Palestinian neighborhoods of Isawiyah (adjacent to the Hebrew University of Jerusalem campus on Mount Scopus) was developed. This was done in an attempt to provide the legal basis for any future development, by producing a zoning plan that would be used for issuing building permits. This would guarantee the legal growth of the neighborhood without the threat of housing demolition (Ron and Cohen-Blankshtain, 2011; Cohen-Blankshtain et al., 2013).

In another case, the organization has been attempting to assist the Palestinian residents of Beit Safafa, a Palestinian village divided in the 1948 war between Israel and Jordan. After the 1967 war, the village was reunited. However, its community is now split along residency status – some are citizens of Israel while others are East Jerusalemites and therefore have only residency status. Bimkom has been involved in trying to stop the construction of a major highway through the village. The highway's development would cut the community in two and therefore its people, and Bimkom is trying to promote Beit Safafa's underground development through a tunnel (N. Hasson, 2013).

Beit Safafa is a unique example of a Palestinian community that survived the Arab–Israeli war and is active in what Israel considers West Jerusalem. However, in West Jerusalem, most of the communities that once housed Arab populations (prior to 1948) are now home for Jews. These include historically significant areas such as Baka, Musrara, and Ein Kerem, which retain many of the original Arab houses with their unique architectural features. Their original Arab inhabitants are the forgotten ghosts of these communities. The Arab residents prior to the 1948 war have been fundamentally erased from the social and historical urban fabric, although not from the physical urban landscape or from Palestinians' memory.

One organization in Israel has taken on the task of remembering the remnants of these Arab communities. Zochrot (Hebrew for remember) is an Israeli–Palestinian non-profit devoted to remembering what happened to the Arab community as a result of the 1948 war and motivating Israel to be accountable for its actions. It views Israel as a colonial power vis-à-vis the Palestinian community. As the executive director of the organization put it, Israeli resistance to remembering and owning the problems associated with Israel's violent beginnings is powerful.

> There was an Arab village of Malcha. The Jewish people now living in the homes of the former residents don't know anything about the history of the place as an Arab village pre 1948. . . . Names like Malcha are Arabic names. But these Arabic names have become part of the Hebrew language. . . . The Palestinian memory is totally absent. Efforts to bring it up are often rejected very strongly. (Interview, 2008)

Jewish Israelis' rejection of the memories of Arab residents is, in part, a political reaction. Israeli acknowledgment of former

Arab residents fuels the cry for a Palestinian demand for their right of return (Rempel, 1999). For some Palestinians touring these lost places, collecting testimonies from the original residents and preserving some evidence (or recreating a linkage to the past by signposting) is about historic justice. *Zochrot*, the act of remembering, is directly linked to the battle over their identity and belonging as residents of the city regardless of their nationality. It is an expression of a Palestinian right to the city and of the right to the Jerusalem that was theirs before the State of Israel.

But remembering these former Arab villages is also a way to present an alternative narrative of Israel's 1948 war of independence. For Palestinians, as we have seen, this was the Nakba (or disaster, in Arabic) – the destruction of the Palestinian landscape during the war (Falah, 1996).

Zochrot attempts to reconstruct memory of and belonging to forgotten places with respect to Palestinian collective identity in Israel. In a way, Zochrot symbolically challenges Israel's spatial expansion in East Jerusalem. It refuses to see the outcome of the 1948 war as final and unchangeable. Instead it implicitly (and sometimes explicitly) advocates a pluralistic Jerusalem, one shared between Jews and Palestinians. This kind of symbolic resistance questions Israel's legitimacy over Jerusalem and its singular ownership over memory and place making.

Conclusion

Despite Israel's attempts to control East Jerusalem, Palestinians' struggle over East Jerusalem is both evident and ongoing. Their resistance in Arab Jerusalem is neither dormant nor silent. The Palestinian challenge to Israeli authority is visible and takes on varied forms of opposition in daily life, sometimes very violent ones.

Palestinians' continued life in Jerusalem and ability to retain their residency status may be viewed as a triumph. It is a victory for the Palestinians of East Jerusalem to stay in their homes and remain present as citizens of Jerusalem. They could leave for Ramallah or Bethlehem, and many have done so. But many have stayed. And they have stayed for a reason. For Palestinians to remain in East Jerusalem in spite of the oppressive treatment of Israel is a significant form of resistance.

From Israel's perspective, the Palestinians of East Jerusalem are the others – strangers and outsiders in their own city. The metaphor associated with their daily lives is that they must walk between the raindrops, that is, an impossible feat. Palestinians must walk between the raindrops to coexist as East Jerusalemite Palestinians under Israeli rule and to maintain their identity, needs, and dreams. One Palestinian business man from Ramallah whom we interviewed told us that the best strategy for Palestinian resistance is actually being patient. He explained that sometimes what power and might cannot achieve, time will. According to this perspective, the only thing Arab Jerusalem needs to do is manage to stay in place and wait for demography to work. Over time, Palestinians living in East Jerusalem will increase in numbers. They will have their say; Jerusalem will not be partitioned or divided. Eventually all of Jerusalem will be Palestinian.

6

Downtown Place Making and Growth in Israeli Jerusalem

Introduction

Although Jerusalem may be one of the most well-known places on earth, it is less known as a city. Yes, a city – the kind of city that picks up the garbage (or not), that provides the infrastructure to get people to work and back, that protects its residents from ordinary crimes and raw sewage, and that has schools, grocery stores, and, most important of all, coffee shops. Jerusalem inspires with its holy places and millennial historical events. But at the end of the day (and the beginning), its people – Jewish, Christian, Muslim, and other – live the stuff of plain old ordinary lives. Jerusalem may provide residents a special kind of redemption after they die. But while they are alive on this earth and living in Jerusalem, the specialness of Jerusalem recedes into the background and the normal work of urban development holds sway.

To be sure, Jerusalem's development may appear to be anything but normal. It was not until the mid–nineteenth century that development began to occur outside the Old City walls. Jerusalem was reticent about expansion. Development was slow, with its economy tied to religious activity and its growth stymied by its frontier status. Jerusalem's development has never been typical, and its conflict over settlements, nationalism, identity, and statehood make it special – more special than it sometimes would like to be. Imagine that settlements were not the stuff of political conflict but instead were the exclusionary environmentally unfriendly places known as suburbs in the United States. What if the spatial segregation of secular Jews, the Haredim, and Palestinians could be tackled with laws of affirmative, fair housing and promises of equal opportunity? What if people's identity and what they represent were less prominent and instead making money prevailed? In a place like Jerusalem, this could be called progress.

Despite its social and political troubles, Jerusalem's politicians and leaders have been trying to free up some development from ideology. This push to have Jerusalem recognize its potential as a money-making engine has not come out of nowhere. Making places make money, and lots of it, is a more recent innovation of global capital.

Out of global capitalism have come global cities. Fundamental to development and redevelopment of global cities has been revalorization – the creation of new economic value from places that have deteriorated and lost their value, that have been devalorized (Harvey, 2000; N. Smith, 2002). Although capitalism continues to rely on the production and circulation of commodities, it now also profits from urban development. Gentrification and downtown development are fueled by the potential for profit underwritten and subsidized by governments who view their role as promoting private sector activity in the city. This is the neoliberal city (Brenner and Theodore, 2002).

The watchword of the neoliberal city is that it provides the requisite infrastructure and support for the private sector to invest in and make money from urban development. With the rise of the neo-liberal city, public–private partnerships have come to structure government support of the private sector (Hackworth, 2007). Today urban development explicitly relies on the public sector to manage investment opportunities and to make money from development itself. The role of government in the neoliberal city is to support real estate development – office building, housing complexes, and so on. The neoliberal city is about urban development and ensuring that development investment activities are both safe and profitable. The public sector explicitly underwrites development and ensures predictable profits.

Although Jerusalem has embraced the neoliberal turn, it faces a different set of challenges from a more normal and conventional city. Its growth has been politically driven, both implicitly and explicitly. For over forty years, the growth of Jerusalem has been motivated as a takeover operation, not a money-making venture. True, money has been made for some. But profit was not an explicit goal. West Jerusalem's post-1948 development was intended to put an Israeli Jewish stamp on Jerusalem – to build a new (West) Jerusalem as the capital of its new Jewish state, Israel. Following the 1967 war and its territorial gains, the construction of new Israeli neighborhoods was designed to link East and West Jerusalem, and reestablish the capital city's status as the central urban node in the country. Israeli decision makers seized this moment to unify the city. Large infrastructure investments, economic incentives, and new housing opportunities were part of a strategic plan. The goal was not to simply take over the space that had been conquered, but to turn a frontier city in the country's periphery into a thriving metropolis under Israeli control. Politics was primary to Jerusalem's expansion, but its economic development also played a prominent role.

From Israel's perspective, Jerusalem's growth was and remains politically tied to the establishment, growth, and continued viability of the nation. For people who have spent their lives in and around cities devoid of such explicit political objectives, Jerusalem's spatial structure may appear a bit odd. Its downtown is a mix of all sorts of land use and is devoid of tall buildings, without much density. Of course, in Jerusalem (as the song goes), "when you're alone and life is making you lonely, you can always go downtown." But first you have to find it. In what we are calling normal places, downtowns are the hubs, where economic, political, and social life begins (Robertson, 1995, 1999; Birch, 2002). But this has not been the case in Jerusalem, where government has been housed more or less in the outskirts of West Jerusalem, where businesses are in Tel Aviv or safely protected in guarded shopping malls, and where people are afraid that going and being downtown might be a life-threatening activity. Unlike the downtown in the song made famous by Petula Clark, in Jerusalem's downtown, everything's not waiting for you. Therefore in its recent incarnation as a neoliberal city, Jerusalem has been at work attempting to transform itself into a safe and attractive place for investment and to become a wealth-generating urban enterprise.

After years of outward growth as the sole development strategy, Jerusalem's development actors have advanced another approach that also favors inward growth. Jerusalem's ethno-national growth machine has been promoting a new development path that is oriented toward the center of the city, not the periphery. It supports the development of small vacant places within urban neighborhoods called infill development. It is promoting land-use intensification through the development of high-rise residential structures. It focuses on large-scale urban renewal projects which gut old buildings and refurbish them for new development.

Jerusalem's urban development schemes continue to develop its periphery with a politicized suburban growth approach while also focusing on developing central places and its long-ignored downtown. This chapter explores contemporary urban development in Israeli Jerusalem by focusing on the city's changing growth trajectory. It examines Jerusalem's contemporary activities around inner-city business and commercial development and a move toward what is called densification – creating denser, more centrally located, and wealthier residential land. It also explores tensions in housing policy in Jerusalem around affordability and development for the wealthy.

The first part highlights the historical context for these activities and examines the emergence of Jerusalem's original growth trajectory and how it is different from typical metropolitan growth dynamics. The second part discusses the role of specific planning initiatives that have seen public investment directed at attracting private sector involvement when previously none existed. The third part describes three redevelopment projects in downtown

Jerusalem: the Jerusalem Western Entrance Quarter, the urban quarter of Mamilla, and the Machane Yehuda market place.

Jerusalem's Growth

Between 1948 and 1967, Jerusalem was divided between two countries, Jordan and Israel. Jerusalem became two cities separated by barbed-wire fences and walls (Lustick, 2004; Klein, 2005). For Israel, the formation of a divided city triggered the immediate need to shift urban growth westward.

With Jerusalem as its capital, Israel introduced a planning approach that created a new city adjacent to the Old City but physically both separate and disconnected from it. A new Government District, the "Capitol," was developed in and around Givat Ram at the western edge of the city (Shapiro, 1973). This immense urban national center comprised government offices, a new Hebrew University campus (the Edmond J. Safra Campus), the National Library, museums, and the Knesset building. As with capital cities around the world, the government played a dominant role in directing this type of urban development.

Yet Jerusalem had other development issues, particularly housing problems. During the 1950s and early 1960s, immigrants, largely Holocaust survivors and Jews from Muslim countries in Asia, Africa, and the Middle East, moved to the city in large numbers. Israel needed to provide housing solutions. Immigrants were housed in temporary refugee camps made up of tents and tin shacks. Some immigrants were moved to former Palestinian villages and neighborhoods that had been taken over in the 1948 war, while others were housed in newly built public housing super-block apartment buildings. The post-1948 West Jerusalem was a poor border city (Dumper, 1997; M. Benvenisti, 1998).

Jerusalem's development activities changed dramatically with the 1967 war. The capture of East Jerusalem profoundly influenced the city's development trajectory. With the 1967 war, Israel gained control over both parts of Jerusalem. To unite the two areas, Jerusalem embarked on a strategy of urban expansion. The decision to engage in urban expansion seems particular to Israel, although this was experienced by cities almost everywhere. This was the classic debate over whether to prioritize suburbanization or the redevelopment of the inner city (Jackson, 1985; Fishman, 1987; Beauregard, 2006).

On the surface, Jerusalem's development direction seemed similar, where housing investments moved outward, encouraging house-deprived city residents to go and live at the urban/suburban fringe. But Jerusalem's development trajectory was different, different in terms of sources of capital, housing design and density, and the political goals of metropolitan expansion. Israel used public money, control, and land ownership for shaping development.

Accelerated development and growth in Israeli Jerusalem was geared outward without any significant upgrading of the city center or investment in Palestinian commercial and residential areas. Although Jerusalem's development patterns looked like classic economic disinvestment from the urban core to the fringe, its expansion was less economic and more political. Since 1967, most of Jerusalem's metropolitan growth has taken the form of non-contiguous urban sprawl, development that has been largely motivated by the politics of the conflict – to gain permanent control over East Jerusalem and parts of the West Bank. Yet settlement policy is also housing policy. By constructing settlements, Israel has built a huge amount of new housing.

The housing component of settlement development around Jerusalem is often overlooked. The mayor of Ma'ale Adumim, one of Israel's largest settlement/cities in the West Bank, explained that settlements deliver subsidized housing to Jerusalemites. By moving to settlements like Ma'ale Adumim, people view themselves as making cost-effective economic decisions not political ones:

People who move to Ma'ale Adumim are not ideologically settlers. Many are young couples that want a new place to live. They are interested in a better quality [of life and housing] than the one in Jerusalem. And residents and investors pay fewer taxes than in Jerusalem. (Interview, 2008)

The head of the regional council of Gush Etzion, another major settlement, also believed that settlements operated to construct needed housing. By building new housing, settlements also fulfill a huge pent-up demand for affordable housing in Jerusalem:

> There is no housing in Jerusalem. . . . Jerusalem is a poor city. It has to grow to the suburbs. Now the future of Jerusalem is outside of the municipal boundaries of Jerusalem. . . . [Another] type of subsidy for a place the government wants to develop is providing money in the form of infrastructure . . . making housing cheaper. (Interview, 2007)

As housing policy, Jerusalem's growth has been similar to the suburban housing strategy used in many North American cities. It offers cheap housing to the people who move out of the central city.

To be sure, Jerusalem's urban expansion, settlements and suburbs alike, has not been like the suburbanization of American cities. Jerusalem's post-1967 neighborhoods were not urban bungalows filled with family rooms and multiple bathrooms. This new housing has been of high quality and located in well-planned communities. Jerusalem's housing expansion in the form of settlements and suburbs worked to solve problems of poor, overcrowded, and deteriorating housing conditions.

By the late 1990s, Jerusalem's growth was at a crossroads. The conflict continued to motivate Jerusalem's metropolitan development. Israeli governments were obligated to further advance spatial expansion and suburban growth, fueling the myth of an undividable, ever-growing greater metropolitan Jerusalem.

But there were demands to develop Jerusalem's central place. This turn to redevelop central cities was not unique to Jerusalem. But Jerusalem's situation represented political complexities as well as generic urban problems like a limited tax base, poverty, and massive inequality. Jerusalem wants to be a global player too, like Tel Aviv, but also like Barcelona or Glasgow – an attractive place for capital investments. Jerusalem's leaders perceived a need to redevelop the city, improve its competitive position locally and internationally, and encourage urban investment and reinvestment. Like every other city on the planet except for those in North Korea, Jerusalem wants to join the global economy.

Planning and Public Investment in Jerusalem

There are three issues that have dominated the direction of Jerusalem's development. The first is security and the risk associated with large-scale development in a city plagued with violence. The second is the location of land free for housing development within a city containing little vacant land and overflowing with social antagonisms between different groups. The third issue is the management of transportation in a city that is old with narrow streets, is reliant on tourism, and has a poor local population dependent on public transit.

The Barrier/Fence/Wall

Jerusalem's security issues are more extensive than in other cities. Even in a post-9/11 world where threats of terrorism are everywhere, its security risk for terrorism remains at the top of the charts. Cities across the globe continue to prepare for what-if scenarios. But Jerusalem's experiences with terrorism are not hypothetical. Although one is safer from pickpockets there than in Barcelona, in Jerusalem people consistently and legitimately worry about being physically safe. Daily life is structured around protecting oneself from covert attacks and random violence.

Terrorism in the form of bombs on buses, in restaurants, and in other public places has plagued Jerusalem (Savitch, 2005; Kliot and Charney, 2006; Benmelech and Berrebi, 2007; Hazam and Felsenstein, 2007). Tourism plummeted in Jerusalem when terrorism was at its peak during the Second Intifada (2000–5). The years after the 2014 Gaza War are also predicted to be low points for tourism and the Jerusalem economy.

Terrorism is bad for local economies because people stay away from unsafe places. But terrorism also prevents the initiation of many economic development activities because these require capital investment, not just by government but by private investors too. For investors of capital, predictability and perceptions of predictability are the hallmarks of profitability, particularly when it comes to urban redevelopment, and terrorism is the essence of unpredictability. Therefore encouraging capital investment requires reducing terrorism.

To reduce terrorism, Israel has built a security barrier around the perimeter of the country as well as the city of Jerusalem. Although the construction of this barrier/fence/wall is largely intended to protect people, not simply investment capital, its broader and longer-term effects have been economic. At least until the 2014 Gaza War, the barrier/fence/wall has been a major boon for development in Jerusalem. Although people debate whether it has directly reduced the incidence of terrorist activities, it is perceived as being responsible for the decline in terrorism.

In some ways, the barrier/fence/wall is like other strategies that produce a more predictable urban investment landscape. A popular US urban strategy has been Hope VI, a 1990s policy that tore down US central city high-rise public housing and replaced it with low-rise housing that blended into a more middle-class urban landscape. By reducing the volume of crime and poverty, Hope VI has created new markets for urban development by making neighborhoods containing public housing safe for investment. Hope VI has expelled poor public housing residents and has returned urban land to capitalism (Goetz, 2013).

The barrier/fence/wall is, in some ways, a kind of Hope VI for Jerusalem – a policy that appears to make investment in Jerusalem safer for capitalism. By ridding neighborhoods of high-rise public housing, Hope VI reduced fears of crime and violence in urban neighborhoods. In Jerusalem, the barrier/fence/wall appears to have achieved something similar. As a result, it has encouraged large-scale investment in the very places where bombs appeared routine. Urban development in Jerusalem is ubiquitous. Massive numbers of cranes now decorate the city's skyline.

The Safdie Plan and the Push against Jerusalem's Expansion

Jerusalem's development has been a major concern of Israel, with two issues largely dominating the growth agenda – population and land. Since the beginning of the State of Israel, the politics around population and land have been steered and manipulated to facilitate national and local political aspirations. Israel's national political agenda has been geared toward spatially expanding Jerusalem for housing increasing numbers of Jews and for strengthening Israelis' demographic dominance over the city.

The local urban agenda, on the other hand, has focused on the need to strengthen the socioeconomic base of Jerusalem and manage more conventional urban challenges, such as growth management, infrastructure investments, and housing prices. These challenges were compounded in the early 1990s with the massive immigration of people from the former Soviet Union.

As should now be obvious, for Israel Jerusalem is an ethnonational political tool. This national political agenda required Jews to dominate Jerusalem. Jerusalem became the residential destination for many Jews. But it also needed more space in which to house these Jews. This need set in motion the Safdie Plan, a planning agenda that was ultimately politically defeated in 2007.

Initiated in 1998, the Safdie Plan was the creation of famed architect Moshe Safdie. Its intent was to expand the municipal boundaries of Jerusalem. But rather than expand it over the Green Line into the West Bank, the Safdie Plan was to expand Jerusalem westward into what already was Israel.

This project called for the construction of twenty thousand new housing units, commercial and industrial space in the Jerusalem Hills, a largely undeveloped area that has some suburbs but is still mostly rural. The Safdie Plan was to build on adjacent woodland within this area, ultimately engaging in the activity of paving paradise and putting up that proverbial parking lot.

Although the politics of the Safdie Plan were to shift Jerusalem's development away from the West Bank, its urban development push was more in line with a conventional urban development agenda. The Safdie Plan was a vision of a contemporary and more cosmopolitan Jerusalem. As a *Haaretz* reporter explained, the discourse around the plan had changed

> from a concern with the demographic problem to helping Jerusalem with its urban problems. . . . The idea was to reverse trends of negative immigration. Keep the city alive with social diversity. Keep up the middle class. . . . The most important thing was that Safdie [Plan] would save the city. [The plan's advocates] also realized . . . Arabs were behind the [separation] fence. Jews felt more secure and saw demographics as less of a problem. So the idea shifted to the one of how to keep young people from leaving Jerusalem. (Interview, 2007)

Originally, the Safdie Plan was initiated by two central government bodies, the Israel Land Administration and the Jerusalem Development Authority, and supported and promoted by the entrepreneurial and pro-growth Mayor Ehud Olmert. With this kind of backing, the Safdie Plan was considered to be a fait accompli. For most urban onlookers, it was destiny.

Nonetheless, a feisty group of environmentally oriented groups led by the Society for the Preservation of Nature in Israel (SPNI) decided to fight the plan. To the surprise of many, in early 2007 the mayor of Jerusalem recommended killing the development. This ultimately led to its defeat.

Although a win for Israeli's environmentalists, the Jerusalem mayoral tabling of the plan was simply political, not progressive. As explained by the head of the Jerusalem Development Authority,

> the death of the Safdie Plan is a huge tragedy. . . . [Its] rejection is one of the horrors of the city in recent years. . . . The mayor decided that to gain another term, he needed more popularity from the seculars. So he decided to cater to the Greens. He has no vision, only political vision. (Interview, 2008)

In practice, however, the defeat of the plan was achieved by a coalition of stakeholders, namely Israel's environmental movement, the SPNI, and the Jerusalem public, who filed around sixteen thousand objections against the plan. Naomi Tzur, head of

Sustainable Jerusalem and Director of the Jerusalem SPNI at the time, explained why this group believed stopping the plan was so important:

> The Safdie Plan was essentially giving up on the city. It was derived from not being able to plan in other parts of the city. It was based on a false premise, that there is no room to build housing in the city. It was also based on the false need that Jerusalem needs to increase its Jewish population. (Interview, 2007)

The defeat of the plan in 2007 has effectively created what may be considered a Green Belt around the city that has limited its outward expansion. The municipality is now forced to consider other growth options, namely infill and intensification, as the new urban scheme for developing Jerusalem. As the municipality's chief planner explained: "The city is growing and needs to provide new housing units. It is very clear the only way to go, in the absent of the ability to spread outwards, is to redevelop, densify, intensify . . . replacing existing buildings with new ones" (interview, 2012). He further explained that the underlying motivation was to focus on development downtown: "We want to stimulate urban revitalization and economic development of the inner city. The downtown is essential for Jerusalem's growth."

Post-Safdie, Jerusalem's contemporary neoliberal development schemes are promoting large-scale urban renewal programs. Unlike the United States, where public housing is in the center of the city, Jerusalem is focusing on razing and redeveloping former public housing estates at the urban fringe. In the center of Jerusalem, the main redevelopment goals have been to add new residential units to existing built-up areas, introduce new land uses and new populations into aging neighborhoods, and improve the use of urban infrastructure.

Jerusalem's urban redevelopment activities are not that different from those of other cities caught up in the quest for profits from what is called urban regeneration; likewise, urban renewal in Jerusalem is a money-making strategy intended to upgrade and reintegrate decaying built-up areas into the urban fabric. Like elsewhere, the focus on profit over people has bloomed in an escalating national housing crisis, where housing has become less affordable to many social groups in society (Marom, 2013; Alfasi and Fenster, 2014). When we asked a major private developer why get into renewal projects, he replied, "We do business. Anything that has a business side to it . . . it's interesting for us. . . . [As long as] we're gonna make money" (interview, 2014). Jerusalem's relative newness to the urban regeneration scene makes it a player deserving of study.

Together, the barrier/fence/wall and the defeat of the Safdie Plan have rerouted development inward – enabling Israel to focus on Jerusalem to essentially call the question on what the city is and will be. This has transformed Israel's ethno-national growth machine's emphasis of spatial expansion into a state-sponsored neoliberal agenda which also favors intensification and regeneration of the city center and development of large-scale projects throughout the city (Yacobi, 2012; Charney and Rosen, 2014; Alfasi and Ganan, 2015).

Transportation

Two major development projects around mass transit have structured the path and location of real estate development. These are Tel Aviv–Jerusalem fast rail and the JLR.

The Tel Aviv–Jerusalem fast rail will connect the city of Tel Aviv and the Ben Gurion International Airport to Jerusalem. By connecting Jerusalem to the Tel Aviv economic hub, the train is intended to transform Jerusalem's position from a frontier city to an integrated part of Israel's high-tech and business economy. This transportation initiative, still years from completion, is anticipated to eventually make the now separate Jerusalem and Tel Aviv metropolitan areas into one metropolitan region.

The JLR serves as a mass transit system that improves internal linkage between the neighborhoods of East and West Jerusalem (see Figure 6.1). As a sleek modern transit operation that moves through Jewish and Palestinian neighborhoods alike, the JLR is

Figure 6.1   Jerusalem Light Rail, Jaffa Center downtown
(© Anne Shlay)

intended to convey modernity, civilization, and connection to the developed world.

Both of these mega-project developments are tied to the general goal of renewing and expanding Jerusalem's urban core. Planners hope that such infrastructure improvements will increase the number of residents, workers, and tourists in the downtown.

Redevelopment in Downtown Jerusalem

Several large-scale projects have been under development in Jerusalem. These include: (1) the Jerusalem Western Entrance Quarter; (2) the Mamilla Redevelopment Project; and (3) development around the Machane Yehuda market.

The Jerusalem Western Entrance Quarter

The Jerusalem Western Entrance Quarter is intended to redirect new development and to encourage more economic activity in the city's new business corridor. It will eventually contain twelve new skyscrapers, Jerusalem's version of the Docklands, and will be a new business district providing large quantities of office space. Intended to rebrand Jerusalem as a modern metropolis, it is designed to be accessible to Jerusalem's new transit systems.

Mamilla

Mamilla is an urban redevelopment project. It has been a project with a very long history of being redeveloped. The area was first established in the late nineteenth century west of the Jaffa Gate of the Old City. Originally it was a mixed Arab–Jewish urban quarter that served as a business district, an extension of the market place that was located around the Jaffa Gate (Kark, 1991). It contained four major hotels that became the symbols for the international and multi-religious characteristics of the city.

The Mamilla area changed radically in 1947 when rising tensions between the Palestinian and Jewish populations of the city eventually materialized into a full-scale war the following year. By the end of the war (in 1949), Mamilla was in ruins. It became the armistice line between Israel and Jordan that divided Jerusalem and was barricaded by concrete walls (separation walls) and barbed wire. Its location as the border for a divided Jerusalem kept it undeveloped through to the 1967 war.

After the 1967 war, the barricades were rapidly torn down. This was the beginning of Mamilla's forty-year extreme makeover. Redevelopment challenges included historic preservation and economic development. Mamilla was also used as part of the Jerusalem unification project, specifically as a spatial vehicle for reconnecting the Old City with the new Israeli neighborhoods of West Jerusalem (Kroyanker, 1988; Amirav, 2009; Shtern, 2010).

From the mid-1980s until the late 2000s, the Mamilla area

Figure 6.2   Mamilla under construction (© Anne Shlay)

ceased to exist as a neighborhood and became a construction site
(see Figure 6.2). The area now contains three luxury hotels – the
Mamilla Hotel, the David Citadel Hotel, and the Waldorf Astoria
– an office tower, a shopping center comprised of an open mall and
public streets that lead to the Jaffa Gate, and the upscale David's
Village residential gated community (Grant and Rosen, 2009). The
project also includes preservation of some of the historic buildings
(e.g. the French Hospice Saint Vincent de Paul) and construction
of a major underground parking lot.

Mamilla appears to be creating ripple effects across the downtown. The nearby area contains many new condominiums, for
example King David's Crown, King David Residence, Jerusalem
Towers, Jerusalem of Gold, and more. Many of these new residential projects, particularly in the downtown, cater explicitly to
foreign investors. Many foreign Jews, particularly from France
and the United States, have purchased homes in Jerusalem. Some
buy homes in central Jerusalem and concentrate their purchases in

particular neighborhoods, including the German Colony, Baka, and Mamilla. These homes, typically in luxury apartment buildings, are priced for foreigners. Both the high prices and the large volume of these transactions have had considerable effects on the Jerusalem housing market by increasing the price of housing particularly within centrally located neighborhoods and creating real estate bubbles in the city (Loirer, 2007).

The Transforming Market Place

Machane Yehuda has been an important Jerusalemite landmark for more than a century. It is a market place extending over several blocks that operates as an amalgam of stores and stands that sell all sorts of food and house-based paraphernalia to the Jerusalem populace. Established in the late nineteenth century to serve residents of the newly established neighborhoods outside of the Old City, it soon evolved into a local employment center along the major Jaffa road in West Jerusalem. What is happening to development in Machane Yehuda is not part of a grand development scheme. Rather, development and redevelopment are emerging in parts of the surrounding space, while the ultimate goal for the area itself seems to be increasing accommodation for upper-income families and office space.

Machane Yehuda has been a great success as West Jerusalem's most important and central market place. Despite this triumph, the market suffered from neglect and disinvestment. By the 1980s, its aging infrastructure (not to mention its odorousness) made it clear that it was in urgent need of change. In the early 1990s, the market place saw its first major makeover, including refurbished infrastructure, newly paved roads, renovated market stands, upgraded electricity wiring, and a partial enclosure of the market (see Figure 6.3).

Machane Yehuda soon faced another challenge. Escalating security threats during the Second Intifada were brought to the front door of its stores when suicide bombers exploded at the entrance to the market place and on public buses that served it and

Figure 6.3   Machane Yehuda (© Anne Shlay)

the rest of the downtown. As a result, it was heavily fortified. Most of its entrances were closed down. Private security guards, police officers, and soldiers from the Israel Defense Forces (the army) controlled its entrances and patrolled the area. The place was safe, but this condition of hyper-militarization of space took the fun out of visiting the downtown and added an element of anxiety to the shopping experience. Only a few Jerusalemites continued to visit the market during these tense times.

Machane Yehuda's position as an important and popular market place and institution has, however, been buoyed by several changes in the Jerusalem situation and environment. A major change has been the drastically improved security situation for Israelis. At the same time, the city began to improve the accessibility of the area by building the JLR along the Jaffa road. Jerusalem initiated a series of efforts to attract students to live in the area. In addition, there were changes in consumer tastes and there was a growing demand for an urban lifestyle that included pubs, cafés, live music, and more.

An urban policy focus on Machane Yehuda became a huge opportunity for local merchants to transform their businesses and to become an attractive haunt for students and young professionals who now lived in and around the downtown. New businesses previously unthinkable (e.g. stores selling clothing, jewelry, art, Judaica) now blend in with the market's noisy and picturesque streets.

Machane Yehuda has become a more hip place to be. Restaurants and bars often host events including live music, themed special food evenings, food and wine tastings, art exhibitions, and tours for tourists (individuals and groups of many participants) that include bakery tours, cooking workshops, and more. Artists, painters, and sculptors have collaborated to transform the area into a lively urban cultural scene. The market also hosts special events on holiday seasons (e.g. just before Yom Kippur, Tu Bishvat, and Passover).

Adjacent to Machane Yehuda is the Etz Chaim compound – a physical structure with a unique history with Jerusalem. In the early twenty-first century it was first developed as the Etz Chaim Yeshiva (i.e. an Orthodox Jewish institution that focuses on the study of religious texts). In 2008, the Yeshiva sold the site to a developer who planned to use it for extensive commercial and residential development. Two high-rise condominium buildings are being developed alongside an urban plaza and a small park, and it will include a commercial level for businesses, cafés, restaurants, shops, and galleries. Another structure will include a public plaza, a swimming pool, and commercial space. The compound's original historic buildings are to undergo restoration, some to be preserved and one to be renovated as a luxury hotel.

This project exemplifies the recent changes in the area. Old and new coexist along newly commodified spaces. More tourists and residents visit and live in the area. As Machane Yehuda emerges from a base for traditional fruit and vegetable stands to a center catering to a more diverse set of activities, nearby areas are experiencing tremendous development pressures.

The adjacent neighborhoods of Nachlaot, with their distinctive architecture, restaurants, and shops, have become a favorite destination for tourists and college students. This has promoted processes of scattered gentrification that have resulted in growing numbers of affluent groups moving to live in these areas (Hubbard, 2008; D. Smith, 2008).

Conclusion

Jerusalem's downtown development activities reflect attempts by the city's planners and politicians to treat it as if it were a regular city where there is money to be made. And in some ways, they appear to be succeeding. The most recent Jerusalem development activities are not geopolitically driven, but are commercial and economic. Jerusalem is trying to build up its business districts and attract people to its downtown areas for entertainment and shopping.

Jerusalem is working at building hubs around entertainment, shopping, and offices. None of these developments approximate the more traditional downtown, in part because they are scattered around various parts of the city. But when Petula Clark sang in "Downtown" that "everything's waiting for you," she did not specify that it was all waiting in one place. Possibly, Jerusalem's commercial planning activities reflect contemporary development patterns associated with the multi-centered postindustrial city. Although Jerusalem has been around for millennia, its development trajectory has always been unusual and off the beaten path.

While maintaining its focus on building settlements in the West Bank and in East Jerusalem, Jerusalem is systematically toiling at downtown commercial development. If you read any international newspaper, you will see headlines about the building of more settlements. Yet at the same time and parallel to these political struggles, Jerusalem is attempting to act and develop like a normal city – one devoid of extreme conflict, divisions, walls, and antagonisms.

There is a Jerusalem that wants to be normal even if the profitability of central city real estate is not a sure thing. Ultimately, these in-town developments may not succeed in economically integrating and building up Jerusalem's commercial activities. Yet in true neoliberal style, Jerusalem wants to be the consummate new town in town and for its workers to pick up some takeout on their way home from the office. Jerusalem wants to be about shopping for that new dress, a pair of shoes, and some earrings to match. It wants to be about listening to blues or jazz, getting a drink or coffee at a nice-looking café, and finding that perfect restaurant. Being urban is no longer just about density; it is about lifestyle, and Jerusalem has lifestyle to burn.

If Chicago, New York, and Miami can make money from real estate development, so should Jerusalem. Jerusalem is no different. In the United States, people will pay top dollar to be by the lakefront, to be in Manhattan, to be close to the ocean. In Jerusalem, rich foreign Jews will pay millions of shekels to be able to walk to the Kotel and feel its holiness on any given Shabbat. There may not be gold in them hills but there are more than a few shekels in a King David Street location that is adjacent to all of the holy places and the Mamilla shopping mall.

This epitomizes Jerusalem's expression of neoliberalism, which is to be able to embrace the real estate market in all of its glory. The government is not just building transportation arteries, sewers, and waterways. It is building Jerusalem's very capacity to live and breathe as a city and urban land market. Who is it for? Contemporary Jerusalem is a feature of global capitalism like everywhere else.

Jerusalem pretends it has a normal market. But the market only works because it is barricaded in by the latest security equipment and technology. Jerusalem in many ways is the ultimate neoliberal city because walking around it in its contemporary form is only possible because of public investment – in the military, settlements, and the barrier/fence/wall. Jerusalem's neoliberal city is a product of its ethno-national growth coalition – the Jerusalem growth machine.

7

Conclusion

People call Jerusalem the holy city because it is the place most consistently linked with the origins of three of the world's most significant religions: Islam, Christianity, and Judaism. It is in Jerusalem where it is said that Jesus carried the cross on which he died, that the Prophet Muhammad launched his journey to heaven, and that Judaism's First and Second Temples were constructed. Jerusalem's Old City is not simply old; it is an ancient urban wonder. Yes, we will always have Paris, but long before that city became a universal symbol of romantic love, Jerusalem had already achieved its status as the place for the love of God. Carnal joys can be found the world round, but Jerusalem delivers spiritual devotion. For those concerned with heaven on earth or in some afterlife, Jerusalem is the real deal. Jerusalem has been a source of salvation for literally thousands of years.

Yet in the here and now, Jerusalem is deeply obsessed and splintered along ethno-national, political, class, and religious fault lines. In many ways it is the poster child for contested space, and is arguably the ultimate divided city-region. Living in Jerusalem and understanding its complexity is like taking a very long rollercoaster ride. A rollercoaster ride is an intense experience and a terrifying yet exhilarating wake-up call. Likewise, the experience of Jerusalem makes people feel alive, gets the adrenalin going, but also overloads the senses. Take in the diversity of people, the primeval versus contemporary land uses, its ungainly geography, conflicts between everyone, the mixture of sacred and profane, and the consistently out-of-control politics. The cumulative effect is perhaps not for the faint of heart, but is is nothing short of "wow."

Moshe Amirav (2009) argues that policy makers who attempt to deal with the city's challenges and complexities get possessed by a type of mental illness called "the Jerusalem syndrome," a kind of obsessive compulsion that projects all cares and concerns about the world onto Jerusalem and, by default, all of that city's issues and problems. Despite intense world-wide difficulties and the challenges of globalization, Jerusalem has become a, if not the, central international preoccupation of so many political leaders who have unsuccessfully worked to promote dialogue and peace talks between Israelis and Palestinians.

Back in the hopeful days of the late 1970s, US President Jimmy Carter miraculously achieved a peace agreement between Israel and Egypt, inspiring many to work at resolving longstanding conflicts over Jerusalem. Look over the list of US presidents and their respective secretaries of states who became Jerusalem junkies: Ronald Reagan and George Shultz; George Bush and James Baker; Bill Clinton, Warren Christopher, and Madeleine Albright; George Bush, Colin Powell, and Condoleezza Rice; Barack Obama, Hillary Clinton, and John Kerry. Add to this list the host of advocacy organizations and religious institutions across the United States. Now include the diplomats, politicians, army generals, journalists, and academics from all over the world. No city, we submit, gets the same political and international attention as Jerusalem.

From the perspective of countries containing enormous cities with enormous problems, the disproportionate focus on Jerusalem may seem unfair. But for reasons that may not be entirely reasonable, Jerusalem is special. And more than being the opiate for the masses, Jerusalem is political. Jerusalem politics are not isolated internal squabbles germane to the local. Jerusalem's requisite political maneuvering gets the juices flowing for battle in the ultimate international contact sport. More than any other place, Jerusalem is about politics.

But neither of us are politicians. We are social scientists who focus on cities. We study cities by applying conventional social science methods and techniques with the goal of objectively collecting the data from which our findings are derived. With this methodological goal in mind, we lay out a caveat with some trepidation. We are emotionally involved and deeply invested in Jerusalem. We live, breathe, and dream this city. At times this intense intellectual voyage has wreaked emotional havoc with our seemingly rational selves. Jerusalem is a master at breaking down one's defense mechanisms, particularly the ones that define us as social scientists.

For social scientists like us who are not religious and do not have an avowed political point of view, studying Jerusalem is more than an intellectual challenge. We have found it difficult to maintain an analytical perspective on Jerusalem because it is not a rational place. Even losing our analytical capacity for a moment has led us to question whether we could pull off what we started to do. But at the end, we think that we have succeeded in maintaining perspective. Although we have emerged from this experience with psychological scarring, we think we have largely stayed on course.

We think that we "get" Jerusalem because we accept the limitations of ourselves as social scientists. People believe that Jerusalem, the holy city, is the city of God, or Gods, depending on your religious point of view. But the passion and intensity of religious feeling feed into political feelings and actions. How can one consistently analyze these claims, claims that are sometimes spiritual, fanatical, polemical, or all three in various combinations? Analyze Jerusalem? Are you crazy? Yes, we are. You cannot successfully study Jerusalem unless you are on the edge, because the emotionality and place attachment associated with this place demand feelings on the part of the researcher. How else can you possibly understand this place? The challenge is not with being on the edge but to avoid falling off of it.

The rational (and at the same time possibly futile) purpose of this book has been to foster an accessible yet complex understanding of Jerusalem. We wanted to provide people with a guide to the complexity of the Jerusalem situation, not to simplify it. We wrote this book because of what we learned after eight years of research and teaching about Jerusalem. What we learned was not about Jerusalem per se but more specifically about what people seemed to know about Jerusalem. We learned that many people have a one-dimensional understanding and an overly simplistic sense of the Jerusalem situation, and that this perpetuates the conflict.

When it comes to the Jerusalem conflict, many people have a clear, if not overbearing, sense of the right and the wrong, the good and the bad, and the good and bad guys associated with it. Yet these judgments and deeply held convictions often appear based on crude assumptions combined with a paucity of evidence. People profess informed political positions on Jerusalem without knowing much about it. On one of the most important cities in the world, people's positions are shaped by ideology and group membership, not analysis. Knee-jerk positions may work for some political situations, but for Jerusalem too much is at stake. For Jerusalem we wanted people to conclude less but know more, to have more information to make better, more informed decisions somewhere down the road.

What is rational in our goals for this book is our desire to increase the quality of information about Jerusalem, not to necessarily foster any particular political opinions about it. The credo of science is to provide facts, not to tell people what to do with these facts. We decided that we could provide information that would ultimately allow people to analyze Jerusalem and not simply reduce it to a series of slogans. We believe that good policy even around something as volatile as Jerusalem is informed by good analysis.

Coming Home to Jerusalem

Urbanists like to measure and rank urban environments. What are the largest urban centers? Which places have the most population? What are the most powerful urban centers? Where is wealth concentrated? The most important cities seem to get grouped into these categories: world cities, great cities, global cities, and mega-cities.

Yet Jerusalem is typically absent from all these rankings. Indeed, at best, in Israel it is Tel Aviv, the economic hub, that is mentioned as having global characteristics (Alfasi and Fenster, 2005, 2009; Fenster and Yacobi, 2005). Jerusalem is neither Rome, nor Mecca, having, as we have seen, a population of less than a million. Yet its persona looms large.

We thought that concluding with a short journey to Jerusalem would help give a feel for the city and provide a sense of its emotional complexity and of the sensations that grip us as we move across its terrain. This is our Jerusalem, where every stop on the journey speaks to questions over social and political ownership but also makes it apparent why owning this nutty place may actually be important.

Our journey is in the form of a tour with short stops – stations in the everyday life of Jerusalem. Imagine that you have just landed in Tel Aviv's Ben Gurion Airport with a mere twenty-four hours to spend in Jerusalem. It is Friday morning and we meet just outside of the arrival gate.

On the way to Jerusalem, visitors begin to realize just how small this place is. The ride from Tel Aviv to Jerusalem takes forty minutes. Getting to Jerusalem involves a choice of two highways. Immediately the geopolitical game is on. Either we take Highway 1, a road located within the boundaries of pre-1967 (post-1948) Israel. Alternatively, we can drive on Highway 433, a road that goes through the West Bank territory taken by Israel in 1967 and deemed the apartheid road because it was closed for many years to Palestinians. We have barely approached Jerusalem but already the choices mark one's politics.

We arrive in Jerusalem. It is Friday noon. On our way to Jerusalem's famous market, Machane Yehuda, we see the shining silver light rail train as it moves though what seems like ancient construction. We also see lots of new construction along the Jaffa road corridor with massive cranes dotting the city's skyline. The market is packed with people and it is busy and loud with vendors, ordinary shoppers, and tourists, many getting what they need for Shabbat dinner and to carry them over the next twenty-four hours when most Jerusalem stores are closed.

Meanwhile, just about one mile away in East Jerusalem, Muslim believers gather to pray and listen to religious leaders talk in mosques. Friday is also Youm-Al-Juma'a (for Islam, this is the equivalent day to Judaism's Saturday and Christianity's Sunday).

We keep driving. We pass the newly built urban quarter of Mamilla. Mamilla used to be the no man's land dividing East and West Jerusalem prior to the 1967 war. Now it consists of luxury housing, hotels, and the large Mamilla shopping mall.

We arrive at the Notre Dame complex, a Christian hotel, conference and pilgrimage center, and suite of restaurants located across the street from the Old City. Parking signs are in English and Arabic with no apparent signs in Hebrew. The complex's security guards are Palestinian, and for the first time since arriving in the city, Israeli sovereignty is in question.

We drive on to the Hebrew University on Mount Scopus. The university is located on land that has been part of Israel since 1947. Does this make our visit to the university politically neutral? We are afraid not. To get to the university requires driving through Arab Jerusalem and on land deemed occupied territory. We pass by several famous East Jerusalem hotels, including the American Colony (historically rich) and the Ambassador Hotel (which is frequented by Palestinian politicos).

From Arab Jerusalem we enter the neighborhood of the French Hill. The French Hill, as noted above, is a largely Jewish Israeli neighborhood located on East Jerusalem annexed land after the 1967 war, built as part of the effort to unify East and West Jerusalem. Although viewed as part of Jerusalem by Israel, it is considered by the international community to be a West Bank settlement. This is the first type of settlement we see today – one of the new neighborhoods built in the 1970s in East Jerusalem.

We arrive at the Hebrew University. To get there, we cross the Green Line; there is no way of getting there without crossing this invisible boundary. The view from the university is panoramic as well as geopolitical. On this clear day to the east we see the Jordan valley, the Dead Sea, and the Jordan Mountains – a reminder of how close Israel is to adjacent countries.

Also visible is the separation barrier/fence/wall, which walls off various parts of the West Bank from entry to Israel. One of the walled-off places is the Shuafat Refugee Camp, an area Israel annexed and made part of Jerusalem in 1967. This camp is officially home to Palestinian refugees from the 1948 war and now houses an estimated twenty thousand people.

To the east we see Ma'ale Adumim, a large city located across the border from Israel on the West Bank side on land occupied after the 1967 war. This is a second type of settlement that we are seeing on this tour – a settlement type on which there is universal consensus that it actually is a settlement.

From the Hebrew University we continue to the Mount of Olives, a five-minute drive along the mountain ridge. On the way, huge Israeli flags wave proudly from roofs of houses that architecturally look like Arab constructions. In addition to the Jewish homes built on East Jerusalem land claimed after 1967, this is a third type of settlement in Jerusalem. These are individual homes located in the heart of existing Palestinian neighborhoods and occupied by right-wing Israeli Jews. Surrounding these homes are the visible markers of settlements – security cameras, barbed wire, and armed guards.

We make it to the Mount of Olives. Tourists skillfully operate their cameras, attempting to capture the perfect shot, the city at sunset. The vista is breathtaking, a view from east to west. The Old City and Temple Mount are at centre stage – a biblical landscape at the epicenter of a violent conflict.

Our final stop is the Kotel, the foundational wall of the Second Temple located in the Old City. The fastest route is through Arab East Jerusalem. We drive along the barrier/fence/wall that separates the Palestinian neighborhoods of Ras Al Amud (under Israeli control) and Abu Dis (under Palestinian control). This tall concrete wall is the quintessential visual manifestation of Israeli power.

The Palestinian Parliament building is on the outside of the wall, disconnected from the rest of Jerusalem. Although it seems that Israel makes the ultimate decision over what is in or out, there

are evident and visual signs of Palestinian resistance indicating that
Israeli power is not absolute. Some Palestinian flags wave proudly
on the roofs of private homes, and the plethora of graffiti conveys
powerful political messages. We see Palestinian residential construction everywhere. The Israeli government calls this illegal and
most construction is under the constant threat of demolition.

In the Palestinian neighborhood of Ras Al Amud, we pass a
fortified complex with imposing gates and armed private guards.
This Jewish residential complex of around a hundred dwelling
units is known as the Olive Heights complex (in Hebrew, Ma'ale
Hazeytim). It is a gated community located near the old Jericho
road, not far from the Jewish ancient cemetery on the Mount of
Olives. This is the fourth type of Israeli settlement we have seen
today. Also built on East Jerusalem land acquired after the 1967
war, this settlement is neither an entire neighborhood nor a single
home. It has the look and feel of an armed camp.

Then, after a brief ride, we are at the Kotel. We go through
metal detectors and put our bags through X-ray machines to get
into the plaza. For believers, visiting the Kotel is a spiritual experience of joy and excitement. For most Jews, religious or not, it is
evidence of an ancient Jewish existence. The Kotel seems to exude
something in everyone because of its historic and religious significance for Jewish history, its perceived centrality to Jerusalem and
to Israel, and the projection of holiness into the wall itself.

But the everyday experience of the Kotel also reeks of conflict,
conflict between Jews and Palestinians and conflict within the
Jewish community itself. We do not even realize how intense
the security is at the Kotel until we make a brief trip over to
the Christian Church of the Holy Sepulchre, where there is no
(visible) security at all. And at the Kotel, the women in our party
who reach its plaza in sleeveless dresses, shorts, or skirts above the
knee are accosted by the clothing police (a euphemism for women
policing female modesty at the Kotel), who provide material with
which these offenders can cover up. Of course, the segregation of
men and women is foreign to our non-Orthodox Jewish visitors.

Jerusalem has a different feel on Friday evenings. It is the Jewish
Shabbat, and Jerusalem is one of Israel's most religious cities. The

city is quiet; outsiders might think everyone in West Jerusalem is either asleep or at home. The rift between religious and secular Jews, and particularly between ultra-Orthodox Jews and the rest of Jewish Jerusalem, is visible only to the extent that we see a stray car or two making their way down streets that are not blocked off for Shabbat. City Hall is ruled by a coalition of parties and the mayor is historically dependent on the religious parties' support. It is Shabbat now (starting Friday evening after sundown) and many Israelis in Jerusalem go to synagogues, particularly the Orthodox and ultra-Orthodox, but also Jews who consider themselves as traditional (and not secular). This is a great opportunity to get a good night's sleep.

On Saturday morning we visit the Temple Mount, the location of the First and Second Temples. Not only is this Judaism's holiest site, however, as we have noted above it is also where the Al-Aqsa Mosque and the Dome of the Rock are to be found. This area is controlled by the Jerusalem Islamic Waqf, the organization charged with managing these important Islamic collective assets. We take a look but do not engage in any type of religious activity because Jews are not allowed to pray at the Temple Mount. There is no explicit Israeli sovereign presence on the Temple Mount despite its importance to the Jewish people and to the State of Israel.

We decide to visit Bethlehem, the city of Jesus' birth, which is located in the West Bank a mere ten minutes from Jerusalem. The Israeli members of the group cannot go because they are not permitted by Israeli law to visit Area A West Bank localities that are fully under Palestinian control. These include Bethlehem, Ramallah, Nablus, Jericho, and others. So we take a Palestinian bus from the station located just outside Damascus Gate in the Old City.

The bus through Jerusalem passes two large newer neighborhoods with many big cranes and lots of construction taking place. These are Gilo and Har Homa, both built on annexed East Jerusalem land over the Green Line. These neighborhoods, which in a different time and place would be small cities in their own right, look different from the ones we drove through yesterday in East Jerusalem. They appear like fortresses.

The bus goes through the checkpoint at the border without stopping. Palestinians can travel to the West Bank without issue. It is returning to Israel where they face obstacles.

We arrive in Bethlehem and grab a cab. The cab driver speaks English. As the cab drives into Bethlehem, he points out a housing development that we can see in the distance. "See that?," he asks. We answer yes. He says, "That is a settlement. Israel keeps building more and more and more. They keep taking our land. They are building more housing on our land. It never stops." One person asks, "Is that Har Homa?" "Yes," he says. "Israel calls Har Homa a Jerusalem neighborhood. But in Bethlehem and almost everywhere else, Har Homa is a settlement."

When the international media report that Israel is building new housing in Jerusalem settlements, it is largely the building of homes in the Jerusalem neighborhoods of Gilo and Har Homa to which they refer. These represent the fifth set of settlements we see on this tour, which, like the new neighborhoods of the French Hill, are intended to expand and to claim more land as part of a united Israeli Jerusalem.

We take the bus back into Israel and pick up the car in Jerusalem to make our way to the airport. En route, we stop at Ein Karem, a former Palestinian village at the western urban fringe of the city. Ein Karem and its surroundings were captured by Israel in the 1948 war, and served as an immediate emergency housing solution for immigrants and Jewish refugees of World War II. Today all of its former Palestinian inhabitants are gone and Ein Karem is an upscale Jewish residential neighborhood with distinguished Arab architecture amidst a village of restaurants and churches. It is one of the few areas of Jerusalem with places open on Shabbat.

We arrive at the airport. Our plane cannot take off before the end of Shabbat, so we have plenty of time. It is only after we make it into the air that we begin to ask difficult questions about where we have actually been and what it all means.

Notes

Chapter 1 Introduction: The Politics of Space

1 Calculating the size of the Jerusalem metropolitan area is dependent, obviously, on its definition. An Israeli Jewish Jerusalem metropolitan area excludes Palestinian cities. A Palestinian Jerusalem metropolitan area would include Palestinian cities and exclude Jewish ones.

Chapter 3 What Is Jerusalem?

1 Al Quds website (*http://www.alquds.edu/en1/5/2014*).

Chapter 4 Who Is Jerusalem?

1 Three inscriptions – Jewish, Christian, and Muslim – are engraved on the façade of the YMCA building: "The Lord our God the Lord is One" in Hebrew; "I am the Way" in Aramaic; and "There is no God but God" in Arabic (*http://ymca.org.il/aboutus.html*).
2 This part of this chapter provides an overview of demographic trends in Jerusalem. It relies on data publicly available as part of a statistical atlas called *Jerusalem: Facts and Trends 2013*, published by the Jerusalem

Institute for Israeli Studies (Chosen et al., 2013). This atlas is compiled from data provided by the Israel Central Bureau of Statistics and the Municipality of Jerusalem.

3 The Jerusalem residency identification card has no reported nationality. There is a place on the card for a nationality to be identified. But nationality on East Jerusalem Palestinian cards is left blank; they are neither Palestinian nor Israeli.

Chapter 5 The Palestinian Challenge and Resistance in
Arab Jerusalem

1 Orient House website (http://www.orienthouse.org/).

References

Abu El-Haj, Nadia, 2001. *Facts on the Ground: Archaeological Practice and Territorial Self-Fashioning in Israeli Society*. Chicago: University of Chicago Press.

Akram, Susan M., 2002. Palestinian refugees and their legal status: rights, politics, and implications for a just solution. *Journal of Palestine Studies*, *31(3)*, 36–51.

Alatout, Samer, 2009. Walls as technologies of government: the double construction of geographies of peace and conflict in Israeli politics, 2002–present. *Annals of the Association of American Geographers*, *99*, 956–68.

Alfasi, Nurit, and Tovi Fenster, 2005. A tale of two cities: Jerusalem and Tel Aviv-Jaffa in an age of globalization. *Cities*, *22*, 351–63.

Alfasi, Nurit, and Tovi Fenster, 2009. Between the "global" and the "local": on global locality and local globality. *Urban Geography*, *30*, 543–66.

Alfasi, Nurit, and Tovi Fenster, 2014. Between socio-spatial and urban justice: Rawls' principles of justice in the 2011 Israeli protest movement. *Planning Theory*, *13*, 407–27.

Alfasi, Nurit, and Erela Ganan, 2015. Jerusalem of (foreign) gold: entrepreneurship and pattern-driven policy in a historic city. *Urban Geography*, doi: 10.1080/02723638.2014.977051.

Alfasi, Nurit, Shlomit Flint-Ashery, and Itzhak Benenson, 2013. Between the individual and the community: residential patterns of the Haredi population in Jerusalem. *International Journal of Urban and Regional Research*, *37*, 2152–76.

Allegra, Marco, 2013. The politics of suburbia: Israel's settlement policy and the production of space in the metropolitan area of Jerusalem. *Environment and Planning A*, *45*, 497–516.

Allegra, Marco, Anna Casaglia, and Jonathan Rokem, 2012. The political geographies of urban polarization: a critical review of research on divided cities. *Geography Compass*, *6*, 560–74.

Amirav, Moshe, 2007. The disintegration of the Jerusalem unification policy: Palestine–Israel. *Journal of Politics, Economics and Culture*, *14*, 9–15.

Amirav, Moshe, 2009. *Jerusalem Syndrome: The Palestinian–Israeli Battle for the Holy City*. Eastbourne, UK: Sussex Academic Press.

Azaryahu, Maoz, 1996. The power of commemorative street names. *Environment and Planning D*, *14*, 311–30.

Azaryahu, Maoz, 1997. German reunification and the politics of street names: the case of East Berlin. *Political Geography*, *16*, 479–93.

Azaryahu, Maoz, and Arnon Golan, 2001. (Re)naming the landscape: the formation of the Hebrew map of Israel 1949–1960. *Journal of Historical Geography*, *27*, 178–95.

Azaryahu, Maoz, and Aharon Kellerman-Barrett, 1999. Symbolic places of national history and revival: a study in Zionist mythical geography. *Transactions of the Institute of British Geographers*, *24*, 109–23.

Barghouti, Omar, 2009. Derailing injustice: Palestinian civil resistance to the "Jerusalem Light Rail." *Jerusalem Quarterly*, *38*, 46–58.

Bartal, Shaul, 2012. The battle over Silwan: fabricating Palestinian history. *Middle East Quarterly*, *19*, 31–41.

Beaumont, Peter, 2014. Gaza war may be over but Jerusalem is still simmering. *Guardian*, September 26.

Beauregard, Robert A., 2006. *When America Became Suburban*. Minneapolis: University of Minnesota Press.

Benmelech, Efraim, and Claude Berrebi, 2007. Human capital and the productivity of suicide bombers. *Journal of Economic Perspectives*, *21*, 223–38.

Benvenisti, Eyal, 2012. *The International Law of Occupation*. Princeton, NJ and Oxford: Princeton University Press.

Benvenisti, Meron, 1998. *City of Stone: The Hidden Story of Jerusalem.* Berkeley: University of California Press.

Biger, Gideon, 2008. The boundaries of Israel–Palestine past, present, and future: a critical geographic view. *Israel Studies, 13,* 68–93.

Bimkom, 2006. *Between Fences: The Enclaves Created by the Separation Barrier.* Jerusalem: Bimkom, Planners for Planning Rights.

Birch, Eugenie L., 2002. Having a longer view on downtown living. *Journal of the American Planning Association, 68,* 5–21.

Bollens, Scott A., 1998. Urban planning amidst ethnic conflict: Jerusalem and Johannesburg. *Urban Studies, 35,* 729–50.

Bollens, Scott A., 2000. *On Narrow Ground: Urban Policy and Ethnic Conflict in Jerusalem and Belfast.* Albany: State University of New York Press.

Bollens, Scott A., 2007. *Cities, Nationalism and Democratization.* New York: Routledge.

Bollens, Scott A., 2012. *Cities and Soul in Divided Society.* New York: Routledge.

Bowker, Robert, 2003. *Palestinian Refugees: Mythology, Identity and the Search for Peace.* Boulder, CO: Lynne Reinner.

Braier, Michal, 2013. Zones of transformation? Informal construction and independent zoning plans in East Jerusalem. *Environment and Planning A, 45,* 2700–16.

Brenner, Neil, and Nik Theodore, 2002. Cities and the geographies of "actually existing neolibralism." *Antipode, 34,* 349–79.

Brin, Eldad, 2006. Politically-oriented tourism in Jerusalem. *Tourist Studies, 6,* 215–43.

Brooks, Robert D., 2007. The wall and the economy of the Jerusalem governorate. In Robert D. Brooks (Ed.), *The Wall Fragmenting the Palestinian Fabric in Jerusalem,* pp. 27–54. Jerusalem: International Peace and Cooperation Center.

Brooks, Robert D., Rassem Khamaisi, Rami Nasrallah, Amer Hidmi, and Shahd Wa'ary, 2009. *Jerusalem Wall: A Decade of Division and Urban Incarceration – A Survey on the Impact of the Separation Wall on Jerusalem.* Jerusalem: International Peace and Cooperation Center.

Calame, Jon, and Esther R. Charlesworth, 2009. *Divided Cities: Belfast, Beirut, Jerusalem, Mostar, and Nicosia.* Philadelphia: University of Pennsylvania Press.

Charney, Igal, and Gillad Rosen, 2014. Splintering skylines in a fractured city: high-rise geographies in Jerusalem. *Environment and Planning D, 32,* 1088–101.

Chesin, Amir, S., Bill Hutman, and Avi Melame, 1999. *Separate and Unequal: The Inside Story of Israeli Rule in East Jerusalem.* Cambridge, MA: Harvard University Press.

Chiodelli, Francesco, 2012. Planning illegality: the roots of unauthorised housing in Arab East Jerusalem. *Cities, 29,* 99–106.

Chiodelli, Francesco, 2013. Re-shaping Jerusalem: the transformation of Jerusalem's metropolitan area by the Israeli barrier. *Cities, 31,* 417–24.

Choshen, Maya, Michal Korach, Inbal Doron, Yael Israeli, and Yair Assaf-Shapira, 2013. *Jerusalem: Facts and Trends 2013.* Jerusalem: Jerusalem Institute for Israel Studies.

Clarno, Andy, 2008. A tale of two walled cities: neo-liberalization and enclosure in Johannesburg and Jerusalem. *Political Power and Social Theory, 19,* 159–205.

Cohen, Hillel, 2007. *The Rise and Fall of Arab Jerusalem 1967–2007.* Jerusalem: Jerusalem Institute for Israel Studies.

Cohen, Yinon, 2002. From haven to heaven: changing patterns of immigration to Israel. In Daniel Levy and Yfaat Weisspp (Eds), *Challenging Ethnic Citizenship: German and Israeli Perspectives on Immigration,* pp. 36–58. New York: Berghahn Books.

Cohen-Blankshtain, Galit, Amit Ron, and Alama Gadot-Perez, 2013. When an NGO takes on public participation: preparing a plan for a neighborhood in East Jerusalem. *International Journal of Urban and Regional Research, 37,* 61–77.

Cohen-Blankshtain, Galit, and Eran Feitelson, 2011. Light rail routing: do goals matter? *Transportation, 38,* 343–61.

Cohen-Hattab, Kobi, and Noam Shoval, 2014. *Tourism, Religion and Pilgrimage in Jerusalem.* London and New York: Routledge.

Denton, Nancy, 2013. Interpreting US segregation trends: two perspectives. *City and Community, 12,* 156–9.

Dumper, Michael, 1997. *The Politics of Jerusalem since 1967.* New York: Columbia University Press.

Dumper, Michael, 2002. *The Politics of Sacred Space: The Old City of Jerusalem in the Middle East Conflict.* Boulder, CO: Lynne Rienner.

Dumper, Michael, 2014. *Jerusalem Unbound: Geography, History, and the Future of the Holy City*. New York: Columbia University Press.

Falah, Ghazi, 1990. Arabs versus Jews in Galilee: competition for regional resources. *Geojournal, 21*, 325–36.

Falah, Ghazi, 1996. The 1948 Israeli–Palestinian war and its aftermath: the transformation and de-signification of Palestine's cultural landscape. *Annals of the Association of American Geographers, 86*, 256–85.

Fenster, Tovi, and Haim Yacobi, 2005. Whose city is it? On urban planning and local knowledge in globalizing Tel Aviv–Jaffa. *Planning Theory and Practice, 6*, 191–211.

Fishman, Robert, 1987. *Bourgeois Utopias: The Rise and Fall of Suburbia*. New York: Basic Books.

Flint, Shlomit, Itzhak Benenson, Nurit Alfasi, and Yefim Bakman, 2013. Between friends and strangers: Schelling-like residential dynamics in a Haredi neighborhood in Jerusalem. In Lidia Diappi (Ed.), *Emergent Phenomena in Housing Markets*, pp. 103–26. Heidelberg: Physica-Verlag.

Fregonese, Sara, 2012. Beyond the "weak state": hybrid sovereignties in Beirut. *Environment and Planning D, 30*, 655–74.

Friedland, Roger, and Richard Hecht, 2000. *To Rule Jerusalem*. Berkeley: University of California Press.

Gelbman, Alon, and Ofra Keinan, 2007. National and transnational borderlanders' attitudes towards the security fence between Israel and the Palestinian Authority. *GeoJournal, 68*, 279–91.

Gieryn, Thomas F., 2000. A place for space in sociology. *Annual Review of Sociology, 26*, 463–96.

Goetz, Edward G., 2013. *New Deal Ruins: Race, Economic Justice, and Public Housing Policy*. Ithaca, NY and London: Cornell University Press.

Gonen, Amiram, 1995. *Between City and Suburb: Urban Residential Patterns and Processes in Israel*. Avebury, UK: Aldershot.

Gottdiener, Mark M., 1987. Space as a force of production: contribution to the debate on realism, capitalism and space. *International Journal of Urban and Regional Research, 11*, 405–17.

Gramsci, Antonio, 1971. *Selections from the Prison Notebooks of Antonio Gramsci*. Quintin Hoare and Geoffrey Nowell Smith, Trans. and Eds. London: Lawrence & Wishart.

Gramsci, Antonio, 2001. The formation of intellectuals. In Vincent

Leitch (Ed.), *Norton Anthology of Theory and Criticism*, pp. 1135–43. New York: Norton.

Grant, Jill L., and Gillad Rosen, 2009. Armed compounds and broken arms: the cultural production of gated communities. *Annals of the Association of American Geographers*, *99*, 575–89.

Greenberg, Raphael, 2009. Towards an inclusive archaeology in Jerusalem: the case of Silwan/the City of David. *Public Archaeology*, *8*, 35–50.

Greenberg Raanan, Malka, and Noam Shoval, 2013. Mental maps compared to actual spatial behavior using GPS data: a new method for investigating segregation in cities. *Cities*, *36*, 28–40.

Hackworth, Jason, 2007. *The Neoliberal City*. Ithaca, NY: Cornell University Press.

Hadi, Mahdi Abdul, 1996. The ownership of Jerusalem: a Palestinian view. In Karmi Ghada (Ed.), *Jerusalem Today: What Future for the Peace Process?*, pp. 83–96. Reading, UK: Ithaca Press.

Handel, Ariel, 2013. Gated/gating community: the settlement complex in the West Bank. *Transactions of the Institute of British Geographers*, *39*, 504–17.

Harvey, David, 2000. *Spaces of Hope*. Edinburgh: Edinburgh University Press.

Harvey, David, 2003. The right to the city. *International Journal of Urban and Regional Research*, *27*, 939–41.

Hasson, Nir, 2013. Israel rejected plan that would avoid splitting Beit Safafa, documents reveal. *Haaretz*, August 28.

Hasson, Shlomo, 1996. Local politics and split citizenship in Jerusalem. *International Journal of Urban and Regional Research*, *20*, 116–33.

Hasson, Shlomo, 2001. Territories and identities in Jerusalem. *GeoJournal*, *53*, 311–22.

Hasson, Shlomo, 2002. The syntax of Jerusalem: urban morphology, culture and power. In John Eade and Christopher Mele (Eds), *Understanding the City: Contemporary and Future Perspectives*, pp. 278–304. New York: Blackwell.

Hazam, Shlomie, and Daniel Felsenstein, 2007. Terror, fear and behaviour in the Jerusalem housing market. *Urban Studies*, *44*, 2529–46.

Herzog, Hanna, 2005. On home turf: interview location and its social meaning. *Qualitative Sociology*, *28*, 25–47.

Horowitz, Dan, and Moshe Lissak, 1989. *Trouble in Utopia: The Overburdened Polity of Israel.* Albany: State University of New York Press.

Hubbard, Phil, 2008. Regulating the social impacts of studentification: a Loughborough case study. *Environment and Planning A, 40,* 323–41.

International Peace and Cooperation Center, 2007. *Jerusalem on the Map.* Jerusalem: International Peace and Cooperation Center.

Israel Defense Forces, 2003. *Fence Against Terror.* Available at: https://www.youtube.com/watch?v=qOh9N33DxWk.

Jabareen, Yosef-Rafeq, 2010. The politics of state planning in achieving geopolitical ends: the case of the recent master plan for Jerusalem. *International Development Planning Review, 32,* 27–43.

Jackson, Kenneth, T., 1985. *Crabgrass Frontier: The Suburbanization of the United States.* New York and Oxford: Oxford University Press.

Jefferis, Danielle C., 2012. Institutionalizing statelessness: the revocation of residency rights of Palestinians in East Jerusalem. *International Journal of Refugee Law, 24,* 202–30.

JTA, 2013. No Christmas trees in Israeli parliament, speaker decides. *Haaretz,* December 22. Available at: http://www.haaretz.com/news/national/1.564860.

Kallus, Rachel, 2004. The political role of the everyday. *City, 8,* 341–61.

Kaminker, Sarah, 1997. For Arabs only: building restrictions in East Jerusalem. *Journal of Palestine Studies, 26,* 5–16.

Kark, Ruth, 1991. *Jerusalem Neighborhoods: Planning and By-Laws (1855–1930).* Jerusalem: Magnes Press.

Khalidi, Rashid, 2007. *The Iron Cage: The Story of the Palestinian Struggle for Statehood.* Boston, MA: Beacon Press.

Khalidi, Rashid, 2010. *Palestinian Identity: The Construction of Modern National Consciousness.* New York: Columbia University Press.

Klein, Menachem, 2003. *The Jerusalem Problem: The Struggle for Permanent Status.* Gainesville: University Press of Florida.

Klein, Menachem, 2004. Jerusalem without East Jerusalemites: the Palestinian as the "other" in Jerusalem. *The Journal of Israeli History, 23,* 174–99.

Klein, Menachem, 2005. Old and new walls in Jerusalem. *Political Geography, 24,* 53–76.

Klein, Menachem, 2008. Jerusalem as an Israeli problem – a review of forty years of Israeli rule over Arab Jerusalem. *Israeli Studies, 13(2),* 54–72.

Klein, Menachem, 2010. *The Shift: Israel–Palestine from Border Struggle to Ethnic Conflict.* New York: Columbia University Press.

Kliot, Nurit, and Igal Charney, 2006. The geography of suicide terrorism in Israel. *GeoJournal, 66,* 353–73.

Kliot, Nurit, and Yoel Mansfeld, 1999. Case studies of conflict and territorial organization in divided cities. *Progress in Planning, 52,* 167–225.

Kotek, Joël, 1999. Divided cities in the European cultural context. *Progress in Planning, 52,* 227–37.

Kroyanker, David, 1998. *Jerusalem – Conflicts over the City's Physical and Visual Form.* Jerusalem: Jerusalem Institute for Israel Studies (in Hebrew).

Krystall, Nathan, 1998. The de-Arabization of West Jerusalem 1947–1950. *Journal of Palestine Studies, 27,* 5–22.

Lefebvre, Henri, 1991. *The Production of Space.* Translated by Donald Nicholson-Smith. New York: Wiley-Blackwell.

Lefebvre, Henri, 1996. *Writings on Cities.* Translated and edited by Eleonore Kofman and Elizabeth Lebas. New York: Wiley-Blackwell.

Levy Report, 2012. *Report on the Status of Building in Judea and Samaria Area.* Jerusalem: The State of Israel. Available at: *http://www.pmo.gov. il/Documents/doch090712.pdf (in Hebrew).*

Loirer, Yonatan, 2007. *Data Concerning "Ghost Apartments" in Jerusalem.* Jerusalem: Kiryata.

Lieberson, Stanley, 1981. *A Piece of the Pie: Black and White Immigrants since 1880.* Berkeley: University of California Press.

Logan, John R., and Harvey L. Molotch, 1987. *Urban Fortunes: The Political Economy of Place.* Berkeley and Los Angeles: University of California Press.

Logan, John R., and Harvey Molotch, L., 2007. *Urban Fortunes: The Political Economy of Place.* Second revised edition. Berkeley and Los Angeles: University of California Press.

Lustick, Ian S., 2004. Yerushalayim, al-Quds and the Wizard of Oz: facing the problem of Jerusalem after Camp David II and the al-Aqsa Intifada. *The Journal of Israeli History, 23,* 200–15.

McKenzie, Steven L., 2002. *King David: A Biography*. Oxford: Oxford University Press.

Mann, Barbara E., 2011. *Space and Place in Jewish Studies*. New Brunswick, NJ: Rutgers University Press.

Marcuse, Peter, 1993. What's so new about divided cities? *International Journal of Urban and Regional Research*, *17*, 355–65.

Margalit, Meira, 2001. A chronicle of municipal discrimination in Jerusalem. *Palestinian–Israel Journal*, *7(1)*, 32–40.

Marom, Nathan, 2013. Activising space: the spatial politics of the 2011 protest movement in Israel, *Urban Studies*, *50(13)*, 2826–41.

Masry-Herzalla, Asmahan, and Eran Razin, 2014. Israeli–Palestinian migrants in Jerusalem: an emerging middleman minority. *Journal of Ethnic and Migration Studies*, *40*, 1002–22.

Mayer, Arno J., 2008. *Plowshares into Swords: From Zionism to Israel*. London and New York: Verso.

Merrifield, Andy, 2002. *Metromarxism: A Marxist Tale of the City*. New York and London: Routledge.

Mizrachi, Yonathan, 2012. *Archeology in the Shadow of Conflict*. Jerusalem: Emek Shaveha.

Molotch, Harvey L. 1976. The city as a growth machine: toward a political economy of place. *American Journal of Sociology*, *82*, 309–32.

Montefiore, Simon, 2012. *Jerusalem: The Biography*. New York: Vintage Books.

Morris, Benny, 2008. *1948. A History of the First Arab–Israeli War*. New Haven, CT: Yale University Press.

Nasrallah, Rami, 2003. Divided cities: trends of separation and integration. In Abraham Friedman and Rami Nasrallah (Eds), *Divided Cities in Transition*, pp. 25–50. Jerusalem: Jerusalem Institute for Israel Studies.

Nasrallah, Rami, 2005. Transformations in Jerusalem: where are we heading? In Michèle Auga, Stephan Stetter, Shlomo Hasson, and Rami Nasrallah (Eds), *Divided Cities in Transition: Challenges Facing Jerusalem and Berlin*, pp. 205–25. Jerusalem: Friedrich Ebert Stiftung, International Peace and Cooperation Center, and Jerusalem Institute for Israel Studies.

Nasrallah, Rami, 2007. The Jerusalem separation wall: facts and political implications. In Robert D. Brooks (Ed.), *The Wall Fragmenting the*

Palestinian Fabric in Jerusalem, pp. 13–26. Jerusalem: International Peace and Cooperation Center.

Nusseibeh, Sari, 2008. Negotiating a city: a perspective of a Jerusalemite. In Tamar Mayer and Suleiman Ali Mourad (Eds), *Jerusalem: Idea and Reality*, pp. 198–204. New York: Routledge.

Owais, Abdalla, 2008. Transformations between East Jerusalem and its neighborhoods. In Omar Yousef, Rassem Khamaisi, Abdalla Owais, and Rami Nasrallah (Eds), *Jerusalem and Its Hinterland*, pp. 53–65. Jerusalem: International Peace and Cooperation Center.

Parmenter, Barbara, 1999. City on the Hill. *Planning Forum, 4(5)*, 4–11.

Peled, Yoav, 1992. Ethnic democracy and the legal construction of citizenship: Arab citizens of the Jewish state. *American Political Science Review, 86*, 432–43.

Pullan, Wendy, and Maximillian Gwiazda, 2009. "City of David": urban design and frontier heritage. *Jerusalem Quarterly, 39*, 29–38.

Pullan, Wendy, Philipp Misselwitz, Rami Nasrallah, and Haim Yacobi, 2007. Jerusalem's road 1: an inner city frontier? *City, 11*, 176–98.

Pullan, Wendy, Maximillian Sternberg, Lefkos Kyriacou, Craig Larkin, and Michael Dumper, 2013. *The Struggle for Jerusalem's Holy Places.* New York: Routledge.

Purcell, Mark, 2002. Excavating Lefebvre: the right to the city and its urban politics of the inhabitant. *GeoJournal, 58*, 99–108.

Purcell, Mark, 2003. Citizenship and the right to the global city: reimagining the capitalist world order. *International Journal of Urban and Regional Research, 27*, 564–90.

Reich, Ronny, Eli Shukron, and Omri Lernau, 2007. Recent discoveries in the City of David, Jerusalem. *Israel Exploration Journal, 57*, 153–69.

Reiter, Yitzhak, 2008. *Jerusalem and Its Role in Islamic Solidarity.* New York: Palgrave Macmillan.

Reiter, Yitzhak, 2013. Narratives of Jerusalem and its sacred compound. *Israel Studies, 18*, 115–32.

Rempel, Terry, 1999. Dispossession and restitution in 1948 Jerusalem. In Salim Tamari (Ed.), *Jerusalem 1948: The Arab Neighborhoods and their Fate in the War*, pp. 189–237. Jerusalem: Institute of Jerusalem Studies and Badil Resource Center.

Reuveny, Rafael, 2003. Fundamentalist colonialism: the geopolitics of Israeli–Palestinian conflict. *Political Geography, 22*, 347–80.

Robertson, Kent, 1995. Downtown redevelopment strategies in the United States: an end-of-the-century assessment. *Journal of the American Planning Association*, *61*, 429–36.

Robertson, Kent, 1999. Can small-city downtowns remain viable? A national study of development issues and strategies. *Journal of the American Planning Association*, *65*, 270–83.

Ron, Amit, and Galit Cohen-Blankshtain, 2011. The representative claim of deliberative planning: the case of Isawiyah in East Jerusalem. *Environment and Planning D*, *29*, 633–48.

Rose-Redwood, Reuben, Derek Alderman, and Maoz Azaryahu, 2010. Geographies of toponymic inscription: new directions in critical place-name studies. *Progress in Human Geography*, *34*, 453–70.

Rosen, Gillad, and Eran Razin, 2008. Enclosed residential neighborhoods in Israel: from landscapes of heritage and frontier enclaves to new gated communities. *Environment and Planning A*, *40*, 2895–913.

Rosen, Gillad, and Anne B. Shlay, 2014. Whose right to Jerusalem? *International Journal of Urban and Regional Research*, *38*, 935–50.

Sa'di, Ahmad, and Lila Abu-Lughod, 2007. *Nakba: Palestine, 1948 and Claims of Memory*. New York: Columbia University Press.

Said, Edward W., 1995. Projecting Jerusalem. *Journal of Palestinian Studies*, *XXV*, 5–14.

Sassen, Saskia, 1994. *Cities in a World Economy*. Thousand Oaks, CA: Pine Forge Press.

Sassen, Saskia, 2001. *The Global City: New York, London, Tokyo*. Princeton, NJ: Princeton University Press.

Sasson Report, 2005. *Summary of the Opinion Concerning Unauthorized Outposts*. Jerusalem: Israeli Ministry of Foreign Affairs. Available at: *http://www.mfa.gov.il/mfa/aboutisrael/state/law/pages/summary%20of%20opinion%20concerning%20unauthorized%20outposts%20-%20talya%20sason%20adv.aspx*.

Savitch, Hank V., 2005. An anatomy of urban terror: lessons from Jerusalem and elsewhere. *Urban Studies*, *42*, 361–95.

Shapiro, Shahar, 1973. Planning Jerusalem: the first generation, 1917–1968. In David Amiran, Arie Shachar, and Israel Kimhi (Eds), *Urban Geography of Jerusalem*, pp. 139–53. Berlin: De Gruyter.

Shavit, Ari, 2013. *My Promised Land: The Triumph and Tragedy of Israel*. New York: Spiegel and Grau.

Sherwood, Harriet, 2013. The new Jerusalem. *Guardian*, July 27. Available at: *http://www.theguardian.com/world/2013/jul/27/the-new-jerusalem*.

Shiblak, Abbas, 1996. Residency status and civil rights of Palestinian refugees in Arab countries. *Journal of Palestine Studies*, *25*, 36–45.

Shlay, Anne B., and Robert P. Giloth, 1987. The social organization of a land-based elite: the case of the failed Chicago 1990 World's Fair. *Journal of Urban Affairs*, *9*, 305–24.

Shlay, Anne B., and Gillad Rosen, 2010. Making place: the shifting Green Line and the development of "greater" metropolitan Jerusalem. *City and Community*, *9*, 358–89.

Shmueli, Deborah F., and Khamaisi Rassem, 2011. Bedouin communities in the Negev. *Journal of the American Planning Association*, 77, 109–25.

Shoval, Noam, 2007. Transformation of the urban morphology of Jerusalem: present trends and future scenarios. In Shlomo Hasson (Ed.), *Jerusalem in the Future: The Challenge of Transition*, pp. 90–120. Jerusalem: Floersheimer Institute for Policy Studies.

Shoval, Noam, 2013. Street naming, tourism development and cultural conflict: the case of the Old City of Acre/Akko/Akka. *Transactions of the Institute of British Geographers*, *38*, 612–26.

Shtern, Marik, 2010. *In Foreign Fields: Interaction Patterns between Israelis and Palestinians in Mixed Commercial Zones in Jerusalem*. Jerusalem: Floersheimer Institute for Policy Studies.

Silver, Hillary, 2010. Divided cities in the Middle East. *City and Community*, *9*, 345–57.

Singer, Rachel, and Rachel Bickel, 2014. Which way to go? Women's walking decisions and ultra-Orthodox enclaves in Jerusalem, *Gender, Place & Culture*, doi: 10.1080/0966369X.2014.939153.

Slae, Bracha, 2013. Demography in Jerusalem's Old City. *Jerusalem Post*, January 13.

Smith, Darren, 2008. The politics of studentification and "(un)balanced" urban populations: lessons for gentrification and sustainable communities? *Urban Studies*, *45*, 2541–64.

Smith, Neil, 2002. New globalism, new urbanism: gentrification as global urban strategy. In Neil Brenner and Nik Theodore (Eds), *Spaces of Neoliberalism: Urban Restructuring in North America and Western Europe*, pp. 88–103. New York: Blackwell.

Smooha, Sammy, 1997. Ethnic democracy: Israel as an archetype. *Israel Studies*, 2, 198–241.

Stein, Yael, 1998. *The Quiet Deportation Continues: Revocation of Residency and Denial of Social Information of East Jerusalem Palestinians*. Jerusalem: HAMOKED Center for the Defense of the Individual and B'Tselem.

Strom, Elizabeth, 2008. Rethinking the politics of downtown development. *Journal of Urban Affairs*, 30, 37–61.

Tamari, Salim, 1999. *Jerusalem 1948: The Arab Neighborhoods and their Fate in the War*. Jerusalem: Institute of Jerusalem Studies.

Thawaba, Salem, and Hussein Al-Rimmawi, 2012. Spatial transformation of Jerusalem: 1967 to present. *Journal of Planning History*, 12, 63–77.

Tobin, Jonathan S., 2014. Where apologies are needed. *Commentary*, July 7. Available at: *http://www.commentarymagazine.com/2014/07/07/where-apologies-are-needed-terror-palestinians-israel/*.

Tzfadia, Erez, 2005. The ethno-class trajectory of new neighborhoods in Israel. *GeoJournal*, 64, 141–51.

Vesselinov, Ellena, Matthew Cazessus, and William Falk, 2007. Gated communities and spatial inequality. *Journal of Urban Affairs*, 29, 109–27.

Wallach, Yair, 2011. Trapped in mirror-images: the rhetoric of maps in Israel/Palestine. *Political Geography*, 30(7), 358–69.

Wari, Shahd, 2011. Jerusalem: one planning system, two urban realities. *City*, 15, 457–72.

Weber, Max, 2009. *From Max Weber: Essays in Sociology*. Edited by H.H. Gerth and C. Wright Mills. New York: Routledge.

Weizman, Eyal, 2007. *Hollow Land: Israel's Architecture of Occupation*. London: Verso.

Yacobi, Haim, 2007. The NGOization of space: dilemmas of social change, planning policy, and the Israeli public sphere. *Environment and Planning D*, 25, 745–58.

Yacobi, Haim, 2012. God, globalization and geopolitics: on West Jerusalem's gated communities. *Environment and Planning A*, 44, 2705–20.

Yiftachel, Oren, 1991. State policies, land control, and an ethnic minority: the Arabs in the Galilee region, Israel. *Environment and Planning D*, 9, 329–62.

Yiftachel, Oren, 1998. Planning and social control: exploring the dark side. *Journal of Planning Literature*, 12, 395–406.

Yiftachel Oren, 2006. *Ethnocracy: Land and Identity in Israel/Palestine.* Philadelphia: University of Pennsylvania Press.

Yiftachel, Oren, and Haim Yacobi, 2002. Planning a bi-national capital: should Jerusalem remain united? *Geoforum, 33,* 137–45.

Yiftachel, Oren, and Haim Yacobi, 2003. Urban ethnocracy: ethnicization and the production of space in an Israeli "mixed city." *Environment and Planning D, 21,* 673–93.

Young, Iris, 2004. Five faces of oppression. In Lisa Heldke and Peg O'Connor (Eds), *Oppression, Privilege, and Resistance,* pp. 37–63. Boston, MA: McGraw-Hill.

Zertal, Idith, and Akiva Eldar, 2007. *Lords of the Land: The War over Israel's Settlements in the Occupied Territories, 1967–2007.* New York: Nation Books.

Index

Al-Aqsa, 18, 54, 69, 94, 157, 193
Al-Aqsa Intifada, *see* Second Intifada
Al Quds, 41–2, 47, 88, 93-4
Al Quds University, 41–2, 75, 131, 133, 140
Arab villages, 51, 162
Arafat, Yasser, 155
archaeology, 5–6, 53, 55, 84, 96
Armenian Quarter, 3, 19, 81
Ashkenazim, 27, 98, 103, 108–9, 120
assimilation, 1, 15, 88, 126, 135, 156

Bethlehem, 25, 72, 76, 93, 98, 132, 138, 163, 193–4

center of life, 73, 81, 130
Chicago School of sociology, 92, 116, 159
Christian holidays, 104
Christian Quarter, 3, 19, 81
Christianity, 3, 6, 10, 19, 31, 33, 50, 80–1, 9–5, 98–9, 103–6, 125, 164, 185, 190
Church of the Holy Sepulchre, 19, 94, 192

city as growth machine, 16, 23, 31, 34-5
    Israeli growth machine, 44, 176
    Jerusalem growth machine, 24, 35–6, 43–4, 87, 167, 184
City of David, 4–6, 54, 79, 83–5, 118
concentrated poverty, *see* poverty
conflict
    Arab–Israeli, 43, 47, 68, 139
    Palestinian–Israeli/Jewish, 2–5, 9, 13–16, 43, 79, 81, 84, 87, 110, 136–7, 139, 192
contested space, 5, 43, 114, 185

diaspora,
    Jewish, 33, 50, 59, 92, 114, 123–4, 133, 144
    Palestinian, 33, 125, 133–4
divided city, 7, 16, 25, 31, 37–8, 41, 44, 52, 111, 168, 185
Dome of the Rock, 10, 18, 94, 157, 193
downtown, 11, 166–7, 175, 179, 181–3

E1, 71–2
El'ad, 5, 7, 25, 79–80, 84–5
elections
  local, 127–8, 146, 148–51
  national, Israeli, 127, 146, 150
  national, Palestinian, 154, 157
Ethiopian immigrants, 12, 98–9, 103, 108–9
Etz Chaim, 182
everyday life, 11–12, 22, 31–2, 42–5, 98, 106, 111, 130, 137–8, 141–2, 189

facts on the ground, 6, 26, 57, 61, 96
First Intifada, see Intifadas

geopolitics, 2, 33, 35, 51, 66, 75, 86, 118, 124, 131, 136, 154, 183, 189, 190
Gilo, 71, 193–4
Gramsci, Antonio, 29–31
Greater Palestine, see Palestine
Green Line, 21–3, 45, 48, 51–5, 60, 62, 66, 77, 97, 110, 117, 173, 190, 193
growth coalition, 34–5
growth machine, see city as growth machine
Gush Etzion, 67, 170
G'vat Ze'ev, 67

Haifa, 101–2
Har Homa, 71–2, 193–4
Haram al-Sharif, 54, 94, 157–8
Haredi, see ultra-Orthodox
Hebrew University, 20–2, 27, 41, 89, 160, 168, 190–1
Holocaust, 47, 119, 135, 168
Holy Basin, 45, 79, 84
Husseini, Faisal, 152–3

immigration, 1, 12, 27–8, 32, 59, 61, 100–1, 107–9, 125–6, 134–5, 168, 173, 194
Independence Day, 58
Intifadas, 15, 68, 82, 138, 151–4
  First Intifada 68, 151–4

Second Intifada 69, 74, 110, 158, 171, 180
Ir David, see City of David
Islam, 6, 8, 54, 80, 92–5, 103, 125, 157, 185, 190
Islamic Waqf, 157–8, 193
Israeli Arabs, 125–7, 138

Jerusalem
  Arab, 42, 51–2, 59–60, 72, 103, 111, 129, 138–49, 151–4, 156–7, 160, 162–3, 190
  East, 14, 16–17, 25–7, 33, 41–2, 45, 48, 51–3, 57–61, 73, 75, 77–9, 81, 83, 85–6, 88, 90, 97, 101, 103, 111–12, 117–18, 125, 127–31, 137–50, 152–7, 159–63, 166, 168–9, 176, 183, 190–3, 196
  Israeli, 17, 20, 22, 83, 103, 111, 141, 145, 167, 169, 194
  Jewish, 42, 51, 68, 140, 142, 146, 193
  metropolitan area, 25–6, 35, 61–2, 97, 101, 117, 169–70
  municipality, 20, 44, 77, 79
  Palestinian, 78, 112, 132
  West, 27, 48, 51–2, 57, 59–60, 81, 85, 90, 97, 111, 115, 141, 143–4, 146, 161, 166–8, 176, 178, 180, 190, 193
  Yerushalayim, 47, 88, 93
Jerusalem Light Rail, 46, 85–6, 89, 144, 189
Jerusalem of memory, 52–4, 79, 86–7
  Arab/Palestinian, 52–4, 88, 138, 140
  Jewish/Israeli, 53–4, 83–4
Jerusalem Unification Day, 30
Jerusalemites, 6, 44, 100, 104, 169, 181
  Arab/Palestinian, 73–4, 112, 127–8, 135, 141, 146–7, 149–50, 154, 156, 159, 161, 163
  Israeli/Jewish, 22, 44, 146
  secular, 2, 116
Jewish Quarter, 3, 19, 50, 81–2

Jordan, 20–1, 27, 47–8, 50–2, 54, 57, 63, 82, 111, 134, 139, 143, 160, 168, 178
 Hashemite Kingdom, 47
Judaization of space, 5, 17, 54
Judea and Samaria, 36, 43, 64, 66, 110, 118

Knesset, 52, 74, 127, 168
Kotel, 18, 50–1, 60, 82–3, 122, 158, 184, 191–2
 Wailing Wall, 59
 Western Wall, 8, 50, 82, 94, 122, 158

Lefebvre, Henri, 31–3, 43
Levy Report, 64
Logan, John, 31

Ma'ale Adumim, 66–7, 72, 169, 191
Machane Yehuda, 27, 168, 177, 180–2, 189
Mamilla, 3, 57, 168, 177–80, 184, 190
Marcuse, Peter, 37
Mizrahim, 27, 90, 98, 103, 108–9, 120
Molotch, Harvey, 31, 33–4
Mount Scopus, 21, 57, 89, 160, 190
Muhammad, *see* Prophet Muhammad
Muslim Quarter, 2, 18–19, 81–2

Nakba, 15, 48, 58, 140, 162
National Religious, 36, 43, 105, 118–20, 122–3
neoliberalism, 17, 109, 184,
Nusseibeh, Sari, 133, 140

occupation, 14, 54, 65, 67–8, 115, 133, 146, 151
Old City, 2–5, 8, 18–20, 47–8, 50–2, 54, 60, 75, 77, 79–82, 84, 94, 111, 115, 118–19, 122, 157, 164, 168, 178, 180, 185, 190–1, 193
Olmert, Ehud, 155, 174
Orient House, 52, 128, 152–3
 Oslo Agreements, 14, 17, 42, 68–9, 71–2, 78, 128–30, 133, 139, 145, 151, 153–6

Palestine, 47–8, 58, 69, 72, 78–9, 82, 96, 123, 125–6
Palestine Liberation Organization (PLO), 133, 152–3, 155
Palestinian Authority, 41–3, 68, 69, 75, 128, 133, 150, 153, 155–6
Palestinian Parliament, 41–2, 75, 131, 191
planning, 26, 34, 59, 71, 85, 91, 116, 144, 160, 167–8, 173, 183
political parties, 103, 110, 120, 133
 poverty 1, 2, 9, 39, 99–100, 113, 130, 136, 170, 172
 production of space, 16, 20, 31Prophet Muhammad, 6, 10, 94, 185

Ramallah, 25, 45, 72, 98, 128–9, 132, 134, 138, 155, 163, 193
refugees,
 camp, 48, 51, 54, 126, 134, 168, 191
 Jewish, 133, 194
 Palestinian, 33, 48, 51, 53–4, 58, 67, 126, 128, 133–4, 155, 191
right to the city, 20, 26, 32, 137, 149, 162
Russian immigrants, 12, 98, 108–9, 126 135

Safdie Plan, 25, 173–6
Sasson Report, 63–4
Second Intifada, *see* Intifadas
secular Israelis, 86, 104
secular Jerusalemites, 2, 100, 116
secular Jews, 11, 27, 30, 33, 67, 82, 92, 105–6, 109, 113, 115–17, 142, 165, 193
secular neighborhoods, 11, 27, 116, 121
secular settlers, 66
secular tourists, 11
secular Zionism, 36, 122
security barrier/fence/wall, 17, 25, 41–3, 45, 74–9, 81, 96, 98–9, 103, 112, 114, 125, 127, 130–1, 139, 159, 172, 176, 184, 191
 apartheid wall, 46, 74

security barrier/fence/wal (*cont.*)
  security (separation) barrier, 16, 44, 46, 74, 77, 159, 172
  security (separation) fence, 46, 74
  security (separation) wall, 16, 44, 74–5, 159, 178, 191
separation barrier/fence/wall, *see* security barrier/fence/wall
settlements, 8, 12, 15, 17, 20, 25–6, 35–6, 43–5, 58–60, 62–7, 69, 71–2, 75–6, 79, 82, 87–8, 98, 101, 110–11, 116–18, 122, 129–31, 136, 143–4, 146, 151, 160, 165, 169–70, 183–4, 190–2, 194
settlers, 25, 36, 66, 68, 82, 84, 110, 118–19, 122
Sharon, Ariel, 74, 77
  government, 75
Silwan, 4–6, 79, 84–5, 119
spatial politics, 13, 15–17, 20, 23, 38, 61

Tel Aviv, 101–2, 132, 167, 170, 176, 189
Temple Mount, 18, 54, 60, 94, 157–8, 191, 193
terrorism, 13, 17, 69, 74, 76, 86, 155, 171–2
tourism, 5, 10, 17, 171
transportation, 26, 144, 171, 176, 184
  public, 85, 90

ultra-Orthodox, 2, 11–12, 27, 33, 36, 66–7, 90, 99–101, 103, 105–7, 109–10, 113, 116, 119–23, 136, 148, 193
unification, 52, 57, 59, 85, 146
  of Jerusalem, 50, 55, 57–9, 65, 85, 111, 115, 141–2, 144–5, 151, 178
  politics of, 17
Unification Day, 30
United Nations, 15, 48, 50–1, 58, 65, 82
wars
  1948 War, 15–16, 48, 50–1, 57, 60, 63, 82, 107, 112, 115, 125, 140, 160–2, 168, 191, 194
  see also Nakba
  1967 War (Six-Day War), 4, 9, 15, 20, 52, 54, 59, 62, 75, 101, 115, 134, 160, 166, 168, 178, 190–2
  1973 War (Yom Kippur War), 15
  1982 and 2006 Lebanese Wars, 15
  2008 and 2014 Gaza Wars, 15, 138, 145, 171–2
West Bank, 14, 25, 33, 35–6, 41, 45, 52–4, 62–6, 69, 71–2, 75–7, 82, 86, 98, 101, 110, 115–16, 118–19, 125, 128–30, 134, 137, 139, 146–7, 151, 153–6, 169, 173, 183, 189–91, 193–4
Women of the Wall, 82, 122, 124

Young Men's Christian Association (YMCA), 93

Zionism, 14, 25, 28, 36, 58–9, 65, 106, 115, 118–20, 133